T0203036

Lecture Notes of the Institute for Computer Sciences, Social Informatics and Telecommunications Engineering

520

The LNICST series publishes ICST's conferences, symposia and workshops.

LNICST reports state-of-the-art results in areas related to the scope of the Institute.

The type of material published includes

- Proceedings (published in time for the respective event)
- Other edited monographs (such as project reports or invited volumes)

LNICST topics span the following areas:

- General Computer Science
- E-Economy
- E-Medicine
- Knowledge Management
- Multimedia
- Operations, Management and Policy
- Social Informatics
- Systems

Muthoni Masinde · Sabine Möbs ·
Antoine Bagula

Editors

Emerging Technologies
for Developing Countries

6th EAI International Conference, AFRICATEK 2023
Arusha, Tanzania, December 11–13, 2023
Proceedings

 Springer

Editors
Muthoni Masinde ⓘ
Department of Information Technology
Central University of Technology, Free State
Bloemfontein, South Africa

Sabine Möbs ⓘ
Baden-Wuerttemberg Cooperative State
University
Stuttgart, Germany

Antoine Bagula ⓘ
Department of Computer Science
University of the Western Cape
Cape Town, South Africa

ISSN 1867-8211   ISSN 1867-822X (electronic)
Lecture Notes of the Institute for Computer Sciences, Social Informatics
and Telecommunications Engineering
ISBN 978-3-031-63998-2   ISBN 978-3-031-63999-9 (eBook)
https://doi.org/10.1007/978-3-031-63999-9

This Springer imprint is published by the registered company Springer Nature Switzerland AG
The registered company address is: Gewerbestrasse 11, 6330 Cham, Switzerland

If disposing of this product, please recycle the paper.

Preface

We are delighted to present the proceedings of the sixth European Alliance for Innovation (EAI) International Conference on Emerging Technologies for Developing Countries (AFRICATEK 2023), co-organized with the Nelson Mandela African Institution of Science and Technology in the scenic locale of Arusha, Tanzania. This edition, dedicated to unravelling the complexities and potential of smart cities within the context of developing nations, particularly Africa, showcases the pivotal role of technology in addressing the unique challenges and tapping into the untapped potential of these regions.

AFRICATEK 2023 brought together a vibrant community of scholars, researchers, practitioners, and innovators from Africa and across the globe, engendering a fertile ground for the exchange of innovative ideas, research findings, and practical insights aimed at harnessing technology for sustainable development across the continent. Reflecting the multifaceted nature of technological evolution, the conference explored a wide array of themes, from smart city frameworks and technological innovations to contextually relevant design approaches and smart applications critical for Africa's progress in sectors such as education, healthcare, agriculture, and urban planning.

The compilation of rigorously selected papers, enriched by four keynote addresses, encapsulates the discourse on the transformative impact of technologies like the Internet of Things (IoT), artificial intelligence (AI), and data analytics on societal advancement. This volume not only highlights the synergetic fusion of traditional practices with modern technological solutions but also illustrates the transformative potential of these innovations in driving socio-economic growth, enhancing environmental sustainability, and improving governance and healthcare services across the continent.

Our heartfelt appreciation goes out to the organizing and technical program committees for their exceptional dedication and expertise, which were pivotal to the success of the conference. We extend our gratitude to our partners, sponsors, and all participants, whose invaluable contributions were instrumental in the realization of this significant event. The collaborative endeavours and insights gained at AFRICATEK 2023 embody our collective commitment to accelerating the integration of cutting-edge technologies in developing areas, paving the way for a future where such innovations are integral to achieving prosperity and equity.

The insights and outcomes of AFRICATEK 2023, documented in these proceedings, highlight the exciting, albeit challenging, path toward technological empowerment in developing regions. This scholarly record is envisioned not just as a compilation of research but as a beacon guiding future endeavours in research, innovation, and policy formulation, aimed at exploiting the full spectrum of emerging technologies for the betterment of society. We hope that this volume will inspire continuous dialogue, collaboration, and action, furthering the journey towards realizing the full potential of technology in shaping the futures of developing nations.

December 2023

Muthoni Masinde
Sabine Möbs
Antoine Bagula

Organization

Steering Committee

Imrich Chlamtac   University of Trento, Italy

Organizing Committee

General Chair

Muthoni Masinde   Central University of Technology, Free State, South Africa

General Co-chair

Verdiana Grace Masanja   Nelson Mandela African Institution of Science and Technology, Tanzania

TPC Chairs

Muthoni Masinde   Central University of Technology, Free State, South Africa

Antoine Bagula   University of the Western Cape, South Africa

TPC Co-chair

Sabine Moebs   Baden-Wuerttemberg Cooperative State University, Germany

Web Chair

Adeyinka Akanbi   Central University of Technology, Free State, South Africa

Publicity and Social Media Chair

Judith Flora   St. Augustine University of Tanzania, Tanzania

Workshops Chair

Elisha Markus   Central University of Technology, Free State,
                                  South Africa

Sponsorship and Exhibit Chair

Muthoni Masinde   Central University of Technology, Free State,
                                  South Africa

Publications Chair

Bankole Awuzie   University of Johannesburg, South Africa

Panels Chair

Wesley Doorsamy   University of Leeds, UK

Tutorials Chair

Regina Pohle-Fröhlich   Niederrhein University of Applied Sciences,
                                  Germany

Demos Chair

Ntima Mabanza   Central University of Technology, Free State,
                                  South Africa

Posters Chair

Joyce Nabende   Makerere University, Uganda

Local Chairs

Verdiana Grace Masanja   Nelson Mandela African Institution of Science
                                  and Technology, Tanzania
Mussa Dida   Nelson Mandela African Institution of Science
                                  and Technology, Tanzania

Technical Program Committee

Adeyinka Akanbi	Central University of Technology, Free State, South Africa
Amon Taruvinga	University of Fort Hare, South Africa
Antoine Bagula	University of the Western Cape, South Africa
Attlee Munyaradzi Gamundani	Namibia University of Science and Technology, Namibia
Bankole Awuzie	University of Johannesburg, South Africa
Celestine Iwendi	University of Bolton, UK
Deogratias Shidende	DHBW Heidenheim, Germany
Devotha Nyambo	Nelson Mandela African Institution of Science and Technology, Tanzania
Dirk Reichardt	DHBW Stuttgart, Germany
Donal Fitzpatrick	National Disability Authority, Ireland
Ramadhan Sinde	Nelson Mandela African Institution of Science and Technology, Tanzania
Elisha Markus	Central University of Technology, Free State, South Africa
Emmanuel Manasseh	Nelson Mandela African Institution of Science and Technology, Tanzania
Ferdinando Kahenga	Esisalama Academy, Tanzania
Fungai Bhunu Shava	Namibia University of Science and Technology, Namibia
Gerald Muriithi	Central University of Technology, Free State, South Africa
Gemin Peter Iyakurwa	Nelson Mandela African Institution of Science and Technology, Tanzania
Guillaume Nel	Central University of Technology, Free State, South Africa
Gugulethu Zuma-Netshiukhwi	Agricultural Research Council, South Africa
Irina Tal	Dublin City University, Ireland
James Njenga	University of the Western Cape, South Africa
Johannes Freudenmann	DHBW Karlsruhe, Germany
Judith Leo	Nelson Mandela African Institution of Science and Technology, Tanzania
Katja Wengler	DHBW Karlsruhe, Germany
Kennedy Njenga	University of Johannesburg, South Africa
Leandra Jordaan	Central University of Technology, Free State, South Africa
Marco Zennaro	International Centre for Theoretical Physics, Italy
Mateus Jovita	Namibia University of Science and Technology, Namibia

Contents

Smart Infrastructure and Urban Management

Comprehensive Review of Smart Parking Occupancy Prediction Models in Nairobi City: Strengths, Weaknesses, and Research Gaps

Josephine Tanui, Solomon Mwanjele Mwagha(✉), and K. Cheruyoit Wilson

Taita Taveta University, Voi, Kenya
soproltd@gmail.com

Abstract. An in-depth analysis of smart parking occupancy prediction models in contemporary cities is presented in this research. The paper identifies key research gaps while methodically analyzing the strengths, flaws, and resilience of existing models. Priority was given to the models' precision and efficacy in addressing the city's growing parking issues. An extensive analysis of these models demonstrated that they help to manage to park effectively because of their properties including real-time data integration and great forecast accuracy. On the other hand, several restrictions and flaws have been found, including issues with data accessibility, a lack of generalizability, and the complexity of certain advanced models. These findings emphasized the value of creative and situation-specific responses. The findings demonstrated the urgent need for further study, notably in the fields of data integration, scalability, interpretability, cost-effectiveness, and user centered methods for smart parking models. These flaws are now being addressed to build a comprehensive smart parking system that is tailored to the particular urban dynamics of Nairobi. They also provide a framework for future study. Our project's ultimate goal is to significantly improve Nairobi's urban mobility and parking management, and machine learning will be a key instrument in this transformation process.

Keywords: Literature Review · Nairobi City · Occupancy Prediction · Parking Management · Smart Parking · Traffic Management · Urban Mobility · Urban Planning

1 Introduction

While cities continue to grow and car ownership becomes more common, the task of managing parking spaces becomes more difficult. Inadequate parking management can result in air pollution, traffic congestion, and lost time [1]. However, parking space utilization can be optimized with the help of smart parking systems that use cutting-edge technology, resulting in a superior parking experience. Accurate parking occupancy predictions are critical for intelligent parking system efficiency, allowing proactive management and effective resource allocation [2].

M. Masinde et al. (Eds.): AFRICATEK 2023, LNICST 520, pp. 3–20, 2024.
https://doi.org/10.1007/978-3-031-63999-9_1

Smart parking systems can simplify the process of locating vacant parking spaces and enhance the productivity of parking enforcement officers. These systems operate by precisely forecasting parking occupancy in real-time, resulting in more efficient utilization of resources and well-informed choices for drivers and parking operators [2]. Although there are several approaches to predicting parking occupancy, each technique has its unique advantages and limitations.

1.1 Smart Parking Occupancy Prediction

Accurate forecasting of parking space occupancy is essential for efficient parking space management. To optimize resources and make proactive decisions, park managers must have this information [3]. Additionally, this helps reduce traffic congestion, enhance the parking experience, and allocate resources effectively. The use of intelligent parking systems has created a significant demand for intelligent prediction of parking space occupancy in cities.

A lot of research papers have delved into diverse modeling strategies, data collection techniques, and predictive factors to augment the accuracy and dependability of occupancy estimates [4]. Smart parking occupancy prediction systems can now be expanded with technological breakthroughs such as the Internet of Things, data analytics, and cloud computing. Nevertheless, forecasting parking lot occupancy is a complex task that relies on multiple factors, including the day and time of the week, weather conditions, and parking lot location [5].

1.2 Multivariate Logistic Regression

The statistical model of multivariate logistic regression has gained widespread popularity for its effectiveness and interpretability in predicting binary outcomes [6]. This technique involves studying the relationship between multiple predictor variables and a binary outcome, thereby offering valuable insights into the factors that influence park occupancy. By accurately estimating the probability of occupancy, logistic regression enables parking managers to plan and allocate resources more efficiently [7, 8].

In smart parking, multivariate logistic regression is frequently used to forecast parking occupancy and enhance parking management techniques [9]. The logarithmic chance of park occupancy and the predictor variables, however, are assumed to be linearly related [10]. The predictor variables are therefore considered to be independent of one another [5].

1.3 Ordinary Least-Squares Regression

Ordinary least squares regression (OLS) is a well-established technique for parameter estimation and inference in linear regression [11]. Although OLS regression was originally developed for continuous outcome variables, it can be adapted for binary outcomes within the framework of logistic regression. The use of OLS in the context of multivariate logistic regression enables robust parameter estimation and model interpretation using the theoretical foundations and statistical properties of OLS regression [12]. Although

OLS regression is a widely used technique, it has some limitations when applied to smart parking occupancy prediction [13], which assumes a linear relationship between the predictor variables and the outcome variable [14].

1.4 Robustness and Challenge

Developing a robust occupancy prediction model requires addressing potential challenges arising from real-world parking datasets [15]. Outliers, influential observations, and violations of model assumptions can affect the accuracy and reliability of the model. To overcome these challenges, robust regression techniques and data transformations can be used, increasing the robustness of the model and ensuring accurate predictions [16].

Concerns include user adoption and behavior, integration and interoperability, integration and data security, privacy and data security, and dynamic parking situations [17]. For the implementation and operation of smart parking systems to be effective, it is essential to address these resiliency and obstacles. To guarantee the system's dependability, accuracy, and user happiness, a mix of technological advancements, good planning, collaboration amongst stakeholders, and continuous monitoring and development is needed.

2   Statement of the Problem

Nairobi, Kenya is a thriving metropolis that faces an ongoing urban challenge related to transportation congestion. Residents and visitors in general increasingly experience this issue daily, and it poses a significant barrier to efficient urban mobility. The struggle to find a parking spot in the congested city streets is at the core of this problem. Accurately estimating parking availability in Nairobi is the major difficulty of this work. This is a challenging computational problem with significant effects on urban transportation. It is crucial to find a solution in a city that is expanding quickly since every minute spent seeking parking causes traffic to back up.

Technology- and data-driven smart parking systems are developing as viable answers to Nairobi's urban transportation issues. These solutions promise to ease traffic, lower pollution, and enhance urban life in general. They serve as the watchdogs of effective municipal transportation by directing drivers to open parking places in real-time. Implementing intelligent parking systems is a fundamentally computational difficulty. It is difficult to anticipate parking occupancy accurately because of several dynamic and interconnected elements. This covers the hour of the day, the day of the week, the location, and any outside activities.

The complexity of these factors requires a sophisticated computational approach. In this computational snafu, machine learning emerges as our promising solution. Robust Multivariate Logistic Regression, in particular, takes center stage, providing a sophisticated tool for calculating parking space availability. Its ability to manage nonlinearity and multivariate interactions is perfectly suited to the complexities of city mobility. The benefits of using machine learning to anticipate parking occupancy are threefold.

First, it saves drivers time by directing them to available parking spaces rather than circling and looking. Second, it has the potential to cut traffic congestion and emissions dramatically, contributing to a more sustainable urban transportation ecosystem. Predicting parking occupancy accurately in Nairobi is a significant computational issue. It is at the crossroads of technology and urban design, presenting a viable answer to the city's traffic problems. Utilizing the power of machine learning, specifically logistic regression, we aim to address this difficulty and contribute to the growth of Nairobi's urban mobility, paving the way for a more efficient, sustainable, and livable city.

3   Objectives

The primary objectives of this study are; to conduct a thorough literature review of smart parking occupancy prediction models in Nairobi City, to evaluate the strengths and weaknesses of these models, and to identify research gaps that warrant further investigation in future studies.

4   Related Studies

Related studies of proposed and developed models is as described in Table 1 below.

Table. 1. Proposed models and their methodologies.

No	Title Model	Algorithm Used	Description	Year
1	Blockchain-Based Parking Solutions	Blockchain technology for secure transactions	Blockchain is explored for secure and transparent payment and booking systems in smart parking	(2010)
2	Machine Learning-Based Time Series Analysis	Time series analysis with machine learning (e.g., LSTM, ARIMA)	Time series analysis models with machine learning components are used to forecast parking space availability	(2010)
3	Reinforcement Learning for Parking Space Allocation	Reinforcement Learning	Uses reinforcement learning techniques to optimize parking space allocation and reduce congestion	(2016)
4	Fuzzy Logic-Based Smart Parking System	Fuzzy Logic	Implements fuzzy logic for decision-making in a smart parking system, considering factors like occupancy and vehicle arrival rates	(2017)

(continued)

Table. 1. (*continued*)

No	Title Model	Algorithm Used	Description	Year
5	Edge Computing for Smart Parking	Edge Computing and Machine Learning	Implements edge computing with on-site data processing and machine learning for real-time parking predictions and management	(2021)
6	Blockchain-Enabled Parking Management	Blockchain (for data security and transparency)	Utilizes blockchain technology for secure and transparent parking transactions and data management	(2022)

4.1 Parking Solutions

Parking solutions refer to a variety of tactics and tools used to address parking-related problems including a lack of parking, traffic, and the effective use of parking spots. Citations are formal notifications or fines delivered to car owners who breach parking restrictions and are one component of parking solutions [19]. Based on a variety of variables, parking solutions may be divided into numerous different categories. These groups reflect diverse strategies for addressing parking-related issues to enhance convenience, effectiveness, and sustainability in urban settings.

4.2 Predictive Modelling for Smart Parking Occupancy

The development and implementation of data-driven strategies to anticipate and estimate parking space availability in real-time are components of predictive modeling for smart parking occupancy [11, 20]. To predict smart parking occupancy, several predictive modeling techniques have been investigated. Based on historical data, real-time sensor data, and other pertinent variables including weather, events, and time of day, these models seek to anticipate parking occupancy.

4.3 Parking and Parking System in Nairobi City

The development and implementation of data-driven strategies to anticipate and estimate parking space availability in real-time are components of predictive modeling for smart parking occupancy [11, 20]. To predict smart parking occupancy, several predictive modeling techniques have been investigated. Based on historical data, real-time sensor data, and other pertinent variables including weather, events, and time of day, these models seek to anticipate parking occupancy. To create prediction models for smart parking occupancy, regression approaches, machine learning algorithms, and statistical techniques have all been extensively used [11].

5   Nairobi County Transport Management

The county government of Nairobi does not have an extensive park management system. However, it has established several rules that are occasionally disregarded by users, which has an impact on the effectiveness and efficient movement of traffic in urban regions, particularly during busy periods when the central business district is crowded [17]. Nairobi, like many other cities across the world, looked at a range of smart parking solutions to address the difficulties related to parking congestion. Smart parking concepts and technologies have been tested and implemented to improve parking management and the quality of urban mobility in general.

Attempts have been made to address parking management issues all across the world throughout the years. A parking management system was suggested as a solution to Nairobi's parking issues, and it is a crucial component of the county's economy that directly affects productivity. As a result, it contributes significantly to profitability, productivity, and overall performance. The parking regulations as listed in [17]. It is also illegal to park on private property without the owner's or another person with legal access to the property's consent. Trailers cannot be parked on public roadways unless they are connected to a vehicle that can push or pull them.

5.1   Nairobi County Government Traffic and Transport Management

Since 1980, both the quality of road traffic and public transportation have decreased [9]. This is due to a lack of discipline among drivers and pedestrians, insufficient public transit due to the large population, an increase in the number of automobiles, insufficiently enforced laws, and an increase in the number of cars [19]. The district's congestion is anticipated to be decreased via the construction of highways and bypasses. Roundabout elimination and other vehicle parking choices outside the primary business district are other suggested strategies to reduce traffic congestion [18]. Table 2 below lists some of the parking lots in Nairobi's central business district that are managed by the two primary agencies, along with their capacities.

Table 2. Showing Nairobi parking lots

Location	Capacity	Authority in Charge
Sunken Car Park	243	County Government
Nairobi Law Courts	220	County Government of Nairobi
Gichamu Lane	80	Private
KICC Grounds	300	Private
Kenyatta Avenue near Laico Regency	180	Private

(continued)

Table 2. (*continued*)

Location	Capacity	Authority in Charge
Utalii Street	70	Private
Intercontinental Hotel open-air parking	70	Private

The modern underground structure is a creative way of providing motorists with additional, convenient, and secure parking spaces within the city center such as an innovative parking facility at the Holy Family Minor Basilica.

5.2 Aspects of Urban Logistics and Parking in Nairobi City

Parking and urban logistics are essential elements of urban planning and management. They contribute significantly to the smooth running of cities and the improvement of urban residents' quality of life. Nairobi, like many other African towns that are developing quickly, presents specific challenges and possibilities related to parking and urban logistics. Drivers utilize a variety of applications, like Google Maps, to find parking spaces and navigate to their destinations, among other things. The essential aspects of Nairobi's parking and urban logistics are listed in Table 3 below.

Table 3. Showing key features of Nairobi's urban logistics and parking in Nairobi City

Key Aspects	Finding/Challenge/Measures	Source
Parking Scarcity	Nairobi faces a shortage of parking spaces, especially in the central business district (CBD). This leads to illegal parking and traffic congestion	[24]
Smart Parking Solutions	Nairobi has started implementing smart parking solutions that use technology, such as sensors and mobile apps, to help drivers find available parking spaces and make payments	[18]
Accessibility and Safety	Ensuring that parking facilities are accessible to all, including people with disabilities, and providing adequate security are essential considerations	[24]
Urban Planning	Urban planners must carefully consider the impact of parking on the city's landscape and overall urban development, aiming for sustainable and efficient use of space	[14]
Informal Parking	Informal parking attendants are common in Nairobi. Formalizing and regulating this sector is important for both parking management and employment	[17]

(*continued*)

Table 3. (*continued*)

Key Aspects	Finding/Challenge/Measures	Source
Parking Fees and Regulations:	Parking fees and regulations, including metered parking and time limits, are used to manage parking demand. These policies need to be enforced effectively	[17]
Mixed-Use Parking Facilities	Due to space constraints, Nairobi is exploring mixed-use parking facilities that incorporate commercial or residential spaces along with parking infrastructure	[25]

5.3 Parking Lots in Nairobi City

Urban transportation difficulties must be addressed, thus technology advancements that move cities toward sustainable smart cities are essential. Offering effective parking services to its citizens is a huge problem for Nairobi County [14]. Lack of knowledge of available parking lots and the easiest ways to get there are some of these difficulties.

The average time spent by vehicles looking for parking is 32 min, according to a 2011 IBM parking survey. About 9,500 parking spots are managed by the Nairobi County Council in the city's commercial hub. On an average peak day, nearly 10,000 automobiles use this parking lot, which is located on Taifa Road, Sunken Car Park (243 spaces), Law Courts Park (220 spaces), and street parking [19].

In comparison to the number of vehicles, each of the county's two off-street parking areas has a capacity of just 700 autos each day. Despite district administrations' advice that people park at their own risk, city drivers complain of additional payments of Kshs 250 to 450 for parking boys who park every day for safety reasons [19] (Fig. 1).

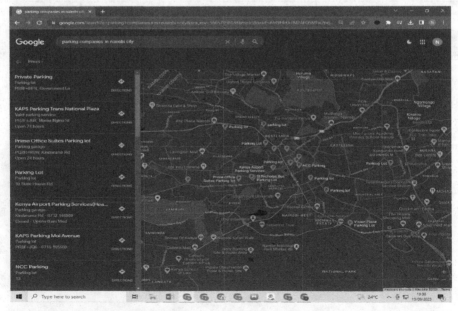

Fig. 1. Showing the Google Map location for some of the Parking Lots within Nairobi CBD

6 Parking Solutions in Nairobi City

On-street, off-street, or buildings—which may be private or public—are all options for parking. Parking is quite dynamic; a parking lot may be engaged and in the next 10 min the lot is unoccupied. According to the IBM worldwide parking study conducted in 2011 [20], finding a parking place, particularly in densely populated metropolitan areas, has become a daily struggle for many drivers. According to a 2010 IBM poll, more than a quarter of drivers got into a parking lot-related argument with another driver, and nearly six out of ten drivers gave up looking for one.

According to this study, almost 30% of a city's traffic is caused by automobiles that circle the neighborhood seeking for an empty parking space. Driving about while seeking parking took on average between 31 and 40 min globally, while drivers in Nairobi took an average of 31 min to find a parking space. Different Parking Guidance Information Systems (PGIS) have been developed to address the difficulties associated with finding parking spaces, but they frequently function as standalone systems in designated areas and, as a result, only disseminate information to a small number of users or selected users, potentially missing out on potential new users. Due to erroneous or outdated information given, these systems' utilization is still low after their installation [21].

6.1 Smart Parking Management System

This technique makes use of several different technologies, most notably the deployment of wireless parking meters installed on sturdy platforms with sensing and communication capabilities, reducing parking conflicts and enabling drivers to get real-time parking information at their destinations [22]. Many systems are not clever enough to assist drivers in finding a desired parking place in congested regions, and can occasionally make the issue worse if they give the wrong information to the drivers [23].

Detailed information on parking availability and utilization would allow drivers to make better real-time decisions on the use of parking lots and roadside parking [23]. To make these systems smarter, Rashid, [23], proposed a Reservation-based Smart Parking System (RSPS) that not only broadcasts real-time parking prices based on parking availability but also provides reservation service as part of a user-targeted service.

6.2 Intelligent Transport Systems (ITS)

ITS aims to provide innovative solutions to the transport sector by application of various technologies such as car navigation, traffic signal control, automatic number recognition, and speed cameras. In the car parking industry, ITS objective is to extract and recognize vehicle registration numbers from car images using various machine learning algorithms, process the image data, and utilize the information for parking lot access records [23]. Using this technology, information regarding parking-free spaces can be relayed to users in real-time.

ITS would be categorized in the line of image acquisition and processing to determine whether parking lots have objects on them and if there are objects, the image processing can judge whether it is a vehicle or not. Collating this data, the number of parking spaces available is relayed to the control center. The ITS and the smart parking management system may have a drawback called multiple-user-chasing-single-space [23]. This is a phenomenon whereby a parking lot has very few parking spaces available during busy hours and more drivers struggle for fewer parking spaces causing severe congestion.

6.3 ZKTeco Smart Parking Systems

ZKTeco Smart Parking Systems is the perfect solution for the growing need for safe parking spaces in Kenya's cities and towns. As the economy and living standards improve, more vehicles are hitting the roads, making the Automatic Number-Plate Recognition (ANPR) device the ideal solution for a convenient and safe user experience from the entrance to the parking space [23]. The ZKTeco Parking Solution offers a range of License Plate Recognition Products (LPR), Ultra-High Frequency (UHF) Products, Parking Barrier Products, and Parking Guidance Products, perfect for busy and high-volume parking.

Installed LPR Cameras detect when vehicle license plates enter the designated area, and customers can easily follow indications to the available parking bays with the help of indicating lights, guidance displays, and the vehicle search kiosk. With the Zkteco Car Park Solution, drivers can search for their vehicles via the vehicle search kiosk, which integrates with the car park system and can detect where and when cars are parked in real-time. Customers can simply enter their car plate number to see their vehicle on the 2D map and the shortest path to it.

7 Establishing the Gap

The parking management system currently in use in Nairobi County has made strides in digitization, specifically in e-payment. However, these efforts have primarily focused on increasing revenue and reducing industry corruption, rather than addressing the issue of finding convenient parking spaces. Implementing a similar system in the Central Business District, which is a bustling business hub, would be an ideal testing ground for its success. If proven effective, this system could be replicated in other areas with high amounts of daily vehicle traffic and parking demands.

After conducting a thorough literature review, it has become clear that a research gap exists in the development of a robust Ordinary Least-Squares (OLS) based Multi-variate Logistic Regression Model for predicting smart parking occupancy in Nairobi city. This gap is due to the unique challenges associated with predicting smart parking occupancy, including limited data availability and data sparsity.

8 Methodology

Within this research, we provide a detailed account of the methods used to thoroughly investigate the Smart Parking Occupancy Prediction Models (SPOPM) concept. Our study employed specific inclusion criteria to gather pertinent information on SPOPM. These criteria required that the reviewed studies were focused on peer-reviewed articles or conference papers, published in English, and specifically pertained to the development or evaluation of smart parking occupancy prediction models in Nairobi city. The analysis incorporated reputable publishers such as Routledge Taylor & Francis Group, IEEE Xplore, ScienceDirect, Springer Link, ACM Digital Library, Hindawi, Nairobi County, KEBS, UoN Digital Repository, JKUAT Digital Repository, KU Digital Repository, and MOI University Digital Repository, among others.

The methodology employed in this paper is rooted in the research method detailed in reference [21]. The paper review process was broken down into three distinct phases, namely planning, review, and results. During the planning phase, guidelines were established to facilitate the effective search of review materials. The review phase was dedicated to developing rigorous guidelines for constructing search strings aimed at identifying relevant review materials from various repositories. This phase yielded initial results, garnered pertinent research papers, and sifted through possible contributions. Subsequently, the chosen documents were subjected to thorough scrutiny during the results phase. A snapshot of the methodology utilized in this study is depicted in Fig. 2 below.

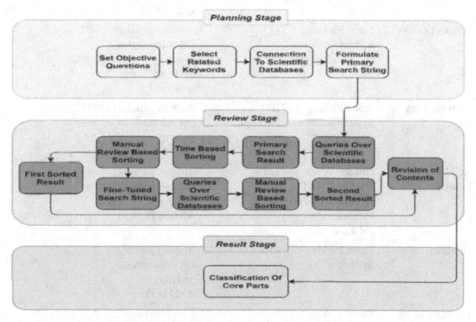

Fig. 2. Showing the Research method in detail

8.1 Data Collection

A systematic literature search was performed using reputable databases, focusing on publications from the year 2008 to the year 2023. The search utilized keywords search strings such as "Urban Mobility, Smart Parking", "Parking Management", "Occupancy Prediction", "Nairobi City Traffic", "Urban Planning", Traffic Management and related terms. A table of query results from different formulated strings over various scientific databases was drawn.

Table 4. Query results from different formulated strings over various scientific databases

Scientific Database	Primary Search String	Primary Search String Result	Modified Search String	Modified Search String Result
Routledge Taylor & Francis Group	"Smart" AND "Parking" AND "Solutions" AND "Sensors" AND "Method"	97	(((smart parking) OR autonomous parking) AND IoT)	185
IEEE Xplore	((((smart parking) AND systems) AND methods) AND networks)	167	(((smart parking) OR autonomous parking) AND intelligent sensors)	294
ScienceDirect	Smart Parking System/Solutions	153	(((smart parking) OR autonomous parking) AND intelligent sensors)	389
Springer Link	Smart Parking System/Solutions	200	(((smart parking) OR autonomous parking) AND IoT)	977
ACM Digital Library	"Smart" AND "Parking" AND "Solutions" AND "Sensors" AND "Method"	121	(((smart parking) OR autonomous parking) AND IoT)	169
Hindawi	Smart Parking System	416	(((smart parking) OR autonomous parking) AND IoT)	0
Nairobi County	Smart Parking System/Solutions	12	Smart Parking AND IoT AND intelligent sensors	2
KBS	Smart Parking System/Solutions	3	Smart Parking AND IoT AND intelligent sensors	0
UoN Digital Repository	Smart Parking System/Solutions	7	Smart Parking AND IoT AND intelligent sensors	6

(continued)

Table 4. (*continued*)

Scientific Database	Primary Search String	Primary Search String Result	Modified Search String	Modified Search String Result
JKUAT Digital Repository	Smart Parking System/Solutions	9	Smart Parking AND IoT AND intelligent sensors	4
KU Digital Repository	Smart Parking System/ Solutions	4	Smart Parking AND IoT AND intelligent sensors	3
MOI University Digital Repository	Smart Parking System/ Solutions	5	Smart Parking AND IoT AND intelligent sensors	1

To compile information regarding smart parking systems and solutions, we carefully selected reputable journal publishers and conducted a comprehensive analysis of both global and local research as shown in Table 4 above. The resulting insights were pivotal in shaping the fundamental components of this paper and identifying the latest technological advancements in the realm of smart parking systems. The scarcity of parking spots during peak hours is a widespread concern for large cities, causing individuals to waste precious time searching for a spot or sitting in long queues, ultimately leading to traffic congestion. To tackle this issue, a multitude of researchers have proposed innovative smart parking solutions and systems, utilizing various technologies to alleviate this challenge.

9 Analysis of the Findings

Quantitative and qualitative data analysis methods were employed. Statistical metrics, including publication trends, model types, and performance metrics, were collected and analyzed.

9.1 Publication Trends

From Table 5 below, the analysis revealed a steady increase in the number of publications related to smart parking prediction models in Nairobi City over the past decade. A total of seventy-nine (79) relevant studies were identified and included in this review (Fig. 3).

Table 5. Year-Wise Literature Frequency in Kenya

Year	2008	2009	2010	2011	2012	2013	2014	2015	2016	2017	2018	2019	2020	2021	2022	2023
Freq	0	0	0	0	0	1	3	4	7	9	6	11	8	16	12	2

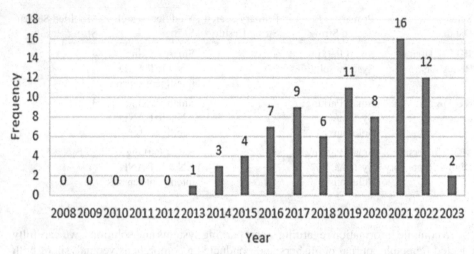

Fig. 3. Showing a Bar graph for the Year-Wise Literature Frequency in Kenya

9.2 Model Types

Related studies of proposed and developed models identified in the reviews are summarized in Table 6 below.

Internationally, Predominantly, machine learning techniques were used out of the seven selected models, including regression (14.29%), fuzzy logic (14.29%), Reinforcement Learning (14.29%), and blockchain (28.57%). Data collection primarily relied on IoT devices, and sensors as buzzing technologies of the current era, where all devices are interconnected with one another through the internet. On the local scene, these technologies are yet to be fully adopted and implemented.

Table 6. Proposed models and their methodologies.

No	Title Model	Algorithm Used	Description	Year
1	Blockchain-Based Parking Solutions	Blockchain technology for secure transactions	Blockchain is explored for secure and transparent payment and booking systems in smart parking	(2010)
2	Machine Learning-Based Time Series Analysis	Time series analysis with machine learning (e.g., LSTM, ARIMA)	Time series analysis models with machine learning components are used to forecast parking space availability	(2010)
3	Reinforcement Learning for Parking Space Allocation	Reinforcement Learning	Uses reinforcement learning techniques to optimize parking space allocation and reduce congestion	(2016)
4	Fuzzy Logic-Based Smart Parking System	Fuzzy Logic	Implements fuzzy logic for decision-making in a smart parking system, considering factors like occupancy and vehicle arrival rates	(2017)
5	Edge Computing for Smart Parking	Edge Computing and Machine Learning	Implements edge computing with on-site data processing and machine learning for real-time parking predictions and management	(2021)
6	Blockchain-Enabled Parking Management	Blockchain (for data security and transparency)	Utilizes blockchain technology for secure and transparent parking transactions and data management	(2022)
7	Regression Models	OLS	Use of mathematical formula to interpret parking spaces	(2022)

9.3 Strengths

The review found several strengths in the existing models, including effective use of historical parking data as indicated in Table 2 above, incorporation of weather conditions, and successful implementation of machine learning algorithms as indicated in Table 6 above.

9.4 Weaknesses

Considering the data provided in Table 4, it is evident that almost all of the reviewed papers chose only ML approaches that employ linear models. Weaknesses identified include limited consideration of real-time traffic data, inadequate attention to urban planning factors, and an over-reliance on linear models especially for technologies in Table 6 above. In Nairobi city, these technologies are still at an infant stage.

10 Conclusion

Nairobi city serves not only as the Kenya nation's capital but also as a significant trade and business hub in the East Africa region. Nonetheless, challenges related to inefficient road utilization, encompassing illegal on-street parking, limited public transportation options, and low parking rates within the central business district, often impede the smooth operation of the Nairobi Metropolitan Region as a central business hub. Previous research and parking surveys have consistently emphasized the critical importance of implementing efficient parking solutions to meet future parking demands. Thus, involving end-users in both the design and evaluation processes becomes paramount as this approach ensures that smart parking solutions can be tailored precisely to meet the unique needs and preferences of the target demographic, aligning the solutions closely with the group's specific requirements.

11 Recommendations

To enhance the smart parking system in Nairobi, these recommendations must be implemented:

- Conduct a real-world test of the system in collaboration with local officials, parking managers, and technology suppliers to ensure its success.
- Invest in enhancing data quality to improve parking availability predictions. This requires improved sensor technology, data validation methods, and maintenance procedures.
- Continuously update and refine machine learning models to ensure their accuracy. Regular updates based on fresh data and evolving urban conditions are essential.
- Explore potential connections between the smart parking system and other smart city initiatives, such as public transportation and traffic control.
- Integrate sustainability measures, such as solar-powered sensors or electric car charging stations, to support environmental objectives.
- Work with local authorities to create legislation and incentives that encourage the use of smart parking solutions. Clear policies are essential to expanding these systems in Nairobi and beyond.

References

1. Buehler, R., Pucher, J., Gerike, R., Götschi, T.: Reducing car dependence in the heart of Europe: lessons from Germany, Austria, and Switzerland. Transp. Rev. **37**(1), 4–28 (2017). https://doi.org/10.1080/01441647.2016.1177799
2. Cao, X., Cui, X., Yue, M., Chen, J., Tanikawa, H., Ye, Y.: Evaluation of wildfire propagation susceptibility in grasslands using burned areas and multivariate logistic regression. Int. J. Remote Sens. **34**(19), 6679–6700 (2013). https://doi.org/10.1080/01431161.2013.805280
3. Corry, M., Porter, S., McKenna, H.: The redundancy of positivism as a paradigm for nursing research. Nurs. Philos. **20**(1), e12230 (2019). https://doi.org/10.1111/nup.12230
4. Gettelman, A., Rood, R.B.: Model Evaluation, pp. 161–176 (2016). https://doi.org/10.1007/978-3-662-48959-8_9
5. Bala, H., Anowar, S., Chng, S., Cheah, L.: Review of studies on public acceptability and acceptance of shared autonomous mobility services: past, present and future. Transp. Rev. **2**(11), 1–27 (2023). https://doi.org/10.1080/01441647.2023.2188619
6. dos Reis, C., Silveira, T., Romano, C.A., Gadda, T.M.C.: Loyalty and public transit: a quantitative systematic review of the literature. Transp. Rev. **42**(3), 362–383 (2022). https://doi.org/10.1080/01441647.2021.1991032
7. Cohen, T., Cavoli, C.: Automated vehicles: exploring possible consequences of government (non)intervention for congestion and accessibility. Transp. Rev. **39**(1), 129–151 (2019). https://doi.org/10.1080/01441647.2018.1524401
8. Sidorchuk, R., Mkhitaryan, V., Skorobogatykh, I., Stukalova, A., Lukina, V.: Modeling of the need for parking space in the districts of Moscow metropolis by using multivariate methods. J. Appl. Eng. Sci. **18**(1), 26–39 (2020). https://doi.org/10.5937/jaes18-23911
9. Alsafery, W., Alturki, B., Reiff-Marganiec, S., Jambi, K.: Smart car parking system solution for the Internet of Things in smart cities. In: 2018 1st International Conference on Computer Applications & Information Security (ICCAIS), pp. 1–5 (2018). https://doi.org/10.1109/CAIS.2018.8442004
10. Jusat, N., Zainuddin, A.A., Sahak, R., Andrew, A.B., Subramaniam, K., Rahman, N.A.: Critical review in smart car parking management systems. In: 2021 IEEE 7th international conference on smart instrumentation, measurement, and applications (ICSIMA), pp. 128–133 (2021). https://doi.org/10.1109/ICSIMA50015.2021.9526322
11. Piccialli, F., Giampaolo, F., Prezioso, E., Crisci, D., Cuomo, S.: Predictive analytics for smart parking: a deep learning approach in forecasting of IoT data. ACM Trans. Internet Technol. **21**(3), 1–21 (2021). https://doi.org/10.1145/3412842
12. Awaisi, K.S., Abbas, A., Khattak, H.A., Ahmad, A., Ali, M., Khalid, A.: Deep reinforcement learning approach towards a smart parking architecture. Clust. Comput. **26**(1), 255–266 (2023). https://doi.org/10.1007/s10586-022-03599-y
13. Padeiro, M., Louro, A., da Costa, N.M.: Transit-oriented development and gentrification: a systematic review. Transp. Rev. **39**(6), 733–754 (2019). https://doi.org/10.1080/01441647.2019.1649316
14. Mei, Z., Zhang, W., Zhang, L., Wang, D.: Real-time multistep prediction of public parking spaces based on Fourier transform–least squares support vector regression. J. Intell. Transport. Syst. **24**(1), 68–80 (2020). https://doi.org/10.1080/15472450.2019.1579092
15. Hirsch, J.A., Stratton-Rayner, J., Winters, M., Stehlin, J., Hosford, K., Mooney, S.J.: Roadmap for free-floating bike-share research and practice in North America. Transp. Rev. **39**(6), 706–732 (2019). https://doi.org/10.1080/01441647.2019.1649318
16. Hosseinzadeh, A., Algomaiah, M., Kluger, R., Li, Z.: Spatial analysis of shared e-scooter trips. J. Transp. Geogr. **92**, 103016 (2021). https://doi.org/10.1016/j.jtrangeo.2021.103016

17. Nairobi County Government. Nairobi City County Public Road Transport and Traffic Management Bill. Nairobi County Gazette Supplement, pp. 25–26 (2019)
18. Nairobi County Government. Nairobi County Integrated Development Plan. Nairobi: Nairobi County Government (2014)
19. Winnie Mitullah, T.M.: Role of ICT in local government. University of Nairobi, Nairobi (2008)
20. IBM (2011). IBM. https://www-03.ibm.com/press/us/en/pressrelease/35515.wss. Accessed 21 Aug 2023
21. Yanjie, J., Amy, G., Philip T.: Design the parking guidance information for the drivers (2012)
22. Hongwei, W.: A reservation-based smart parking system. Lincoln, Nebraska, s.n. (2011)
23. Keseru, I., Randhahn, A. (eds.): Towards User-Centric Transport in Europe 3. Springer, Cham. (2023). https://doi.org/10.1007/978-3-031-26155-8
24. Nairobi Metropolitan Services. Roads, Transport and Public Works (2022). https://www.nms.go.ke/?page_id=220. Accessed 24 Aug 2023

An Internet of Things and Smart Cities Frameworks Implementation in Municipalities: A Systematic Literature Review

Moabi Kompi(✉)

Central University of Technology, Welkom 9460, RSA
mkompi@cut.ac.za

Abstract. Recent years have seen an exponential growth in Internet of Things (IoT) frameworks and smart city frameworks. In many countries, local governments are seeking smart solutions, particularly in these frameworks where IoT innovation, development, and implementation profoundly influence the environment, economy, people, living, governance, and mobility. Internet of Things (IoT) frameworks and smart city implementation in municipalities are comprehensively reviewed and analyzed in this paper. This review is designed to identify, describe, and synthesize research findings on IoT and smart cities frameworks deployments in various municipalities. Databases such as Google Scholar and Web of science were utilized to acquire articles relevant to this study's objectives by scanning their titles, abstracts, introductions, and conclusions. To obtain related data, skimming and reading full texts were used to conduct a comprehensive literature review. For a more comprehensive understanding of current research and practice, 39 relevant studies were systematically reviewed. A variety of IoT technologies, communication protocols, and machine learning applications are discussed in this study. In addition to exploring smart city implementation frameworks adopted globally, the study sheds light on a variety of key areas of interest, including mobility, governance, economy, people, living, and the environment. The findings indicate that digital technologies play an increasingly important role in both providing insights into the evolving IoT and smart city landscape within municipalities globally as well as influencing and improving the quality of life for citizens.

Keywords: Frameworks · Internet of Things · Machine Learning · Smart Cities · Systematic Literature Review

1 Introduction

In the era of rapid development and technological advancement, the concept of smart cities has emerged as a transformative approach to address the complex challenges posed by urban living (Ezugwu et al. 2021). Smart cities leverage digital technologies, data analytics, and innovative frameworks to create efficient, sustainable, and livable urban environments (Lai, et al. 2020). As part of smart cities designs, designers utilize mobile

M. Masinde et al. (Eds.): AFRICATEK 2023, LNICST 520, pp. 21–36, 2024.
https://doi.org/10.1007/978-3-031-63999-9_2

cloud computing, electronic objects, networks, sensors, and machine learning technologies for the different components to interact and communicate with one another. This integration of Internet of Things (IoT) technologies and smart city implementations has garnered substantial attention from researchers, practitioners, and policymakers alike (Siokas et al. 2021). This paper presents a comprehensive exploration of these two interconnected realms, aiming to provide a holistic understanding of their significance, applications, and potential for reshaping modern municipalities in the form of a systematic literature review (Keshavarzi et al. 2021).

Considering the rollout of technology, smart cities, contemporary municipal development, and a planning concept, can provide municipal gains. Likewise, a smart city allows data exchange, interaction, and combining services whenever and wherever necessary. To increase the efficiency and effectiveness of service delivery and management, governments all over the world increasingly rely on information and communication technologies (ICTs) (Din et al. 2019). ICT-based innovation would revolutionize and rewire the traditional ways of managing municipal systems through the application of ICTs in smart cities, which will enhance urban infrastructures technologically and improve the quality of life and solve sustainability concerns. As development accelerates, harnessing the power of IoT has become crucial for addressing municipal challenges such as traffic congestion, energy consumption, and environmental sustainability (Mehmood et al. 2017).

Simultaneously, the implementation of smart city frameworks has emerged as a strategic approach to orchestrate municipal development in a holistic manner. Smart city frameworks encompass diverse dimensions, including mobility, governance, economy, environment, and quality of life as shown in Table 1 (Desdemoustier et al. 2019; Giffinger & Kramar 2022). These frameworks guide municipal planners, policymakers, and other stakeholders in aligning their efforts toward creating well-coordinated, resilient, and citizen-centric municipal spaces. Thus, in a series of studies, it was found that empowerment and inclusion of citizens can unlock smart-sustainable municipal development that emphasizes environmental protection and social equity rather than just reinforcing neoliberal forms.

While both IoT technologies and smart city frameworks hold immense potential, their successful integration requires a deep understanding of their intricacies, challenges, and synergies. This paper embarks on a systematic exploration of these areas by conducting a thorough literature review and analysis of relevant studies. The objective is to shed light on the current state of research, identify key trends, and provide insights into the evolving landscape of IoT and smart city implementations within municipalities (Karuri-Sebina & Guya 2020).

Through the examination of literature on IoT technologies, communication protocols, machine learning applications, and real-world smart city initiatives, this study seeks to contribute to the growing body of knowledge in the field. By unveiling the intersection of these two transformative domains, this paper aims to offer a comprehensive perspective on how IoT frameworks and smart city implementations can jointly shape the municipal landscape, improve the quality of life for residents, and foster sustainable municipal development (HamaMurad et al. 2021).

Table 1. Key Dimensions and Primary Indicators for Smart Cities, quoted from Giffinger and Kramar (2022).

Domain	Indicators
Smart Mobility	Public Transport, Technology and Innovation, Sustainability and Environmental Impact and Clean-Energy Transport
Smart People	Education, Population, Inclusion and Creativity
Smart Living	Healthcare, Security and Safety, Culture, and Housing
Smart Governance	E-governance, Internet and Wi-Fi Coverage and Disaster Preparedness
Smart Economy	Start-ups, International Collaboration, Low Poverty Rate and Job Opportunities
Smart Environment	Green Spaces, Air Quality and Low Pollution, Energy Use, Water, Waste Generation and Biodiversity

Planning continues with defining the key research question that will guide this project since the research question influences several steps throughout the entire process. The paper aims to answer the following research question: *What does the literature say about the extent to which and in what ways smart cities frameworks are deployed within municipalities initiatives globally?* Finally, the objectives of the work reported here were for example: To investigate the landscape of IoT frameworks for smart cities and analyze their technological components and communication protocols. To critically assess the applications of machine learning in securing IoT devices and enhancing smart city functionality. To explore different smart city implementation frameworks adopted by municipalities worldwide and analyze their key dimensions for urban development.

2   Methods

This research work follows systematic literature review principles to achieve its purpose and its corresponding objectives, which are presented in the Introduction. Systematic literature review, also known as systematic review, aim at identifying, evaluating, and interpreting all available research relevant to a particular problem, topic, or phenomenon that needs to be addressed, as described by Kitchenham and Brereton (2013). Similarly, systematic literature review is defined as a systematic, explicit, comprehensive, and reproducible method for identifying, evaluating, and synthesizing the body of completed and recorded work of researchers, scholars, and practitioners in Okoli and Schabram (2010). Considering Kitchenham and Brereton (2013) approach to systematic literature review, the present study adopted the systematic literature review methodology to aid in the planning, searching, screening, extracting data, and synthesizing and reporting of findings.

2.1 Searching Strategy for the Literature

To provide a comprehensive picture, various academic databases, digital libraries, and search engines from both academic and open access sources have been explored as the first step. Among the databases investigated were some renowned online scientific databases, including Web of Science, Scopus, Institute of Electrical and Electronics Engineers Xplore, AIS (Association for Information Systems Library), Springer, and ProQuest, as well as popular ones like Semantic Scholar, MDPI, and Google Scholar. After several challenges encountered regarding the other mentioned databases, the study adopted the adoption of Google Scholar and Web of Science databases. According to Falagas et al. (2008), Google Scholar has some weaknesses, such as the lack of accurate citations and duplicate references, among others. As an example, they contend that its free access makes it a valuable option for researchers on a budget, integration of the PubMed database, and ability to list the most cited articles first cannot be ignored. The Web of Science, on the other hand, offers better graphics and more detailed citation statistics. Using Boolean search strategies AND, OR operators and advanced search strings, the following search strings were used to retrieve the required research articles from databases.:

((Smart Cities AND Internet of Things) OR (Machine learning AND Internet of Things)), ((IoT AND IoT Security Attacks) OR (machine learning AND IoT AND security)), (Security Issues in IoT Layers AND Security Issues in IoT Architecture), ((IoT AND Smart cities frameworks globally) OR (IoT frameworks AND Smart cities frameworks) OR (smart cities)) and ((IoT) OR (IoT AND municipality)).

Among the papers considered were those published between 2010 and 2023 in journals and conferences which included the previously mentioned phrases and related user studies. The aim was to gather scholarly papers published within the last decade, to ensure that the materials collected are as up-to-date and relevant as possible, and coincide with the digital age, as well as the era when IoT and smart cities are becoming increasingly prevalent.

2.2 Criteria for the Selection

According to Table 2, the results of the articles search process were thoroughly screened using pretest criteria for inclusion and exclusion. Firstly, with the inclusion criteria, considerable effort was made to ensure that only published articles from 2010 until 2023 were considered. This was to ensure that interventions and applications related to IoT frameworks and smart cities frameworks for municipalities were kept up to date and relevant. Secondly, all articles were carefully assessed to make sure they were peer-reviewed articles and that they discuss IoT frameworks implementation in terms of smart cities. Lastly, only those articles that met the criteria of relevance, uniqueness, available online and written in English language were included in the review.

In relation to exclusion criteria, the abstracts of many papers revealed that they did not actually make use of IoT frameworks or did not apply smart city framework concepts to municipalities and were therefore eliminated. Also excluded were studies that did not discuss IoT frameworks, municipalities, smart cities frameworks, or cyber security in smart cities. A similar exclusion applied to IoT framework studies that are not available online, peer-reviewed journals, distinctive, book chapters, or conference papers, and smart cities frameworks within municipalities.

Table 2. Inclusion and exclusion criteria for primary studies.

Inclusion	Exclusion Criteria
Addressed the implementation of IoT and smart cities frameworks for municipalities	Addressed related concepts that were not IoT and smart cities frameworks for municipalities
Published between 2010 and 2023	Published before 2010
Written in English	Non-English publications
Peer-reviewed journal, conference papers and seminal works	Papers that are not peer-reviewed (e.g., proposals, theses, related publications such as book chapters and ongoing projects)
Original publications	Duplicated papers
Publications available online	Publications not available online

2.3 Results of the Search

To collect the relevant papers, the search was performed based on both identified databases as well as keywords, as shown in Fig. 1. It was found that Google Scholar and Web of Science (WoS) databases listed 310 and 120 academic publications respectively and 430 in total, searched between January 2022 and June 2023. 176 articles were excluded from this analysis, since these papers are frequently indexed in multiple databases. Thus, a total of 254 articles were resulting from 218 articles from Google Scholar and 36 articles from WoS. The review of these articles exposed 72 duplicates out of 254, which were removed. This resulted in 182 articles being identified during the identification process. Screening the titles, abstracts, introductions, and conclusions of 182 articles led to the researcher finding that a further 82 articles were of no relevance to the current study. There were therefore 100 remaining articles. During the eligibility stage, all 100 articles were carefully reviewed. This review does not cover 61 of these articles because they address different issues regarding IoT and smart cities frameworks implementations. In summary, 39 articles qualified as meeting the inclusion criteria and definitions in this systematic review.

An overview of the distribution of selected papers by their publication year is shown in Fig. 2. According to the diagram, municipalities are increasingly using IoT frameworks and smart cities frameworks to implement projects, and the two concepts had not been combined until 2010. A significant increase in publications was observed after 2014, with 17 significant papers published in 2021 and 8 in 2022.

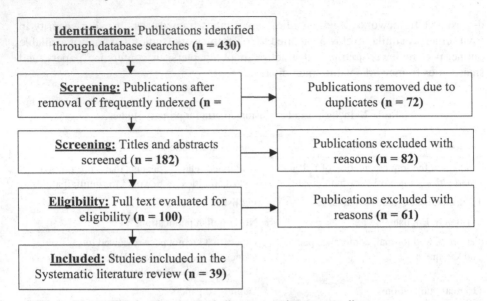

Fig. 1. The systematic literature review process diagram

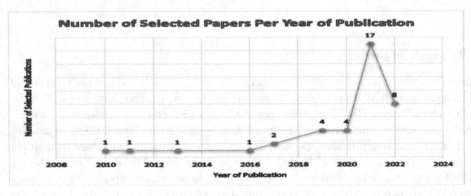

Fig. 2. Line chart depicting the number of published papers per year.

2.4 Extraction of Data

This phase involved analyzing each article individually to determine final inclusion in the systematic literature review, which was a two-part process called screening and eligibility. Each article was screened independently, but a great deal of effort was put into minimizing bias. To determine whether the obtained articles addressed the objective of this study, the first step screening involved scanning the titles, abstracts, introductions, and lastly conclusions. For the second stage eligibility, comprehensive literature reviews were conducted by skimming through and subsequently reading full texts to collect relevant data for a systematic literature review. To carefully assess each study, the following quality assurance criteria were used: what was the application area? What type of data was collected? What methodology was used? Where was the study based? and what type of study was carried out? Accordingly, the articles were categorized according to two primary topics: IoT frameworks for Smart Cities and Smart city implementation frameworks within municipalities globally. Finally, excel spreadsheets were developed to record data systematically and accurately. Table 3 lists the articles classified in each area.

Table 3. Articles classified according to each topic area.

Internet of Things	Implementations Globally
D'Amico, Szopik-Depczyńska, Dembińska, and Ioppolo (2021)*	Bastidas, Bezbradica and Helfert (2017)
Din, Guizani, Rodrigues, Hassan, and Korotaev (2019)	Bellini, Nesi, and Pantaleo (2022)
El-Hajj, Fadlallah, Chamoun and Serhrouchni (2019)	Cisco (2022)
Ghaffar, Alshahrani, Fayaz, Alghamdi, and Gwak (2021)	D'Amico, Szopik-Depczyńska, Dembińska, and Iop-polo (2021)*
Hussain, Hussain, Hassan, and Hossain (2020)	Gheisari, Najafabadi, Alzubi, Gao, Wang, Abbasi, and Castiglione
Imran, Zaman, Imtiaz, Fayaz, and Gwak (2021)	Giffinger and Kramar (2022)
Li, Yang, Yang, Wang, and Wu (2019)	HamaMurad, Jusoh and Ujang (2021)
	Hamzah, Adnan, Daud, Alias, and Dali (2016)
Majid, Habib, Javed, Rizwan, Srivastava, Gadekallu, and Lin (2022)	Khatibi, Wilkinson, Baghersad, Dianat, Ramli, Suhatril, Javanmardi and Ghaedi (2021)
Mokoena and Sebola (2020)	Kourtit (2021)
Nurlan, Zhukabayeva, Othman, Adamova, and Zhakiyev (2021)	Moustaka, Maitis, Vakali, and Anthopoulos (2021)
Qin, Hu, Liu, Witherell, Wang, Rosen, Simpson, Lu and Tang (2022)	Razmjoo, Gandomi, Mahlooji, Garcia, Mir-jalili, Rezvani, Ah-madzadeh and Memon (2022)*
Razmjoo, Gandomi, Mahlooji, Garcia, Mirjalili, Rezvani, Ahmadzadeh and Memon (2022)*	Muthaiyah and Zaw (2021
Shrestha (2022)	Tang, Jayakar, Feng, Huiping and Peng (2019)Tzioutziou and Xenidis (2021)
Siokas, Tsakanikas, and Evangelos (2021)	
Vaigandla, Karne and Rao (2021)	

*   There is more than one issue covered by articles marked with an asterisk.

2.5 Synthesis

A thematic synthesis approach was adopted for this systematic literature review since it covered an array of academic disciplines and fields. A data synthesis approach such as this can be particularly useful for identifying, analyzing, synthesizing, and reporting multidisciplinary datasets, as Cruzes and Dyba (2011) argue. A detailed conclusion was drawn based on the analysis of recurring themes across the included studies to accomplish the study's main objectives. To compare the perspectives and findings from the included studies, the identified IoT frameworks and smart cities framework implementations were seen as starting points. To develop distinct themes from the selected studies, IoT frameworks and smart cities framework implementation and interventions in municipalities served as common concepts.

3   Results

It appears that the number of publications relating to smart cities has increased between 2010 and 2022, according to this systematic literature review. Technological advancements and smart cities are likely to have contributed to this drastic increase. An unusually constant number of publications related to IoT, and smart cities frameworks for municipalities have been published between 2019 and 2023. Following are the sections that detail various applications and aspects of IoT frameworks and smart cities frameworks papers for municipalities. These include IoT frameworks for smart cities and smart city implementations frameworks within municipalities globally.

3.1   IoT Frameworks for Smart Cities

According to the results of this segment, examples of IoT implementations within smart cities fall into a variety of categories, including IoT technologies and machine learning in IoT. By comparing them based on goals, methods, and chronology, this systematic literature review provides a critical analysis of these categories.

IoT Technologies. Some existing IoT technologies and communication protocols utilized to connect physical devices and virtual objects identified by Vaigandla et al. (2021) and Ghaffar et al. (2021) include the following: Bluetooth and Bluetooth Low Energy, which, in contrast to other wireless protocols, is found to be a reliable, afford-able, and low-power protocol that is widely implemented for short-range communications in IoT systems for transferring data wirelessly (Vaigandla et al. 2021). Developed as a global connectivity standard for IoT data networks, Zigbee is a wireless technology allowing for low-cost, security, high scalability, and low-power wireless net-work connections, according to Imran et al. (2021). Similarly, Long Range Wide Area Network (LoRaWAN) is referred to as Low-power, Low-Cost, Mobile, and Secure Wireless Technology by Vaigandla et al. (2021) and Ghaffar et al. (2021), this is due to its ability to optimize for scalable networks with millions of wireless devices with low power consumption and very low cost. Furthermore, it can detect signals under the noise level over long distances, allowing IoT applications to detect low-strength signals.

Machine Learning in IoT. The application of machine learning to real-life problems has become a focus of computer scientists in recent years. As defined by Broderick et al. (2023), machine learning involves detecting patterns in data and using the patterns to predict future data, uncertainty, or making decisions under a certain set of circumstances. For instance, to estimate the transmission effect of innovation, Li et al. (2019) used machine learning. A study by Qin et al. (2022) unearthed that machine learning technologies have demonstrated their effectiveness in a variety of industries, such as computer science, aviation, healthcare, and manufacturing. Corporate management currently uses machine learning methods to optimize production processes (Li et al. 2019). Hussain et al. (2020) identify some of the security related real-world applications that are applicable within machine learning, namely but not limited to: 1) Machine Learning (ML)-based authentication and access control in IoT, 2)ML-based attack detection and mitigation in IoT, 3)ML-based techniques to address Denial of Service (DoS) and Distributed Denial of Service (DDoS) attacks in IoT, 4) ML-based IDS in IoT, and 5)ML-based malware analysis in IoT.

3.2 Smart City Implementation Frameworks Within Municipalities Globally

The application of new technologies has, according to Giffinger and Kramar (2022) become crucial in many dimensions, requiring an increase in energy efficiency, the mitigation of emissions, and facilitating new forms of communication. Hence, many municipalities are embracing new technologies as important tools for municipal development to meet the new challenges comprehensively. The goals, objectives, and indicators of the municipality should be the focus of this (Bastidas, et al. 2017).

European Smart Cities (ESC) approach is a concept developed by Giffinger et al. in 2007 and adapted by Giffinger and Kramar (2022). The duo highlighted six key domains (Smart Mobility, Smart People, Smart Living, Smart Governance, Smart Economy, and Smart Environment) of municipal development in this study. As a result of the ESC approach, municipalities can know how to coordinate better, draw mutual lessons, and exchange best-practice examples (Moustaka et al. 2021), while also tracking progress and planning improvements over time (Giffinger & Kramar 2022). This was to gather insights on data-driven individual city profiles to provide a clear picture of understudied municipalities at different levels of detail, thus effectively leading stakeholders to uncover what smartness means (HamaMurad et al. 2021). The empirical evidence was not only provided in relation to municipality profiles in a differentiated manner because of this approach, but also groups of cities with similar profiles were identified. Likewise, Razmjoo et al. (2022) completed, categorized, and examined research publications based on extensive review of literature that focuses on the problems and solutions of several key sectors that have significant implications for smart cities development, such as public transportation, utilities, street lighting, waste management, public safety, and smart parking. As part of the analysis, they looked at important cities within the European Union (Paris, London, Copenhagen, Barcelona, Amsterdam, and Oslo) and in the USA (Boston, New York, and San Francisco) that are relevant to the IoT. Razmjoo, et al. (2022) provide a summary of a few core ideas related to the three dimensions, presented in Table 4.

Table 4. IoT barriers and appropriate solutions for the development of smart cities, summarized from Razmjoo et al. (2022)

Sectors	Challenges Confronting Municipalities	IoT-led Solutions
Public transport	Private cars create noise in cities, citizens' transportation unmonitored and unsafe; traffic congestion increases CO2 emissions	Smartphones, monitoring sensors can assist in improving the quality of roads
Street lighting	The absence of sensor-equipped streetlights and the presence of defective streetlights	The use of sensors in streetlights, switch to reduce light output, and low-energy bulbs
Utilities	Fuel and electricity wasted, fuel and electricity expenses, smart meters and smart billing, consumption patterns, and limited consumption monitoring	Quality of services improvement by using smart meters, proper consumption patterns, and management services
Smart parking	Parking limited or non-existent, cars parked improperly on the street, and traffic narrows routes	Using drivers' smartphones or embedded sensors to determine location

Through a systematic literature review, D'Amico et al. (2021) created a Smart and Sustainable Logistics in Port Cities framework that holistically integrates a variety of enabling factors, domains, and goals that frame smart and sustainable logistics in port cities. The proposed framework highlights the following enabling factors: Both (1) Ecosystems and (2) Organizations, emphasize an active role and organizational flexible interaction among various stakeholders, including port managers, planners, administrators, entrepreneurs, citizens, couriers, students, port authorities, road and rail transport companies, technology companies, financial institutions, etc., (3) Data and Security, and (4) Policy and Regulation, underscore the complexity of digital technologies, with security levels that encompass data and information from multiple stakeholders. Accordingly, (5) Finance and Funding highlights the importance of tax leverage to trigger worthy logistics developments. Through the support of technology companies such as Cisco, IBM, SAP, Ericsson and Huawei, an in-depth analysis of several pioneering port cities was carried out, including Amsterdam, Rotterdam, Antwerp, Los Angeles, Valencia, Hanan, Montreal, Stockholm, Hamburg, Singapore, etc. (D'Amico et al. 2021). For example, with Cisco Edge Intelligence software, the Port of Rotterdam used a multi-cloud dashboard to analyze, interpret, and refine data from patrol vessels to improve logistics and operations (Tang et al. 2019; D'Amico et al. 2021). Likewise, as part of IBM's logistics infrastructure solutions, sensors, IoT platforms and Augmented Intelligence platforms were integrated into the logistic infrastructures, enabling them to collect, process and provide data on weather, berth availability, and other statistics (Tang et al. 2019; D'Amico et al. 2021). In addition to improvements in information collection, processing, monitoring, analysis and evaluation, the framework enhances the smartness and sustainability of urban and industrial processes by harmoniously integrating mobility, economy, governance, environment, telecommunications, health, safety, and so on, as according to D'Amico et al. (2021) and Bellini et al. (2022).

In their study Muthaiyah and Zaw (2021) developed Overarching Autonomous Learning Framework (OALF), in this model they consider key layers such as acquisition, data, business, and application architectures. Their model addresses the making of a city to being smart, with an emphasis on business architecture having autonomy and self-learning capabilities. According to the pair, smart capabilities need to be able to reason and act independently with very little or no human involvement, to be deemed smart, a device or system must be capable of thinking independently in difficult situations. Two technologies, IoT and artificial intelligence (AI), made this possible (Muthaiyah & Zaw 2021). They used this framework to measure the interest in promoting assessment of social well-being in addition to psychological and emotional well-being among others.

Moreover, Hamzah et al. (2016) created Reconciled Smart City Assessment framework that incorporates, enforces, and improves, the validity of its operations as seen in Fig. 3. In essence, the authors revealed that the development of this framework provides a thorough insight into the assessment of a municipality's smartness that should be based on: (1) six imperative smart city dimensions; (2) the unique main functions of the specific city; (3) the planned/prioritized smart initiatives; (4) actual requirements of the city stakeholders and subsequently smart initiatives of the inhabitants (Hamzah et al. 2016). Meanwhile the concept of municipal resilience can be seen as serving the goal of sustainability and has a similar operational framework as that of smart cities, in terms of operationalizing resilience, the smart city model appears to be instrumental given the importance of the technological dimension (Tzioutziou & Xenidis 2021; Khatibi et al. 2021). According to the finding, resilience thinking is the theoretical background, while smart city solutions are the design requirements, pointing out the specific roles of the two concepts in the emerging integrated framework (Tzioutziou & Xenidis 2021).

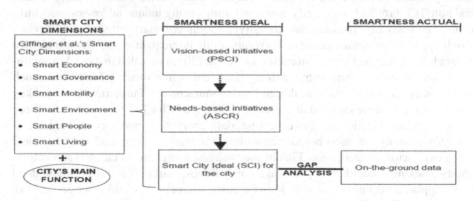

Fig. 3. The Reconciled Smart City Assessment Framework (RSCAF)

4 Discussions

This systematic literature review shows that digital technologies and their frameworks play a fundamental role in the development of a variety of systems and infrastructures for the efficient and effective development of municipalities in different parts of the world as smart city initiatives are undertaken. Such technologies allow better resource management, increased public safety, and improved quality of life for citizens. They also provide opportunities for more sustainable and resilient municipalities. Moreover, they enable data-driven decision making and optimize municipal operations. Despite the study focusing on smart cities frameworks, two major areas where recent scholars have looked were identified, namely: IoT framework implementation for smart cities and smart city implementation frameworks in municipalities around the world.

4.1 IoT Framework Implementation for Smart Cities

According to Vaigandla et al. (2021), Bluetooth and Bluetooth Low Energy are a great tool for smart cities since they are free from open firmware and hardware standards, and they have many advantages over their competitors when it comes to short-range wireless data transmission in IoT systems. BLE has many advantages, including the fact that it does not support open firmware and hardware standards. Zigbee provides seamless Internet connectivity throughout municipalities without sacrificing power or cost, Imran et al. (2021) found. It also enables easy control of thousands of devices, which adds value to the municipalities. In the same light, El-Hajj et al. (2019) on the other hand highlighted the importance to maintenance of data privacy, confidentiality, and secure communication to the IoT architecture, and indicated that sharing of details should respect the privacy of the individual through enforcement of the privacy regulations regarding the collection of data and its storage in memory. As Ghaffar and colleagues (2021) noted, the important aspect of IoT platforms is using the transmission control protocol (TCP) and non-TCP protocols to identify connected things using unique addresses to identify them. The study also revealed that diversifying complementary networks and devices also helps to accelerate adoption; in this regard, both municipalities must have their own network capacities and usage. Moreover, Qin et al. (2022) revealed that machine learning technologies have demonstrated their effectiveness in a variety of industries, such as computer science, aviation, healthcare, and manufacturing. Furthermore, several key security features were outlined in Din et al. (2019) study for IoT-based devices. These features include identity and authentication, data encryption, and secure communication. Additionally, the authors recommend implementing a secure update system, and using two-factor authentication. Finally, they suggest using threat detection and vulnerability assessments to identify potential security issues. Nurlan et al. (2021) highlighted those applications embedded with sensors, software, networks and other related IoT technologies like smart surveillance systems, smart homes and so forth, are associated with smart cities. They emphasized that these technologies provide valuable insights into how municipalities operate, how resources are used, and how citizens interact with their environment. Moreover, they recommend that this data can be used to create more efficient services, improve public safety, and reduce energy consumption. Essentially, Siokas et al. (2021) suggested that policymakers should consider the uncertain social, financial, and cultural environment and the needs of all stakeholders when formulating a policy strategy. Furthermore, they considered the potential implications of the policy on minority groups and vulnerable communities. The policy should also be tailored to the specific needs and conditions of each city. Finally, they posit that policy should be implemented in a way that promotes sustainability and protects human rights.

4.2 Smart City Implementation Frameworks in Municipalities Around the World

The paper identifies and classifies smart city concepts that are used by different municipalities to answer the research question. As well as meeting requirements for smart city development compared to conventional municipal processes, these concepts must also be compatible with the smart city vision and be compatible with it. We then analyze the relationships between these concepts and smart city goals. Several studies included in this research, including Giffinger and Kramar's European Smart Cities (ESC) developed in 2007 and adapted by the same authors in 2022, have identified six key domains of city development (Smart Mobility, Smart People, Smart Living, Smart Governance, Smart Economy, and Smart Environment). Based on the ESC approach, the Planning for Energy Efficient Cities (PLEEC) project has demonstrated that basic conditions like population densities are entirely different in a city like Jyväskylä (a city surrounded by lakes and forests), as opposed to Santiago de Compostela (a touristic Spanish city with a historic center) or Stoke-on-Trent (a city with a long industrial history). Considering that comparing cities based on single characteristics always requires consideration of regional and historic contexts, it is highly advisable not to discuss single indicators, but only the average of combined characteristics at the domain or field level, for a more reliable basis on which strategic policy advice can be formulated. To complement the studies included in this systematic literature review, similar studies have also been conducted in other contexts. For example, after evaluating their framework, namely Smart and Sustainable Logistics in Port Cities, D'Amico, et al. (2021) concluded that the framework can provide the following smart cities areas indicators benefits: Ecosystems and organizations, stakeholders flexible interaction, including port managers, planners, administrators, entrepreneurs, citizens, students, transportation companies, technology companies, financial institutions, data and security, policy, and regulation. As such, a collaborative approach is important for the development of a smart city in the sense of a smart sustainable city, according to them. Similarly, Razmjoo et al. (2022) analyzed, and categorized research publications based on an extensive literature review addressing several key sectors with significant impacts on the development of smart cities, including public transportation, utilities, street lighting, waste management, public safety, and smart parking. Also, a comprehensive analysis of several pioneering port cities, including Amsterdam, Rotterdam, Antwerp, Los Angeles, Valencia, Hanan, Montreal, Stockholm, Hamburg, Singapore, was conducted with the support of technology companies such as Cisco, IBM, SAP, Ericsson, and Huawei (D'Amico et al. 2021). Furthermore, Muthaiyah and Zaw (2021) emphasized the importance of the OALF framework that they say can be used to measure the interest in promoting assessment of social well-being in addition to psychological and emotional well-being among others. Kourtit (2021) recommended that CSF framework can likely assess the livability conditions of but not limited to districts, neighborhoods, or even individual streets in modern cities, to obtain a detailed picture of sustainable, healthy, and safe urban environments, as well as achievements related to health, safety, cohesion, and governance. Gheisari et al. (2021) illustrated how with OBPP, IoT-based smart city devices can be subjected to privacy rules, and abnormal conditions are identified while heterogeneity issues are addressed. Hamzah et al. (2016) examined and investigated RSCAF in further detail, concluding that resilient and smart city frameworks have some fundamental characteristics in common, enabling the development of a unified concept rather than two separate approaches to municipal development.

5 Conclusions

The paper reviews IoT frameworks and smart city frameworks implementation in global municipalities. An elaborate systematic literature review was conducted to highlight the identification, screening, eligibility, and inclusion process, and the results were discussed in detail. Among the 430 works initially extracted, 39 were selected for research based on their relevance to the research question. As a result of the survey of these articles, it is concluded that the integration of IoT frameworks and smart city frameworks will result in a range of innovative smart city concepts, including smart living, smart people, smart economy, governance, and mobility, which are aimed at quality-of-life improvement for citizens. Most of these contributions are noteworthy; however, more work is needed to optimize them, thus opening new research opportunities for those interested in the topic. Through such research, new technologies can be developed, and existing ones can be improved, providing industry and academia with new opportunities. There are no doubt that industrial and academic fields will have a close connection despite any tension. It is shown that smart cities that adopt these technologies and remain interconnected are susceptible to a host of cyber security threats, including privacy and confidentiality breaches, physical threats, vulnerabilities in systems and applications, malware injections, denial of service (DoS), malicious insider threats, and data leaks. Furthermore, these efforts may also provide insights into interdisciplinary approaches that can be applied to other fields.

References

Abdelaziz, A., Mesbah, S.: A review of disaster management frameworks. J. Manage. Inform. Dec. Sci. **24**, 1–10 (2021)

Bastidas, V., Bezbradica, M., Helfert, M.: Cities as Enterprises: a Comparison of Smart City Frameworks Based on Enterprise Architecture Requirements. International conference on smart cities, Cham (2017)

Bellini, P., Nesi, P., Pantaleo, G.: IoT-enabled smart cities: a review of concepts, frameworks and key technologies. Appl. Sci. **12**(3), 1607 (2022)

Broderick, T., Gelman, A., Meager, R., Smith, A.L., Zheng, T.: Toward a taxonomy of trust for probabilistic machine learning. Sci. Adv. **9**(7), 3999 (2023)

Cisco. What Is a Wireless LAN? (2022). https://www.cisco.com/c/en/us/products/wireless/wir eless-lan.html. Accessed 28 June 2022

Cruzes, D.S., Dyba, T.: Recommended steps for thematic synthesis in software engineering. In: 2011 International Symposium on Empirical Software Engineering and Measurement, pp. 275–284 (2011)

D'Amico, G., Szopik-Depczyńska, K., Dembińska, I., Ioppolo, G.: Smart and sustainable logistics of Port cities: a framework for comprehending enabling factors, domains, and goals. Sustain. Cities Soc. **69**, 102801 (2021)

Desdemoustier, J., Crutzen, N., Giffinger, R.: Municipalities' understanding of the Smart City concept: an exploratory analysis in Belgium. Technol. Forecast. Soc. Chang. **142**, 129–141 (2019)

Din, I.U., Guizani, M., Rodrigues, J.J., Hassan, S., Korotaev, V.V.: Machine learning in the Internet of Things: Designed techniques for smart cities. Futur. Gener. Comput. Syst. **100**, 826–843 (2019)

El-Hajj, M., Fadlallah, A., Chamoun, M., Serhrouchni, A.: A Survey of Internet of Things (IoT) authentication schemes. Sensors **19**(5), 1141 (2019)

Ezugwu, A. E., et al.: A novel smart city-based framework on perspectives for application of machine learning in combating COVID-19. BioMed Research International, Landon (2021)

Falagas, M.E., Pitsouni, E.I., Malietzis, G.A., Pappas, G.: Comparison of pubmed, scopus, web of science, and google scholar: strengths and weaknesses. FASEB J. **22**(2), 338–342 (2008)

Ghaffar, Z., Alshahrani, A., Fayaz, M., Alghamdi, A.M., Gwak, J.: A topical review on machine learning, software defined networking, internet of things applications: research limitations and challenges. Electronics **10**(8), 880 (2021)

Gheisari, M., et al.: OBPP: an ontology-based framework for privacy-preserving in IoT-based Smart City. Futur. Gener. Comput. Syst. **123**, 1–13 (2021)

Giffinger, R., Kramar, H.: Benchmarking, profiling and ranking of cities: the 'European Smart Cities' Approach. In: Sylvie, A., Manish, P. (eds.) Place-based Performance Metrics in Building Sustainable Cities. Routledge, Oxfordshire, New York (2022)

Hajjaji, Y., Boulila, W., Farah, I.R., Romdhani, I., Hussain, A.: Big data and IoT-based applications in smart environments: a systematic review. Comput. Sci. Rev. (2021)

HamaMurad, Q.H., Jusoh, N.M., Ujang, U.: Smart city framework reconcile. Open Int. J. Inform. **9**(1), 60–67 (2021)

Hamzah, H., Adnan, Y.M., Daud, M.N., Alias, A., Dali, M.M.: A smart city assessment framework. Jurnal Teknologi **72**(1), 1–6 (2016)

Holmes, W., Bialik, M., Fadel, C.: Artificial Intelligence in Education: Promises and Implications for Teaching and Learning. The Center for Curriculum Redesign, Boston (2019)

Hussain, F., Hussain, R., Hassan, S.A., Hossain, E.: Machine learning in IoT security: current Solutions and Future challenges. IEEE Commun. Surv. Tutor. **22**(3), 1686–1721 (2020)

Imran, M., Zaman, U., Imtiaz, J., Fayaz, M., Gwak, J.: Comprehensive survey of IoT, machine learning, and blockchain for health care applications: a topical assessment for pandemic preparedness, challenges, and solutions. Electronics **10**(20), 2501 (2021)

Karie, N.M., Sahri, N.M., Yang, W., Valli, C., Kebande, V.R.: A review of security standards and frameworks for IoT-based smart environments. IEEE Access **9**, 121975–121995 (2021)

Karuri-Sebina, G., Guya, J.: Discussion paper on a south African approach to smart, sustainable cities and settlements. South African Cities Network (2020)

Keshavarzi, G., Yildirim, Y., Arefi, M.: Does scale matter? an overview of the "Smart Cities" literature. Sustain. Cities Soc. **74**, 103151 (2021)

Khatibi, H., et al.: The resilient–smart city development: a literature review and novel frameworks exploration. Built Environ. Project Asset Manage. (2021)

Kiran, M.B., Wynn, M.G.: The Internet of Things in the corporate environment: cross-industry perspectives and implementation issues. Handbook of Research on Digital Transformation, Industry Use Cases, and the Impact of Disruptive Technologies, pp. 132–148 (2022)

Kitchenham, B., Brereton, P.: A systematic review of systematic review process research in software engineering. Inf. Softw. Technol. **55**(12), 2049–2075 (2013)

Kourtit, K.: City intelligence for enhancing urban performance value: a conceptual study on data decomposition in smart cities. Asia-Pacific J. Region. Sci. **5**(1), 191–222 (2021)

Lai, C.S., et al.: A review of technical standards for smart cities. Clean Techn. **2**(3), 290–310 (2020). https://doi.org/10.3390/cleantechnol2030019

Li, Y., Yang, L., Yang, B., Wang, N., Wu, T.: Application of interpretable machine learning models for intelligent decision. Neurocomputing **333**, 273–283 (2019)

Majid, M., et al.: Applications of wireless sensor networks and Internet of Things Frameworks in the industry revolution 4.0: a systematic literature review. Sensors **22**(6), 2087 (2022)

Mehmood, Y., Ahmad, F., Yaqoob, I., Adnane, A., Imran, M., Guizani, S.: Internet-of-Things-based smart cities: recent advances and challenges. IEEE Commun. Mag. **55**(9), 16–24 (2017)

Mokoena, B.T., Sebola, J.P.: A multi criteria decision urban development framework for land expropriation in south africa: a strategic approach. Int. Arch. Photogram. Remote Sens. Spatial Inform. Sci. **43**, 399–407 (2020)

Moustaka, V., Maitis, A., Vakali, A., Anthopoulos, L.G.: Urban data dynamics: a systematic benchmarking framework to integrate crowdsourcing and smart cities' standardization. Sustainability **13**(15), 8553 (2021)

Muthaiyah, S., Zaw, T.O.K.: Autonomous and adaptive learning architecture framework for smart cities. In: Dash, S.S., Das, S., Panigrahi, B.K. (eds.) Intelligent Computing and Applications, pp. 461–471. Springer, Singapore (2021)

Nurlan, Z., Zhukabayeva, T., Othman, M., Adamova, A., Zhakiyev, N.: Wireless sensor network as a mesh: vision and challenges. IEEE Access **10**, 46–67 (2021)

Okoli, C., Schabram, K.: A guide to conducting a systematic literature review of information systems research. Sprouts: Working Papers on Inform. **10**(26) (2010). http://sprouts.aisnet.org/10-26

Plessis, D.D., Wood, E.: Ramaphosa's Smart City dream becomes 'Reality in the Making.' IMIESA **46**(6), 18–20 (2021)

Qin, J., et al.: Research and application of machine learning for additive manufacturing. Addit. Manuf. **52**, 102691 (2022)

Razmjoo, A., et al.: An investigation of the policies and crucial sectors of smart cities based on IoT application. Appl. Sci. **12**(5), 2672 (2022)

Shrestha, B.: What Is the Difference Between Cat-M1 and NB-IoT? (2022) https://www.iotforall.com/what-is-the-difference-between-cat-m1-and-nb-iot. Accessed 27 June 2022

Siokas, G., Tsakanikas, A., Evangelos, S.: Implementing Smart City strategies in Greece: appetite for success. Cities **108**, 102938 (2021)

Tang, Z., Jayakar, K., Feng, X., Huiping, Z., Peng, R.X.: Identifying smart city archetypes from the bottom up: a content analysis of municipal plans. Telecommun. Policy **43**(10), 101834 (2019)

Tzioutziou, A., Xenidis, Y.: A Study on the integration of resilience and smart city concepts in urban systems. Infrastructures **6**(2), 24 (2021)

Ullah, F.: A beginner's guide to developing review-based conceptual frameworks in the built environment. Architecture **1**(1), 5–24 (2021)

Vaigandla, K.K., Karne, R.K., Rao, A.S.: A study on IoT technologies, standards and protocols. IBMRD's J. Manage. Res. **10**(2), 7–14 (2021)

Accessibility Features for Augmented Reality Indoor Navigation Systems

Frank Samson[1]([✉]), Mussa Ally Dida[1], Judith Leo[1], Deogratias Shidende[2], Godfrey Naman[1], and Sabine Moebs[2]

[1] Nelson Mandela African Institution of Science and Technology, Arusha, Tanzania
{samsonfr,mussa.ally,judith.leo,godfrey.naman}@nm-aist.ac.tz
[2] Duale Hochschule Baden-Württemberg (DHBW), Heidenheim, Germany
{deogratias.shidende,sabine.moebs}@dhbw-heidenheim.de

Abstract. Accessibility plays a pivotal role in developing technological tools that strive to promote inclusivity for users of all abilities. Regrettably, many technological advancements have traditionally disregarded accessibility, assuming homogeneous user abilities or treating it as an afterthought. This paper endeavors to provide a review of accessibility considerations on augmented reality indoor navigation systems, to enhance navigational experiences in indoor learning environments. To achieve this, interviews were conducted with visually impaired individuals, to investigate their existing methods of navigation, identify challenges they face, and uncover potential accessibility features that could enhance indoor navigation systems. Additionally, a literature review was undertaken to explore various accessibility features in the context of indoor navigation systems, including localization technologies and pathfinding algorithms employed in indoor navigation applications. Finally, the paper concludes by offering insights into accessibility features specifically tailored for individuals with visual impairments, to facilitate efficient indoor navigation.

Keywords: Augmented Reality · Indoor Navigation · Accessibility · Visual Impaired

1 Introduction

Individuals with vision and hearing impairments encounter substantial challenges when utilizing indoor navigation systems. It is of supreme importance to incorporate inclusive accessibility features into these systems, thereby significantly enhancing their usability and functionality for people with disabilities [1]. However, the absence of accessibility features in indoor navigation systems implemented in higher learning environments, ultimately leads to significant navigation difficulties for individuals with impairments, hindering their ability to navigate their surroundings with ease [2, 3]. Navigation systems play a crucial role in assisting individuals in moving from one location to another. While outdoor navigation systems have their complexities, indoor navigation systems pose

© ICST Institute for Computer Sciences, Social Informatics and Telecommunications Engineering 2024
Published by Springer Nature Switzerland AG 2024. All Rights Reserved
M. Masinde et al. (Eds.): AFRICATEK 2023, LNICST 520, pp. 37–53, 2024.
https://doi.org/10.1007/978-3-031-63999-9_3

more significant challenges [4]. Challenges of indoor navigation systems are associated with various factors ranging from the complexity of the building map, security concerns, and mostly the technology for its implementation. Technologies for navigation such as Global positioning systems (GPS) are commonly used for outdoor navigation and provide users with accurate position, navigation, and timing information, effectiveness may be limited in indoor environments or areas with obstructed signals [5]. Ultra-wideband (UWB) is a short-range radio technology utilizing radio waves to measure the distance between devices and offers high-precision location tracking with an accuracy ranging from 10 to 30 cm [6, 7]. Infrared technology utilizes tags that emit signals, which can be received and read to identify the source and position of the tagged object. It is commonly used for object tracking or identifying specific locations [7] Also, Wi-Fi, Bluetooth, and Zigbee wireless communication protocols that employ radio fingerprinting and RSSI (Received Signal Strength Indication) propagation can also be utilized for localization purposes [5]. Near-field communication (NFC), which is a technology that enables short-range communication between devices, can be used in combination with other technologies for context-aware applications [8]. Additionally, Radio Frequency Identification (RFID) is a technology that utilizes tags and readers to identify and track objects[7] and an inertial measurement unit (IMU) is a device that integrates sensors such as accelerometers and gyroscopes by analyzing the data from these sensors to determine the position and orientation of an object in space [9–12]. The challenges posed by these technologies are accuracy, coverage, cost, power consumption, and localization principles, which are fundamental to the success of indoor navigation systems [13] Augmented reality (AR), which uses 3-D visualization in real-time access, has been used in different areas, including indoor navigation [14–16] with a promising way of handling these challenges. It has brought precision, localization principles, and accuracy to navigation systems [17]. Consequently, enormous AR applications for indoor navigation with various functionalities have been developed in higher learning environments [16]. However, most of these AR applications do not have accessibility features that support indoor navigation for users with various impairments [18]. The objective of this paper is to review and examine the accessibility features of AR indoor navigation systems in higher learning environments. The remaining sections of this paper cover various related works, encompassing explanations of accessibility, localization technologies, distance distance-finding algorithms, as well as a comprehensive overview of indoor navigation tools. Subsequently, the methodologies employed for identifying accessibility features in an indoor navigation system are outlined. The paper then proceeds with a section dedicated to presenting the obtained results and engaging in a detailed discussion regarding the findings. Finally, the paper concludes by summarizing the main results achieved throughout the study.

2 Related Works

2.1 Accessibility

Accessibility means offering a person with a disability the opportunity to acquire the same information, engage in the same interactions, and enjoy experience as a person without a disability in an equally effective and equally integrated manner [19]. For individuals with disabilities, accessibility entails the use of techniques or technology that enables them to effectively engage and interact with their surroundings. In an educational setting, accessibility means providing education for all individuals, irrespective of their abilities [20]. Scholars have proposed frameworks and models for accessibility for people with disabilities emphasizing accommodation, assistive technology, and inclusion as approaches to address accessibility [16, 21]. Universal design is a framework that places a strong emphasis on accessibility, usability, and inclusion for people with disabilities [22]. This framework can be effectively adopted when developing solutions across various sectors, ensuring that accessibility features specific to each sector are incorporated[23]. Disabilities can vary, resulting in diverse ways for individuals to interact. Various fields have implemented accessibility features by enabling technologies to cater to different disabilities [24, 25]. Visual-disabled people are used to having assistance from a third-party person to help them easily navigate inside a building or with the help of a white cane [26]. Assistive technologies enable individuals with disabilities to embrace life from different perspectives. Technological advancements, such as indoor navigation systems, have significantly enhanced mobility for visually disabled people. These innovations foster a more inclusive environment, enabling disabled individuals to navigate their surroundings and interact with the world more effectively [27–30]. However, in many cases, accessibility is often an afterthought during the development of enabling tools [31, 32]. Assuming that all users are of single ability and can use these technologies leads to numerous accessibility challenges. The development of indoor navigation applications for learning environments should prioritize accessibility as a fundamental feature. This ensures that the application accommodates the needs of all users and promotes social inclusivity and accessibility.

2.2 Localization Technologies

Localization is finding the location of people and places inside the building [17]. Various mechanisms have been employed by indoor navigation systems to track the location of the user's device within a building [5]. These mechanisms are designed to improve accuracy and minimize complexity in navigation systems, with variations in accuracy and implementation cost. Simultaneous Localization and Mapping (SLAM) is one such mechanism that leverages device localization, offering a cost-effective and relatively straightforward implementation. To shed light on the diverse approaches and technologies employed to achieve accurate and efficient tracking in indoor environments, we present various principles and technologies used for location tracking in indoor navigation. Additionally, Table 1 shows a summary of localization methods with their challenges.

2.2.1 Ultra-Wideband

Ultrawideband (UWB) is an emerging technology that holds promise for real-time localization in indoor navigation systems. Its immunity to interference from other signals and low power consumption make it an attractive option [33, 34]. Various arrival mechanisms are employed to calculate the distance between two points on a map, with time of flight and angle of arrival serving as signal strength indicators for precise localization [6]. To achieve better accuracy in tracking location using UWB technology, a minimum of three receivers is typically required, and maintaining a clear line of sight is crucial as depicted in Fig. 1. In tracking the location of UWB tags, pulses of signal are emitted from the tags containing information such as time of flight, timestamp and identification. These signals are then detected by nearby nodes, and the captured data is sent to the source for processing. By determining the measurements of the time of flight, it is possible to obtain the distance and orientation within a short range. However, the usage of UWB can still be hindered by electric interference, which will result in signal weakness.

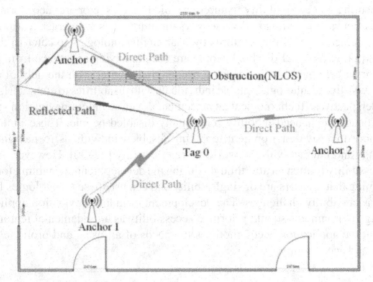

Fig. 1. UWB based on time of arrival. Source [33]

2.2.2 Simultaneous Localization and Mapping (SLAM)

SLAM algorithm helps the devices to realize their position relative to the surrounding environment. The algorithm provides real-time updates to the maps while tracking the location of the device in it. SLAM is made with two fundamental components that include localization and mapping, localization is for determining the device's location on the map, and mapping is for creating the representation of the surroundings relative to where the device is [35]. Various techniques, such as feature-based, keyframe-based, and direct methods, are employed in the SLAM for its effectiveness [36]. In indoor navigation systems, SLAM algorithms rely on different sensor modalities commonly found in these systems, such as RGB cameras, depth sensors, and inertial sensors found in the device containing the system [37]. The algorithm is widely used in tracking the position of an agent on a map for indoor navigation systems and in aligning the virtual object and real object for a better experience [38, 39]. For instance, AR Foundation which is a software development framework developed for AR application development across multiple platforms, supports SLAM for localization and mapping while developing AR applications for navigation [40]. SLAM has two forms or methods for its implementation, which are Visual SLAM (VSLAM) and Laser SLAM (LSLAM) [41]. Visual SLAM uses three-dimensional vision to map and locate objects when neither the surroundings nor the sensor's location is known [42]. Laser SLAM estimates the position and orientation of the robot by utilizing LIDAR sensors to collect 3D point clouds of the surroundings. To measure the distance to objects in the surrounding environment, LiDAR measures the time it takes for beams to reflect to the sensor after they are emitted [43]. Several studies have shown SLAM effective in indoor navigation systems [44–46]. However, the algorithm still faces challenges in indoor environments, such as dynamic objects, low-texture areas, and occlusions [47].

2.2.3 Bluetooth

Bluetooth is the wireless connection type that supports short-range connection up to 10 m between two or more devices [5]. This connection can be managed using software installed in these devices which makes Bluetooth one of the technologies that are used for indoor navigation systems for device location tracking inside the building [48]. Suggested Bluetooth low energy (BLE) which checks the signal strength from the nodes using the receive signal strength indicator (RSSI) and then triangulates the source to identify the position of the device [49]. Implemented BLE indoor navigation using ES P32-Node MCU, different indoor systems have been implemented using the network of Bluetooth devices [50]. BLE has also been used as a location-tracking mechanism together with AR for the implementation of indoor navigation systems [51]. However, the implementation cost of Bluetooth-based indoor navigation systems is higher and there is a challenge signal in mobility caused by interference posed by signals from other devices [5, 50].

2.3 Distance Calculation Algorithms

Navigating from one point of interest to another requires distance calculation and path identification toward that distance. Distance calculation algorithms for identifying short-est paths are used for indoor navigation systems to help the system user navigate from point to point while serving time. Several machine learning-based algorithms, including 2-Nearest Neighbor (2-NN), K-nearest Neighbor, and Euclidean distance-based Weighted K-Nearest Neighbor, have been proposed for predicting the shortest desti-nation point [58–60]. Dijkstra's algorithm is another algorithm used to find the shortest path between points on an indoor navigation system [61, 62]. The algorithm works on weighted points, where each edge has a non-negative weight then it starts by assigning a tentative distance value to every point in the map. The initial point has a distance of 0, and all other nodes are assigned a distance of infinity [61]. A-star algorithm is a search algorithm that searches for the shortest path between the initial point on the map to the destination point on the map, this algorithm has been deployed on indoor navigation for path determination [5, 63]. However, the selection of algorithm to use depends on its efficiency, accuracy, and specific requirements of the system, A-star algorithm is widely suitable for real-time navigation systems. The algorithm works by finding the shortest path, trimming unnecessary paths during the search, and reducing the number of nodes visited which improves its efficiency performance.

Table 1. Localization technologies

Authors	Localization technology	Strength	Challenges
[52]	Bluetooth Beacons	- Precise location indoors - Low power consumption	- Limited range - Requires additional hardware
[53, 54]	VSLAM	- Extract-able Semantic Information - Low Cost - Simple Structure and Diversified Installation Mode	- Dependency on Ambient Light - Computational Load - Dynamic Sensor Performance
[55]	LSLAM	- High Map Construction Precision - Intuitive Map Construction without Cumulative Error	- Limited Detection Range - installation with Structural Requirements - Map Lacks Semantic Information
[56]	UWB	- High accuracy in positioning - Works in indoor environments - Immune to signal interference - Provides real-time tracking	- Requires additional hardware - Limited range - Affected by obstacles
[57]	Wi-Fi Positioning	- Works well indoors - No additional hardware needed	- Accuracy depends on WIFI infrastructure - Limited where there is no power

2.4 Indoor Navigation Tools

Numerous indoor navigation tools have been designed and developed by different researchers, using various algorithms, technology, techniques for localization tracking, and calculation of distance between two different points [64, 65]. However, the challenges for most indoor navigation systems remain, such as accuracy, cost, localization principles, power consumption for the application, and security concerns [5]. Augmented reality and virtual reality have brought about another dimension for data visualization and the creation of virtual spaces for different applications, including navigation systems [66]. The visualization is extended more in augmented reality and gives a better experience by presenting data in 2D and 3D in the field of vision [15]. Different technologies for indoor navigation have been used with implementation on the web platform, mobile phone, or both [67]. Developed an AR indoor navigation application that utilized semantic web technologies to display routes and provide contextual information about the user's environment relied on detecting environmental characteristics and illumination conditions to accurately track user movements [68]. Developed a mobile-based AR indoor navigation system that utilized 2D maps as its foundation relying on 3D markers to aid in navigation [3]. Developed an augmented reality indoor navigation system that leverages Lbeacon and Bluetooth technology on smartphones to determine a user's initial position relative to their destination [69]. Developed a marker-based navigation application using the Vuforia engine. The app uses markers placed at different entrances of a building to identify the user's initial location and destination. However, this developed application did not include accessibility features for people with different impairments, such as vision impairment and hearing impairment, Table 2 shows a feature summary of indoor navigation systems developed using augmented reality.

Table 2. Summary of augmented reality indoor navigation tools

Authors	Problem Addressed	Proposed Solution	Limitations
[68]	Indoor navigation using a 2D map	A marker-based augmented tool for indoor navigation	- The application didn't have 3D features - No accessibility features for people with an impairment
[67]	An Indoor Navigation Methodology for Mobile Devices by Integrating AR and Semantic Web	indoor navigation systems based on Augmented Reality and Semantic Web technologies to present navigation instructions and contextual information about the environment	- Didn't include positioning methods such as Wi-Fi or Bluetooth wireless networks - No accessibility features
[69]	a marker-based navigation application	marker-based navigation application using the Vuforia engine	- Rescanning of the marker each time while moving from one place to another
[3]	an augmented reality indoor navigation system	an indoor navigation system that leverages Lbeacon and Bluetooth technology on smartphones to determine a user's initial position relative to their destination	- Not accessibility features - No advertisements of the surrounding environment - Not enough 3D objects to visualize and enhance the navigation experience
[4]	Indoor navigation system	AtlasMap platform that uses technology fusion that utilizes multiple phone sensors integrated with augmented reality for localization	- Improvement in direction agent - No accessibility features

3 Results

This section presents the findings of the study, which include the results obtained from both the document review and the interviews conducted. The subsection includes results form from document reviews and interviews.

3.1 Indoor Navigation Systems

A literature review was conducted by accessing major research databases to explore articles published about accessibility features in indoor navigation systems. The literature study aimed to answer two research questions: What are accessibility features reported in indoor navigation systems? Which technologies have been used in these indoor navigation systems? To answer these questions, the search query was designed as follows: - Keywords used were "accessibility features", "indoor navigation systems", "Augmented reality navigation", "And Visual impairments". The search query was performed in June 2023, by including relevant keywords and query expressions to generate meaningful and relevant results retrieved from databases such as IEEE, MDPI, and Science Direct with a focus on English-written articles published between 2020 and 2023. This approach aimed to ensure that the study encompassed the most recent research in the field of indoor navigation systems, with a particular emphasis on accessibility features and the incorporation of technologies such as augmented reality navigation. Articles were picked considering their relevance to the study, Table 3 provides the summary of reviewed indoor navigation systems. The review revealed several findings that emphasize the importance of incorporating specific features to address the needs of individuals with vision impairment. Route planning functionalities tailored to their requirements can greatly assist in effective navigation [70]. High contrast and auditory interfaces, along with haptic feedback, enhance accessibility by providing visual and tangible signals [71]. Voice assistance and routed self-learning apps offer personalized and real-time guidance, promoting independent navigation [72]. Audio feedback, text-to-speech (TTS) technology, and voice recognition further augment accessibility by providing spoken instructions, converting text to speech, and enabling hands-free interaction with the system during navigation [73–76]. Suggested an indoor navigation system that makes use of the Atlasmap platform with automated object detection capabilities. Specifically designed for individuals with visual impairments, this system includes a crucial feature of object detection to assist visually impaired individuals during navigation. To enhance the inclusivity and accessibility for users with disabilities, a specialized route specification system was developed that caters to the specific needs and impairments of different users, ensuring they can navigate through the environment with ease and independence [77].

3.2 Interview

The open-ended interview was conducted with five participants, who are leaders representing four centers for people with visual impairments, three males and two females aged between 30 to 45, who have vision disabilities to access the essence of accessibility features for indoor navigation systems. The interview was conducted with ethical consideration and participants were asked for their consent to participate in the interview. Based on the interview responses, it became evident that an ideal application for vision-disabled individuals should offer several key features. Firstly, it should provide accurate and clear audio directions that aid in seamless navigation between various locations. Additionally, the application should possess the capability to distinguish between objects and people, ensuring that navigation instructions are specific and relevant. Moreover, it should be equipped to identify the user's current location and provide notifications regarding the surrounding environment. To enhance convenience, the application should support voice commands as input for navigation instructions. Lastly, it should offer detailed and precise audio guidance, accompanied by comprehensive descriptions, to ensure accurate and reliable navigation assistance. A summary of accessibility features responses that were provided during the interview is shown in Table 4.

Table 3. Summary of reviewed indoor navigation systems

Author	Accessibility feature	Technology used	Localization	Path finding algorithm
[71]	High contrast and auditory interfaces		Bluetooth beacon	K-mean clustering
[72]	vision, sound, and haptics	AR framework	BLE beacons	Beacon fingerprints
[73]	voice interaction, audible warning	ARCore Depth API, Jimmy To's Speech and Text asset for Unity	SLAM	Geolocation and Geocoding APIs
[74]	text-to-speech	iBeacons	Bluetooth module	iBeacons
[75]	Text to Speech, speech recognition	YOLO V3 Algorithm	computer vision	Wearable device
[76]	Object detection	Augmented reality, YOLOv3 object	IndoorAtlas	IndoorAtlas
[78]	turn-by-turn	open-source map data	EMBC22 BLE beacons	Received Signal Strength Indicator (RSSI)
[77]	acoustic and haptic feedback, route planning	Augmented reality	smartphone sensors	GraphHoppe

Table 4. Summary of Interview Response

	Gender	Response
Person one	Male	The application should provide audio assistance during navigation
Person two	Male	The application should have an audio feature and object detection
Person three	Female	The application should have audio feature and voice command functionality
Person four	Female	The application should describe navigation guidance using voice
Person five	Male	The application should be able to tell me where I am using audio

4 Discussion and Conclusion

Our research findings demonstrate that accessibility is an essential feature in application development. Specifically, when designing for individuals with visual impairment, gathering requirements directly from them plays a crucial role in meeting their specific needs and ensuring inclusivity [72]. Voice assistance feedback greatly aided blind individuals in navigating easily by guiding the navigation process using turn-by-turn [78] navigation was an essential feature, as it provided clear directions when reaching the next destination. This aligns with the importance of audio features for providing directions during navigation for individuals with vision impairments. The features suggested such as route planning, high contrast, auditory interface, and haptic feedback vividly show they can help and increase accessibility for visually impaired people in indoor navigation [71, 77]. Additionally, object identification during navigation emerged as a crucial feature that enhances mobility for people with vision disabilities [76].

Incorporating a localization technique in the indoor navigation system helps determine the user's location on the map, facilitating effective navigation. SLAM techniques, which employ localization and mapping algorithms, can be beneficial in accurately identifying the user's location on the map and enabling seamless navigation within indoor spaces as utilized by [73]. Bluetooth beacons have emerged as an additional method for localization by triangulating signals from multiple beacons within indoor spaces to determine users' location and destination [71, 72, 74, 78]. This technique encounters challenges such as signal hindrance, which can sometimes result in inaccuracies during navigation compared to SLAM which relies on a combination of sensor data, such as visual input from cameras or depth information from depth sensors to construct a map of the surroundings.

This paper proposes incorporating specific accessibility features to cater to the needs of visually impaired individuals, ensuring reliable guidance during indoor mobility. These features include utilizing sound and audio assistance to provide auditory cues and directions. By integrating sound-based navigation cues, visually impaired users can receive real-time guidance and feedback, enabling them to navigate the learning environment more effectively. Additionally, for efficient pathfinding within the AR indoor navigation system, we propose utilizing the A-star algorithm which ensures that visually impaired individuals can navigate through the learning environment along the shortest feasible path. A general overview of the proposed system diagram is presented in Fig. 2. The diagram presents an overview of the system, which can be accessed through a user interface on a mobile device such as a smartphone or tablet using the device's camera and creating a digital representation of navigation instructions. The system utilizes the SLAM algorithm to determine the positioning and orientation of the device within the environment, enabling it to localize itself and map the surroundings. To begin using the system, the user enters their destination from their current location. The system then calculates the shortest path and provides feedback to the user for seamless navigation. As the user starts their journey, the system offers visual and audio feedback, providing direction based on the user's preferences. Upon reaching the destination, the user can access a view on the availability status, which is updated by the staff from the web portal.

The analysis of accessibility features for indoor navigation systems, focusing on individuals with vision impairment, has led to recommendations aimed at facilitating their ease of navigation. One of the predominant challenges encountered when incorporating accessibility features into indoor navigation systems is the tendency to assume users' abilities during the design and development stages. Conducting requirement elicitation directly from individuals with disabilities before system development is imperative as it promotes the inclusion of accessibility features and ensures usability for all. Utilizing localization technology and path-finding algorithms holds significant importance in the successful development and implementation of indoor navigation systems. Lastly, it is recommended that more studies should continue to demonstrate the effectiveness of accessibility in AR systems, particularly within learning environments.

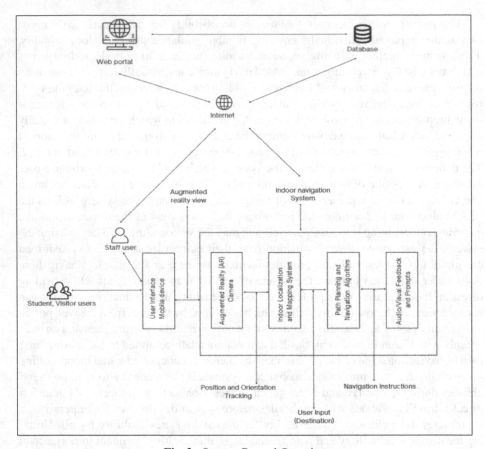

Fig. 2. System General Overview

References

1. Fichten, C., Olenik-Shemesh, D., Asuncion, J., Jorgensen, M., Colwell, C.: Higher education, information and communication technologies and students with disabilities: An overview of the current situation. In: Seale, J. (ed.) Improving Accessible Digital Practices in Higher Education: Challenges and New Practices for Inclusion, pp. 21–44. Springer International Publishing, Cham (2020). https://doi.org/10.1007/978-3-030-37125-8_2
2. Gur Güdükbay, U.: Guido: Augmented Reality for Indoor Navigation Using Commodity Hardware. https://doi.org/10.1109/IV51561.2020.00123
3. Huang, B.-C., Hsu, J., Chu, E.T.-H., Wu, H.-M.: ARBIN: augmented reality based indoor navigation system. Sensors **20**(20), 5890 (2020). https://doi.org/10.3390/s20205890
4. Ng, X.H., Lim, W.N.: Design of a mobile augmented reality-based indoor navigation system. In: 4th international symposium on multidisciplinary studies and innovative technologies, ISMSIT 2020 - Proceedings (2020). https://doi.org/10.1109/ISMSIT50672.2020.9255121
5. Verma, P., Agrawal, K., Sarasvathi, V.: Indoor navigation using augmented reality, pp. 58–63 (2020). https://doi.org/10.1145/3385378.3385387

6. Krishnaveni, B.V., Reddy, K.S., Reddy, P.R.: Indoor tracking by adding IMU and UWB using unscented kalman filter. Wirel. Pers. Commun. **123**(4), 3575–3596 (2022). https://doi.org/10. 1007/S11277-021-09304-3/TABLES/1
7. Arbula, D., Ljubic, S.: Indoor localization based on infrared angle of arrival sensor network. Sensors (Basel) **20**(21), 1–32 (2020). https://doi.org/10.3390/S20216278
8. Olenik, S., Lee, H.S., Güder, F.: The future of near-field communication-based wireless sensing. Nat. Rev. Mater. **6**(4), 286–288 (2021). https://doi.org/10.1038/s41578-021-00299-8
9. Kuang, Y., Yang, Y., Yao, Y.C., Lu, H., Yang, H., Zhang, X.: A method for constructing indoor navigation networks based on IMU. In: ICSMD 2021 - 2nd International Conference on Sensing, Measurement and Data Analytics in the Era of Artificial Intelligence (2021). https://doi.org/10.1109/ICSMD53520.2021.9670853
10. Saez, Y., Montes, H., Garcia, A., Munoz, J., Collado, E., Mendoza, R.: Indoor navigation technologies based on RFID systems to assist visually impaired people: a review and a proposal. IEEE Lat. Am. Trans. **19**(8), 1286–1298 (2021). https://doi.org/10.1109/TLA.2021. 9475859
11. Niroshika, U.A.A., Weerakoon, W.A.G.C.: An interactive virtual mobile assistance for indoor navigation using wireless Beacon technology. In: 2020 IEEE 2nd International Conference on Artificial Intelligence in Engineering and Technology (IICAIET), pp. 1–6. IEEE (2020). https://doi.org/10.1109/IICAIET49801.2020.9257870
12. Elsanhoury, M., et al.: Precision positioning for smart logistics using ultra-wideband technology-based indoor navigation: a review. IEEE Access **10**, 44413–44445 (2022). https:// doi.org/10.1109/ACCESS.2022.3169267
13. Zafari, F., Gkelias, A., Leung, K.K.: A survey of indoor localization systems and technologies. IEEE Commun. Surv. Tutor. **21**(3), 2568–2599 (2019). https://doi.org/10.1109/COMST.2019. 2911558
14. Cankiri, Z.T., Marasli, E.E., Akturk, S., Sonlu, S., Gudukbay, U.; Guido: augmented reality for indoor navigation using commodity hardware. In: Proceedings of the International Conference on Information Visualisation, vol. 2020-September, pp. 708–713 (2020). https://doi.org/10. 1109/IV51561.2020.00123
15. Ekanayake, I., Gayanika, S.: Data visualization using augmented reality for education: a systematic review. In: ICBIR 2022 - 2022 7th International Conference on Business and Industrial Research, Proceedings, pp. 533–537 (2022). https://doi.org/10.1109/ICBIR54589. 2022.9786403
16. Romli, R., Razali, A.F., Ghazali, N.H., Hanin, N.A., Ibrahim, S.Z.: Mobile Augmented Reality (AR) marker-based for indoor library navigation. IOP Conf. Ser. Mater. Sci. Eng. **767**(1), 012062 (2020). https://doi.org/10.1088/1757-899X/767/1/012062
17. Al Delail, B., Weruaga, L., Zemerly, M.J., Ng, J.W.P.: Indoor localization and navigation using smartphones augmented reality and inertial tracking. In: Proceedings of the IEEE International Conference on Electronics, Circuits, and Systems, pp. 929–932 (2013). https://doi.org/10. 1109/ICECS.2013.6815564
18. Eligi, I.: ICT accessibility and usability to support learning of visually-impaired students in Tanzania (2017)
19. Handy, S.: Is accessibility an idea whose time has finally come? Transp. Res. D Transp. Environ. **83**, 102319 (2020). https://doi.org/10.1016/J.TRD.2020.102319
20. Matonya, M.D.: Disability and access in higher education in tanzania: experiences of women with disabilities. Incl. Soc. Just. 293–319 (2020). https://doi.org/10.1163/978900443448 6_020
21. Burgstahler, S., Havel, A., Seale, J., Olenik-Shemesh, D.: Accessibility frameworks and models: Exploring the potential for a paradigm shift. In: Improving Accessible Digital Practices in Higher Education: Challenges and New Practices for Inclusion, pp. 45–72 (2020). https:// doi.org/10.1007/978-3-030-37125-8_3/COVER

22. Heiman, T., Coughlan, T., Rangin, H., Deimann, M.: New designs or new practices? Multiple perspectives on the ICT and accessibility conundrum. In: Seale, J. (ed.) Improving Accessible Digital Practices in Higher Education: Challenges and New Practices for Inclusion, pp. 99–115. Springer International Publishing, Cham (2020). https://doi.org/10.1007/978-3-030-371 25-8_5

23. Burgstahler, S., Havel, A., Seale, J., Olenik-Shemesh, D.: Accessibility frameworks and models: Exploring the potential for a paradigm shift. In: Seale, J. (ed.) Improving Accessible Digital Practices in Higher Education: Challenges and New Practices for Inclusion, pp. 45–72. Springer International Publishing, Cham (2020). https://doi.org/10.1007/978-3-030-371 25-8_3

24. Garcia Carrizosa, H., Sheehy, K., Rix, J., Seale, J., Hayhoe, S.: Designing technologies for museums: accessibility and participation issues. J Enabl. Technol. 14(1), 31–39 (2020). https://doi.org/10.1108/JET-08-2019-0038/FULL/PDF

25. Das, M., Piper, A.M., Gergle, D.: Design and evaluation of accessible collaborative writing techniques for people with vision impairments. ACM Trans. Comput.-Hum. Interact. 29(2), 1–42 (2022). https://doi.org/10.1145/3480169

26. Khan, A., Khusro, S.: An insight into smartphone-based assistive solutions for visually impaired and blind people: issues, challenges and opportunities. Univers. Access Inf. Soc. 20(2), 265–298 (2021). https://doi.org/10.1007/S10209-020-00733-8/TABLES/15

27. Constantinescu, A., Müller, K., Loitsch, C., Zappe, S., Stiefelhagen, R.: Traveling to unknown buildings: accessibility features for indoor maps. In: Miesenberger, K., Kouroupetroglou, G., Mavrou, K., Manduchi, R., Covarrubias Rodriguez, M., Penáz, P. (eds.) Computers helping people with special needs. ICCHP-AAATE 2022. LNCS, vol. 13341. Springer, Cham (2022). https://doi.org/10.1007/978-3-031-08648-9_26/TABLES/1

28. Cheraghi, S.A., Fusco, G., Coughlan, J.M.: Real-time sign detection for accessible indoor navigation. J. Technol. Pers. Disabil. 9, 125 (2021). Accessed June 17 2023. /pmc/articles/PMC8331194/

29. Melfi, G., Baumgarten, J., Müller, K., Stiefelhagen, R.: An audio-tactile system for visually impaired people to explore indoor maps. In: Miesenberger, K., Kouroupetroglou, G., Mavrou, K., Manduchi, R., Covarrubias Rodriguez, M., Penáz, P. (eds.) Computers helping people with special needs. ICCHP-AAATE 2022. LNCS, vol. 13341. Springer, Cham (2022). https://doi.org/10.1007/978-3-031-08648-9_16/TABLES/2

30. Chan, C.S., Shek, K.F., Agapito, D.: The sensory experience of visitors with hearing impairment in Hong Kong Wetland Park based on spatial sensory mapping and self-reported textual analysis. Landsc. Urban Plan. 226, 104491 (2022). https://doi.org/10.1016/J.LANDUR BPLAN.2022.104491

31. Basha-Jakupi, A., Morina, G., Hasimja, D.: J. Access. Design for All. J. Accessib. Des. All 13(1), 94–112 (2008). https://doi.org/10.17411/JACCES.V13I1.369

32. Kamaghe, J., Luhanga, E., Kisangiri, M.: The challenges of adopting m-learning assistive technologies for visually impaired learners in higher learning institution in Tanzania. Int. J. Emerg. Technol. Learn. 15(01), 140–151 (2020). https://doi.org/10.3991/IJET.V15I01.11453

33. Yao, S., Su, Y., Zhu, X.: High precision indoor positioning system based on UWB/MINS integration in NLOS condition. J. Electric. Eng. Technol. 17(2), 1415–1424 (2022). https://doi.org/10.1007/S42835-021-00957-5/TABLES/2

34. Awarkeh, N., Cousin, J.-C., Muller, M., Samama, N.: Improvement of the angle of arrival measurement accuracy for indoor UWB localization. J. Sens. 2020, 1–8 (2020). https://doi.org/10.1155/2020/2603861

35. Li, C., Zhang, X., Gao, H., Wang, R., Fang, Y.: Bridging the gap between visual servoing and visual SLAM: a novel integrated interactive framework. IEEE Trans. Autom. Sci. Eng. 19(3), 2245–2255 (2022). https://doi.org/10.1109/TASE.2021.3067792

36. Karkus, P., Cai, S., Hsu, D.: Differentiable SLAM-net: learning particle SLAM for visual navigation, pp. 2815–2825 (2021)
37. Ayyalasomayajula, R., et al.: Deep learning based wireless localization for indoor navigation. Proc. Ann. Int. Conf. Mobile Comput. Network. MOBICOM **20**, 214–227 (2020). https://doi.org/10.1145/3372224.3380894
38. Zhu, H., Zhao, P., Liu, S., Ke, X.: A SLAM based navigation system for the indoor embedded control mobile robot. In: 2020 4th International Conference on Robotics and Automation Sciences, ICRAS 2020, pp. 22–27 (2020). https://doi.org/10.1109/ICRAS49812.2020.9134926
39. Wu, R., Pike, M., Chai, X., Lee, B.G., Wu, X.: SLAM-ING: a wearable SLAM inertial navigation system. In: Proceedings of IEEE Sensors, vol. 2022-October (2022). https://doi.org/10.1109/SENSORS52175.2022.9967255
40. Chaudhry, T., Juneja, A., Rastogi, S.: AR foundation for augmented reality in unity. Int. J. Adv. Eng. Manage. **3**, 662. https://doi.org/10.35629/5252-0301662667
41. Dai, Y., Wu, J., Wang, D., Watanabe, K.: A review of common techniques for visual simultaneous localization and mapping. J. Robot. **2023** (2023). https://doi.org/10.1155/2023/8872822
42. Qin, Y., Yu, H.: A review of visual SLAM with dynamic objects. Indust. Robot ahead-of-print, no. ahead-of-print (2023). https://doi.org/10.1108/IR-07-2023-0162/FULL/PDF
43. Pan, S., Xie, Z., Jiang, Y.: Sweeping robot based on laser SLAM. Procedia Comput Sci **199**, 1205–1212 (2022). https://doi.org/10.1016/J.PROCS.2022.01.153
44. Long, R., Rauch, C., Zhang, T., Ivan, V., Lam, T.L., Vijayakumar, S.: RGB-D SLAM in indoor planar environments with multiple large dynamic objects. IEEE Robot Autom Lett **7**(3), 8209–8216 (2022). https://doi.org/10.1109/LRA.2022.3186091
45. Bajpai, A., Amir-Mohammadian, S.: Towards an indoor navigation system using monocular visual SLAM. In: Proceedings - 2021 IEEE 45th Annual Computers, Software, and Applications Conference, COMPSAC 2021, pp. 520–525 (2021). https://doi.org/10.1109/COMPSAC51774.2021.00077/VIDEO
46. Keitaanniemi, A., Rönnholm, P., Kukko, A., Vaaja, M.T.: Drift analysis and sectional postprocessing of indoor simultaneous localization and mapping (SLAM)-based laser scanning data. Autom. Constr. **147**, 104700 (2023). https://doi.org/10.1016/J.AUTCON.2022.104700
47. Giubilato, R., Sturzl, W., Wedler, A., Triebel, R.: Challenges of SLAM in extremely unstructured environments: the DLR planetary stereo, solid-state LiDAR, inertial dataset. IEEE Robot. Autom. Lett. **7**(4), 8721–8728 (2022). https://doi.org/10.1109/LRA.2022.3188118
48. Sumer, N.N., Atakli, N., Kucur, O.: Using RSSI-based bluetooth low energy for indoor location detection. In: 5th International Conference on Computer Science and Engineering, UBMK 2020, pp. 83–87 (2020). https://doi.org/10.1109/UBMK50275.2020.9219422
49. Sophia, S., Shankar, B.M., Akshya, K., Arunachalam, A.C., Avanthika, V.T.Y., Deepak, S.: Bluetooth low energy based indoor positioning system using ESP32. In: Proceedings of the 3rd International Conference on Inventive Research in Computing Applications, ICIRCA 2021, pp. 1698–1702 (2021). https://doi.org/10.1109/ICIRCA51532.2021.9544975
50. Alexandr, A., Anton, D., Mikhail, M., Ilya, K.: Comparative analysis of indoor positioning methods based on the wireless sensor network of bluetooth low energy beacons. In: 2020 International Conference Engineering and Telecommunication, En and T 2020 (2020). https://doi.org/10.1109/ENT50437.2020.9431286
51. Lee, H., et al.: Beacon-based indoor fire evacuation system using augmented reality and machine learning. In: Proceedings - 2022 6th IEEE International Conference on Robotic Computing, IRC 2022, pp. 87–90 (2022). https://doi.org/10.1109/IRC55401.2022.00023
52. Bencak, P., Hercog, D., Lerher, T.: Indoor positioning system based on bluetooth low energy technology and a nature-inspired optimization algorithm. Electronics **11**(3), 308 (2022). https://doi.org/10.3390/electronics11030308

53. Theodorou, C., Velisavljevic, V., Dyo, V., Nonyelu, F.: Visual SLAM algorithms and their application for AR, mapping, localization and wayfinding. Array **15**, 100222 (2022). https://doi.org/10.1016/J.ARRAY.2022.100222

54. Zhao, W., Sun, H., Zhang, X., Xiong, Y.: Visual SLAM combining lines and structural regularities: towards robust localization. IEEE Trans. Intell. Veh. 1–18 (2024). https://doi.org/10.1109/TIV.2023.3311511

55. Zhang, F., Liu, J., Kong, X., Sun, Y., Wu, Y., Li, L.: A navigation and mapping method for mobile robots based on 2D laser simultaneous localization and mapping algorithm **12791**, 68–72 (2023). https://doi.org/10.1117/12.3004677

56. Yang, J., Dong, B.S., Wang, J.: VULoc: accurate UWB localization for countless targets without synchronization. Proc. ACM Interact. Mobile Wear. Ubiquit. Technol. **6**(3), 1–25 (2022). https://doi.org/10.1145/3550286

57. Yue, Y., Zhang, Y., Chen, L., Chen, R.: Intelligent fusion structure for Wi-Fi/BLE/QR/mems sensor-based indoor localization. Remote Sens. **15**(5), 1202 (2023). https://doi.org/10.3390/rs15051202

58. Truong-Quang, V., Ho-Sy, T.: Maximum convergence algorithm for WiFi based indoor positioning system. Int. J. Electric. Comput. Eng. **11**(5), 4027 (2021). https://doi.org/10.11591/ijece.v11i5.pp4027-4036

59. Ninh, D.B., He, J., Trung, V.T., Huy, D.P.: An effective random statistical method for Indoor Positioning System using WiFi fingerprinting. Futur. Gener. Comput. Syst. **109**, 238–248 (2020). https://doi.org/10.1016/J.FUTURE.2020.03.043

60. Lee, G., Moon, B.-C., Lee, S., Han, D.: Fusion of the SLAM with Wi-Fi-based positioning methods for mobile robot-based learning data collection, localization, and tracking in indoor spaces. Sensors **20**(18), 5182 (2020). https://doi.org/10.3390/s20185182

61. Ramaneti, K., Mohanty, N., Kumaravelu, V.B.: IoT based 2D indoor navigation system using BLE beacons and Dijkstra's algorithm. In: 2021 12th International Conference on Computing Communication and Networking Technologies, ICCCNT 2021 (2021). https://doi.org/10.1109/ICCCNT51525.2021.9580047

62. Štancel, M., Hurtuk, J., Hulič, M., Červeňák, J.: Indoor atlas service as a tool for building an interior navigation system

63. Kasim, S., et al.: Indoor navigation using A* algorithm. Adv. Intell. Syst. Comput. **549** AISC, 598–607 (2017). https://doi.org/10.1007/978-3-319-51281-5_60/COVER

64. Hayward, S.J., van Lopik, K., Hinde, C., West, A.A.: A survey of indoor location technologies, techniques and applications in industry. Internet of Things **20**, 100608 (2022). https://doi.org/10.1016/J.IOT.2022.100608

65. Kunhoth, J., Karkar, A., Al-Maadeed, S., Al-Ali, A.: Indoor positioning and wayfinding systems: a survey. Hum.-centric Comput. Inform. Sci. **10**(1) (2020). https://doi.org/10.1186/s13673-020-00222-0

66. Liu, Z.J., Levina, V., Frolova, Y.: Information visualization in the educational process: current trends. Int. J. Emerg. Technol. Learn. **15**(13), 49–62 (2020). https://doi.org/10.3991/IJET.V15I13.14671

67. Rubio-Sandoval, J.I., Martinez-Rodriguez, J.L., Lopez-Arevalo, I., Rios-Alvarado, A.B., Rodriguez-Rodriguez, A.J., Vargas-Requena, D.T.: An indoor navigation methodology for mobile devices by integrating augmented reality and semantic web. Sensors **21**(16), 5435 (2021). https://doi.org/10.3390/s21165435

68. Cankiri, Z.T., Marasli, E.E., Akturk, S., Sonlu, S., Gudukbay, U.: Guido: augmented reality for indoor navigation using commodity hardware. In: 2020 24th International Conference Information Visualisation (IV), vol. 2020-September, pp. 708–713 (2020). https://doi.org/10.1109/IV51561.2020.00123

69. Martin, A., John Cheriyan, J.J., Ganesh, J.S., Jayakrishna, V.: Indoor navigation using augmented reality. EAI Endorsed Trans. Creat. Technol. **8**(26), 168718 (2021). https://doi.org/10.4108/eai.17-2-2021.168718

70. Fernando, N., McMeekin, D.A., Murray, I.: Route planning methods in indoor navigation tools for vision impaired persons: a systematic review. Disabil. Rehabil. Assist. Technol. **18**(6), 763–782 (2021). https://doi.org/10.1080/17483107.2021.1922522

71. Upadhyay, V., Balakrishnan, M.: Accessibility of healthcare facility for persons with visual disability. In: 2021 IEEE International Conference on Pervasive Computing and Communications Workshops and other Affiliated Events, PerCom Workshops 2021, pp. 87–92 (2021). https://doi.org/10.1109/PERCOMWORKSHOPS51409.2021.9430998

72. Nair, V., Olmschenk, G., Seiple, W.H., Zhu, Z.: ASSIST: Evaluating the usability and performance of an indoor navigation assistant for blind and visually impaired people. Assist. Technol. **34**(3), 289–299 (2020). https://doi.org/10.1080/10400435.2020.1809553

73. Hayath, T.M., Ravikumar, U.: Voice interactive indoor navigation application for the visually impaired on android phones with real-time obstacle detection using augmented reality with ARCore (2023). https://doi.org/10.36227/TECHRXIV.21897252.V1

74. Choi, B.C., Hareva, D.H., Lukas, S.: Design of blind community assistance devices with indoor positioning system technology. In: 2022 7th International Conference on Informatics and Computing, ICIC 2022 (2022). https://doi.org/10.1109/ICIC56845.2022.10006905

75. Iqbal, A., Akram, F., Ul Haq, M.I., Ahmad, I.: A comprehensive assistive solution for visually impaired persons. In: Proceedings - 2022 2nd international conference of smart systems and emerging technologies, SMARTTECH 2022, pp. 60–65 (2022). https://doi.org/10.1109/SMARTTECH54121.2022.00027

76. Du, P., Bulusu, N.: An automated AR-based annotation tool for indoor navigation for visually impaired people. In: ASSETS 2021 - 23rd International ACM SIGACCESS Conference on Computers and Accessibility (2021). https://doi.org/10.1145/3441852.3476561

77. Richter, J., et al.: Dynamic indoor navigation and orientation system for people with impairments. In: ACM International Conference Proceeding Series, pp. 473–477 (2020). https://doi.org/10.1145/3404983.3410000

78. Striegl, J., Felchow, J., Loitsch, C., Weber, G.: Accessible indoor orientation support by landmark-based navigation. In: Antona, M., Stephanidis, C. (eds.) Universal Access in Human-Computer Interaction: 17th International Conference, UAHCI 2023, Held as Part of the 25th HCI International Conference, HCII 2023, Copenhagen, Denmark, July 23–28, 2023, Proceedings, Part I, pp. 510–524. Springer Nature Switzerland, Cham (2023). https://doi.org/10.1007/978-3-031-35681-0_34

Data Security and Digital Technologies

Adopting Blockchain for Enhancing Data Security and Privacy in Service-Based Digital Platforms: A Case Study of a Distributed Application (Dapp) Global Mission Services

Yves Bizumuremyi[✉], Ntima Mabanza, and Muthoni Masinde

Department of Information Technology, Central University of Technology,
Free State Private Bag X20539, Bloemfontein 9300, South Africa
yvesbizu@gmail.com, {nmabanza,emasinde}@cut.ac.za

Abstract. This research aims to assess the viability of Blockchain technology for improving data security within service-based digital platforms. The methodology includes a literature review to identify blockchain trends and data security problems, surveys to assess possible platform use and user perceptions of online security, and the development of a digital platform prototype for Global Mission Services (GMS). Survey responses are compared statistically to determine user attitudes. The findings show that using the Blockchain-based distributed application (Dapp) platform improves data security significantly. There is significant interest in its implementation, particularly in light of growing concerns about online security. The GMS prototype demonstrates successful missionary service integration while overcoming accessibility barriers. These findings align with previous studies on Blockchain's security benefits, underlining its importance in service-based digital platforms and shared economies. The study emphasises Blockchain's potential in data security and proposes the Ethereum-based Dapp platform as a promising approach to improve security and stimulate greater adoption of service-based digital platforms.

Keywords: Blockchain Technology · Data Security · Shared Economy ·
Missionary Services · Distributed application (Dapp) · Digital Platform ·
Eswatini · South Africa

1 Introduction

A wide range of services are now easily accessible to a larger audience through digital channels because of the expansion of service-based digital platforms in recent years, which has changed how business is conducted [1, 2]. However, this quick transition to the digital age has also increased cyberattacks and unwanted access attempts. These digital platforms manage enormous volumes of private information, raising worries about data security and privacy violations. This problem is especially important in the context of

M. Masinde et al. (Eds.): AFRICATEK 2023, LNICST 520, pp. 57–70, 2024.
https://doi.org/10.1007/978-3-031-63999-9_4

missionary work in Eswatini and South Africa, where essential services are not accessible due to a lack of access to information about these services. Eswatini and South Africa were chosen as case study regions due to their practical accessibility, facilitating precise data collection and direct engagement with missionaries. This approach aims to better understand and address the challenges they encounter in accessing essential services. The paper suggests a novel approach to solve this problem: a decentralised application (Dapp) platform built on the Ethereum Blockchain. Increased confidentiality, immutability, and transparency are all features of this Dapp platform, which combines numerous missionary activities under one digital platform. This platform seeks to improve accessibility and effective resource use while reducing data security and privacy issues by utilising the benefits of blockchain technology.

Blockchain technology has drawn much attention from scientists in several research fields, and it is expected to be crucial in determining the direction of the upcoming wave of digital platforms [3]. Ethereum stands out among the different blockchain frameworks available for its potential to produce Dapps that are reliable, secure, and open [4]. Dapps are naturally resistant to traditional security problems like hacking and data breaches associated with centralised platforms because they are backed by smart contracts and distributed networks [5]. The data security and privacy issues that affect service-based digital platforms, especially those that cater to missionary activities, can be successfully solved by implementing a Dapp platform built on the Ethereum blockchain. This paper describes the creation of such a Dapp platform and emphasises how blockchain technology may be used to improve accessibility, transparency, data security, and privacy protection.

1.1 Objectives

The main objective of this study is to investigate the viability of using blockchain technology to enhance data security and accelerate the uptake and utilisation of service-based digital platforms in Eswatini and South Africa. The study aims to achieve the following specific objectives:

1. Conduct a literature review to identify current trends, concerns, ongoing blockchain technology and data security research, and missionary activities in South Africa and Eswatini.
2. Evaluate the effectiveness of the Dapp platform based on the Ethereum Blockchain in providing trust and data integrity for service-based digital platforms.
3. Develop a prototype of the GMS digital platform that integrates missionary services under a single platform to enhance access and efficient utilisation of the massive resources under the care of missionaries.

2 Literature Review

2.1 Missionaries' Activities

According to Jasmine Senior (2021), Missionaries love and follow Jesus wherever they are while demonstrating love for others throughout their lives. They help communities get better and grow by engaging in missionary work. All around the world, there are missionaries. According to David Maxwell (2014), missionary movements and activities significantly impacted the lives of numerous people worldwide, influencing the course of world history.

Among the many services provided by missionaries in Eswatini and South Africa are those related to health, education, the environment, accommodation and feeding people without homes, drug rehabilitation, helping refugees, early childhood development programs, managing orphanages, stopping human trafficking, communication, and neighbourhood improvement projects. This study focuses on the logistical services travelling missionaries provide to members of their networks as they trade services within their religious group. Many service-based internet platforms today provide specialised services, such as Airbnb and booking.com. Missionaries advertise their services and activities through personal websites or social media. The limitation of this is that the information is not easily found online. The study's findings will be demonstrated on a logistic travel system incorporating all the missionaries' services into one platform.

2.2 Blockchain Technology

Blockchain is a decentralised system built on the concepts of peer-to-peer networks and cryptographic fundamentals like asymmetric encryption and digital signatures. It allows users to communicate and record transactions without restriction or collaboration. In a blockchain architecture, it is possible to choose which valid information is added to the distributor and disseminated across the participant's network using a secure, associated database based on a consensus process [6].

2.2.1 Current Trends in Blockchain Technology and Its Applications in Data Security

The realm of data security has undergone a seismic shift. Thanks to the advent of blockchain technology, which has skyrocketed in popularity over the past several years. Numerous studies have confirmed this game-changing innovation's potent and fast-rising nature within the data protection sphere. This section will delve into many blockchain trends currently observed vis-à-vis applications for securing valuable information.

One of the prevailing trends in blockchain technology is the surge in its utilisation for Dapps. Essentially, Dapps are systemic solutions operating within blockchain networks with immutability, security, and transparency as key facets [7]. Considering Blockchain's dependability and versatility attributes, Dapps can be created effortlessly to safeguard sensitive information while reinforcing safe transactions among users from any location [8].

Another prevailing development in Blockchain Technology pertains to smart contract adoption. These computer programs, also known as self-executing contracts, present possibilities for process automation, such as enforcement and authentication of agreements [9]. Intermediaries or authorities are not required. Smart contracts accomplish data protection and assure transaction execution according to pre-established policies. Deployment of smart contracts can scale down administrative overheads and refine operational efficiencies while mitigating potential technical shortcomings or risks in transactional undertakings [10].

One more trend is that blockchain technology can potentially improve data sharing trust and transparency [11]. Blockchain could be used to build a decentralised network that enables secure data sharing between parties without intermediaries [12]. This is especially useful in low trusts, such as cross-border transactions.

2.2.2 Ongoing Research and Development in Blockchain-Based Solutions for Data Security

Recently, blockchain technology has attracted much attention from researchers due to its potential for data security. Extensive research and development efforts have been invested in exploring blockchain-based solutions for securing sensitive information. One specific area of focus includes creating consensus algorithms that can enhance the scalability and efficiency of blockchain networks [13]. By executing this, more transactions could be efficiently handled concurrently, thus enhancing overall performance.

Another crucial advancement involves developing privacy-preserving technologies for maintaining secure yet anonymous data sharing [14], which adheres to preserving sensitive details. In utilising this innovation, the integrity of all pieces interchanged is secure, while decentralised approaches now ease information management via blockchain technology. Researchers are currently investigating how they can use these advancements in various spheres, such as supply chain management or healthcare, among other aspects [15], to increase data security levels and establish transparency. It all defines an increased efficiency rate plus Secured means towards managing important confidential materials promoting utmost assurance.

2.3 Ethereum

Ethereum [16] is a representative public blockchain using a PoW (Proof of Work) consensus algorithm like Bitcoin. The PoW consensus algorithm is the method blockchain networks use to choose blockmakers from among untrustworthy members. To choose a miner, participants compete to find a hash value that fulfils the desired requirement. The public Blockchain presents the idea of cryptocurrency's economy, which promotes the right consensus by paying the chosen miner in bitcoin. The previous block's integrity is ensured by connecting the newly created block to the previous block using the "previous block hash" found in the block header before being disseminated to the blockchain network's users. The decentralised network continually advances without administrators; all blocks and transactions are publicly available.

Ethereum supports creating and distributing smart contracts [17] for developing DApps. A smart contract is written in Solidity, a Turing completeness language, and recorded in the distributed ledger to ensure the integrity of the results according to automated execution and input [18]. Figure 1 represents the operation of the smart contract in Ethereum. The smart contract made with Solidity is compiled and stored as the EVM (Ethereum Virtual Machine)-bytecode in the ledger. Calling the code through Ethereum clients such as Geth (Go-Ethereum) is executed in the EVM environment.

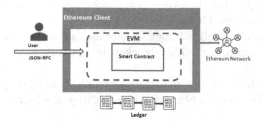

Fig. 1. Ethereum framework architecture

2.3.1 Ethereum Blockchain Mechanism to Ensure the Security of Information

- Cryptography and encryption: These provide security services like confidentiality, non-repudiation, authentication, and authorisation [19].
- Consensus mechanisms: These algorithms determine whether to accept a new block of verified transactions onto the chain [20].
- Timestamp and hashing of the previous block: This safeguards data integrity. Due to consistent and immutable data provenance, the blockchain structure aids in tracking back to a specific transaction [21].

The three initial building blocks of a blockchain are depicted in Fig. 2.

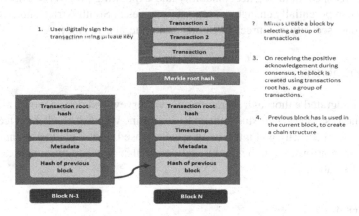

Fig. 2. Building blocks of a blockchain.

Blockchain technology employs a linked list data structure. Transactions are validated by the Blockchain's participant nodes [22]. Each block is hashed to preserve confidentiality and contains a group of legitimate transactions. The chain of blocks that forms, resembling a linked list structure, each holds the hash computed by the preceding block. Every valid transaction is kept track of in every block. The hash value is significantly affected by any hacker effort to alter the data. Each block is guaranteed to be valid by requiring consent from every other node in the chain when a new block is added to the chain [23]. Figure 3 demonstrates this. Any blockchain member can play one of two key roles, which are described below:

Initiate transaction: The Blockchain cannot be active or activated unless the participant starts a transaction. Other blockchain network users then confirm the transaction.

Participants can take on the role of miners by broadcasting and confirming transactions, competing to add a block, and broadcasting new blocks.

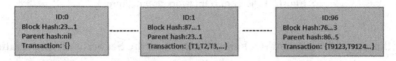

Fig. 3. Blockchain example

The use of blockchain technology in digital platforms such as the GMS platform offers tremendous prospects to improve the existing status of missionary travel. Sensitive data can be securely saved, viewed, and shared only with authorised individuals by exploiting Blockchain's decentralised and transparent characteristics, improving data security and privacy within the missionary ecosystem. Furthermore, Blockchain's immutability and smart contract capabilities enable transparent tracking and verification of resources, encouraging accountability and expediting processes. This disruptive technology can potentially change missionary services in South Africa and Eswatini by increasing data security, resource allocation, and general efficiency.

3   Methodology

This study integrated a thorough literature review, survey, and design works as part of a mixed-methods strategy. This study aimed to determine whether blockchain technology can improve data security and integrity in service-based digital platforms and examine how the GMS platform might be used to deliver vital services to missionaries in South Africa and Eswatini.

3.1   A Literature Review

As mentioned earlier, a mixed methodology was used for this study, including a literature review. A thorough literature study was done to determine the trends, issues, and active research in the areas of blockchain technology and data security in digital platforms. For the aim of this review, electronic databases like IEEE Xplore, ScienceDirect, and Google Scholar were used. Papers that were deemed pertinent to the study's aims and published between 2016 and 2022 made up the review criteria. The main key words were "Blockchain" and "Data Security".

3.2 Survey

Apart from the systematic literature review, surveys were used as part of this study to achieve the research objective. The survey was sent online using Google Forms and distributed to potential GMS platform users through social media such as WhatsApp and email. The collection of data was done in two phases. The first phase aimed at identifying different GMS potential digital platform users around South Africa and Eswatini. This assisted the researcher in learning more about existing missionary centres in South Africa and Eswatini, including the different types of activities conducted by those missionary centres. The second phase aimed at identifying the users online experience with their current website. To get a better understating, in the first phase the survey incorporated questions that sought to collect more detailed information about these missionary centres, such as their details, geographical location, operational data, how long they have been existing, staff number, monthly income, type of services provided, and level of technology adoption (i.e., they had a website or not). In the second phase the survey incorporated question about the perceptions and practices in relation to confidentiality, integrity, and availability within the users' online platforms. The first phase involved 80 missionary centers, with 62 participants completing the survey, and the second phase targeted 50 missionary centers selected based on their website presence and demonstrated knowledge of online security.

Data collected from the survey were examined using R studio 4.0.5. (Team, 2015). Quantitative data from the majority of the questions were imported into Excel for preliminary analysis. Kolmogorov-Smirnov and Shapiro's tests were used to ascertain how the data were distributed. The results were presented using charts and graphs, and the findings were discussed in relation to the study objectives.

3.3 Design Work

This study used a design approach that included the development of a Dapp on the Ethereum blockchain in addition to the literature review and survey method. This Dapp used Ethereum's security and transparency to enable secure and decentralised transactions while resolving issues raised in the survey. The Dapp design, guided by past literature, aims to deliver a well-informed solution associated with research objectives, while also contributing a multi-faceted methodology to issue resolution.

4 Survey Results and Findings

4.1 Selection Results

Geographical Distribution: Most of the missionary centres in the study were in South Africa (95.31%), whereas Eswatini (4.69%) represented a minor part. Most centres (84%) were in Africa, with some also operating in the SADC region and others operating globally (14.1%).

Operational Details: According to the investigation, many of the facilities had been in operation for more than 20 years, demonstrating their longstanding presence. Most centres (40.6%) had between 11 and 20 employees, and 45.3% had monthly income between R 50,000 and R 100,000. The right-skewed distribution of the data indicated the lifetime of most centres. All centres provided workshop and retreat facilities, primarily for religious purposes.

Website Information: Most centres (76.6%) had up and running websites; the others did not. The monthly revenues of centres with websites tended to be more significant, with many of them reaching R 50,000. Increased accessibility and money were strongly connected with website presence. Monthly revenue for a centre was likewise connected with the number of employees.

4.2 Online Security and Website Usage

52% of respondents said they utilised their websites primarily for advertising. Most users (56%), compared to 16% each for tablets and mobile devices, controlled their websites using PCs. The information showed that the experiences of respondents with online security could be summed up as follows:

1. Confidentiality (Mean: 2.996, SD: 0.8525530)
2. Integrity (Mean: 3.144, SD: 0.8038837)
3. Availability (Mean: 2.935, SD: 0.9816742)

In the evaluation of confidentiality, respondents expressed worries about the security of their passwords (mean: 2.74) and the privacy of the internet (mean: 3.92), as well as caution regarding data protection rules (mean: 2.8) and their comprehension of how website owners use their own data (mean: 2.94). Respondents prioritised online business security (mean: 3.32) and paid attention to security during online transactions (mean: 3.14), respectively, regarding integrity. There was space for improvement in the configuration of the available security settings (mean: 2.68), and instances of data compromise were reported (mean: 3.2), even though they demonstrated expertise in configuring digital platform security measures (mean: 3.38). Participants discussed previous incidents of website hacking (mean: 2.92) and prohibited website access (mean: 2.82), with some respondents citing unintentional redirection to alternative websites (mean: 2.8) in terms of availability. These results show the variety of viewpoints and experiences that exist in the field of website usage and online security.

4.3 Selection Findings

Several essential considerations are considered when creating an integrated digital platform for missionary centres. The platform must first and foremost serve a geographically diverse user base predominantly centred in South Africa but also has a regional presence in other regions of Africa and the SADC. Robust data security procedures are therefore required to preserve user data and privacy. The platform must also be flexible enough to accommodate the missionary centres' diverse operational requirements and personnel sizes ranging from 11 to 50 persons. Robust data security and effective team coordination and communication are essential. Additionally, the platform's ability to boost sales through improved online visibility emphasises how crucial it is to design a captivating user interface. These factors combine to create a holistic solution that satisfies the needs of both missionary institutions and visitors while utilising the security and accessibility advantages of blockchain technology, ultimately striving to be a game-changing solution.

4.4 Online Security and Website Usage Findings

According to the survey results regarding online security experience, proper password management is critical from a confidentiality aspect due to worries about online credential security. Passwords that are too simple to remember can jeopardise digital security. As a result, a user-centric platform with strong password tools and security awareness is critical. Users emphasise security in online transactions and configuration, yet data compromises highlight the need for improved protection systems. Incorporating user-friendly security measures can help to build a trustworthy digital ecosystem and increase engagement. Users' experiences with security lapses and outages emphasise the platform's need for robust cybersecurity that constantly enables the system to be online.

5 Prototype Development

The survey was vital in shaping the GMS Digital Platform's requirements. Missionaries from South Africa and Eswatini participated in a survey to understand their needs and services. The survey outcomes outlined key aspects of the platform:

1. **Easy access and Transactions:** The platform must offer user-friendly access and transaction capabilities tailored to missionaries' needs.
2. **Confidentiality:** Robust security measures are crucial to prevent unauthorised access and protect sensitive data.
3. **Data Integrity:** Ensuring reliable data and transactions is vital for user trust.
4. **Availability:** Maintaining seamless access is essential for missionaries' efficiency.

Considering the survey, the following development priorities are recommended:

1. **Data Integrity:** Address user concerns about data reliability.
2. **Confidentiality:** Prioritise password security, data protection, access prevention, and data loss prevention.
3. **Availability:** Enhance platform accessibility.

5.1 Blockchain Implementation in the Prototype to Ensure Data Security

The technology stack for the GMS Digital platform prototype comprises key components aligned with Blockchain. Addressing user requirements, we encompassed four framework components.

1. **Easy Access and Transactional Capabilities:** A user-friendly framework called ReactJS was selected for front-end development. Platform accessibility is improved with ReactJS, which enables smooth user interaction.

2. **Integrity:** Given the high mean score of survey's participants concerned about data integrity, Blockchain technology was critical in tackling the data security issue. Solidity was used to create smart contracts that assure secure transactions. Web3, a JavaScript library, facilitated blockchain integration, as highlighted in Sect. 2, allowing for transparent transactions.
3. **Confidentiality:** Based on the survey results, participants demonstrated the difficulty of using passwords which led to finding a tool that would help resolve the problem. MetaMask emerged as a robust tool, safeguarding user information.
4. **Availability:** Availability is also a crucial concern for the participants based on the results of the survey. To ensure decentralised, secure data storage, Infura IPFS (Inter-Planetary File System) was integrated. IPFS distributes data across nodes, enhancing data security and availability, and reducing the risk of loss or unauthorised access.

5.2 GMS Decentralised Architecture

The platform uses blockchain technology's inherent security capabilities to build a safe and tamper-proof data storage, management, and sharing environment. The Ethereum platform and Web3 client (Ethereum JavaScript API) were utilised in the study's implementation to connect with the front end of smart contracts running on Blockchain.

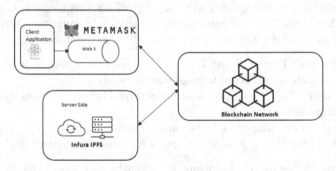

Fig. 4. GMS decentralised architecture

Figure 4 depicts the architecture diagram for the global mission digital platform. The client-side application, or front end, is built with ReactJS to ensure the platform has a user-friendly interface. It is hosted in the distributed network utilising Infura IPFS to ensure availability. The Ethereum blockchain network is used in the backend to ensure distributed server architecture. To ensure proper data protection, each node in the blockchain network retains a copy of the ledger and a smart contract. The platform is built on Ethereum and uses Metamask for authentication. Smart contracts are used for transactions.

5.2.1 System Design

Use Case Scenario: In this use case, Father John Doe and Sister Mary, who are both familiar with the GMS digital platform, serve as the host and guest, respectively. In order to securely verify his identity on the Ethereum blockchain, Father John Doe decides to register his mission centre. He logs in using his Metamask wallet. Then lists accommodation options. Sister Mary logs in at the same time using the same secure method. In search of a suitable place to stay, she clicks on the "Accommodation" feature. She locates a nearby mission with the perfect lodging because she has faith in the platform's specialised services for Catholic missionaries. She smoothly makes a reservation and pays for her stay through the platform's integrated Metamask wallet, securely recording everything on the Blockchain.

Sister Mary uses the platform to interact with other missionaries while on the field, share her community volunteer activities, and market her services. The Blockchain's secure transactions ensure transparent interactions. Father John Doe and Sister Mary each have access to a decentralised, secure, and user-friendly networking and lodging option thanks to the GMS Digital Platform. The platform is well suited to meet the particular requirements of Catholic missionaries working in Swaziland and South Africa since it uses Blockchain, smart contracts, and Metamask integration.

Use Case Diagram

(See Fig. 5).

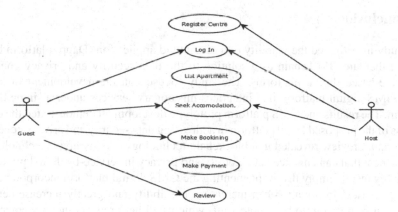

Fig. 5. GMS use case diagram

Class Diagram

The GMS platform's class diagram, shown in Fig. 6, includes the "Center," "Accommodation," "Host," and "Guest" smart contract classes. The figure shows relationship between "Accommodation" and both the "Host" and "Guest" classes as well as one-to-many relationships between "Center" and "Accommodation." While each "Accommodation" corresponds to a single "Center," each "Center" can link to several "Accommodations." Additionally, numerous "Hosts" and "Guests" can be connected to a single "Accommodation," allowing for complex interactions on the GMS platform.

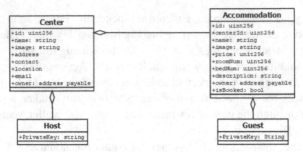

Fig. 6. Class Diagram

5.2.2 Prototype Implementation

The i5 Core processor, 8 gigabytes of RAM, and 250 GB Solid State Drive (SSD) of the laptop used to produce the prototype provided an appropriate balance of processing speed, memory, and storage space for the project's development requirements. ReactJs was used to construct the front end. The testing framework is Truffle, the backend was created in Solidy, and Infura IPFS is being used for distributed storage.

6   Conclusion

This study investigated the viability of a distributed application (Dapp) platform based on the Ethereum Blockchain as a solution to the data security and privacy concerns of service-based digital platforms. The study focused on the development of a prototype GMS digital platform that integrates missionary services under a single digital platform. The results and GMS platform prototype development demonstrated the effectiveness of the proposed Dapp platform in addressing data security and privacy concerns. The literature review revealed that blockchain technology is a disruptive technological advancement that can enhance data security and privacy in service-by digital platforms. The survey results imply that implementing the GMS digital platform incorporating all the missionaries' information can increase accessibility and greatly increase centres' income, enabling them to hire more staff, which will help reduce unemployment and offer greater services to their communities.

7   Limitations and Future Work

This study offered insightful information about the possible uses of blockchain technology for securing service-based digital platforms, but some limitations must be recognised. Firstly, the study's conclusions are based solely on a GMS digital platform prototype case study, which requires additional investigation to determine its potential efficacy and constraints in various scenarios. Secondly, the survey results of the study are based on a small sample number of users. Therefore, future research should also consider employing a bigger sample size to confirm the findings and further understand user perceptions, demands, and concerns related to adopting Dapp platforms. Lastly, the legal and regulatory issues associated with implementing blockchain technology in the shared economy were overlooked. Future studies should investigate the conceivably necessary legal and regulatory frameworks for adopting Dapp platforms in the shared economy and any obstacles to adoption and successful implementation.

References

1. Burnod, P., Dugar-Zhabon, R.: Digital platforms in the B2b market. Mod. Technol. Sci. Technol. Progress **2022**(1), 333–334 (2022). https://doi.org/10.36629/2686-9896-2022-1-333-334
2. Tunggal, A.T.: What is the Cost of a Data Breach in 2022? | UpGuard (2023). https://www.upguard.com/blog/cost-of-data-breach. Accessed 3 April 2023
3. Casino, F., Dasaklis, T.K., Patsakis, C.: A systematic literature review of blockchain-based applications: current status, classification and open issues. Telemat. Inform. **36**, 55–81 (2019). https://doi.org/10.1016/j.tele.2018.11.006
4. Huang, K., Ma, J., Wang, X.: A comparative analysis of bitcoin and ethereum blockchain. In: Proceedings - 2021 2nd international seminar on artificial intelligence, networking and information technology, AINIT 2021, pp. 678–682 (2021). https://doi.org/10.1109/AINIT5 4228.2021.00137
5. Chen, H., Pendleton, M., Njilla, L., Xu, S.: A survey on ethereum systems security: vulnerabilities, attacks and defences. arXiv: Cryptography and Security (2019)
6. Balaskas, A., Franqueira, V.N.L.: Analytical tools for blockchain: review, taxonomy and open challenges. In: 2018 international conference on cyber security and protection of digital services, cyber security 2018, pp. 1–8 (2018). https://doi.org/10.1109/CyberSecPODS.2018. 8560672
7. Verma, S., Dash, S., Joshi, A., Kavita: A detailed study of blockchain and dapps. In: International Conference on Cyber Resilience, ICCR 2022, pp. 1–5 (2022). https://doi.org/10.1109/ ICCR56254.2022.9996003
8. Udokwu, C., Anyanka, H., Norta, A.: Evaluation of approaches for designing and developing decentralised applications on blockchain. In: ACM International Conference Proceeding Series, pp. 55–62 (2020). https://doi.org/10.1145/3423390.3426724
9. Wang, S., Yuan, Y., Wang, X., Li, J., Qin, R., Wang, F.Y.: An overview of smart contract: architecture, applications, and future trends. In: IEEE Intelligent Vehicles Symposium, Proceedings, vol. 2018-June, pp. 108–113 (2018). https://doi.org/10.1109/IVS.2018.8500488
10. Zheng, Z., et al.: An overview on smart contracts: challenges, advances and platforms. Futur. Gener. Comput. Syst. **105**, 475–491 (2020). https://doi.org/10.1016/J.FUTURE.2019.12.019
11. Chowdhury, M.J.M., Colman, A., Kabir, M.A., Han, J., Sarda, P.: Blockchain as a notarization service for data sharing with personal data store. In: Proceedings - 17th IEEE International Conference on Trust, Security and Privacy in Computing and Communications and 12th IEEE International Conference on Big Data Science and Engineering, Trustcom/BigDataSE 2018, pp. 1330–1335 (2018). https://doi.org/10.1109/TRUSTCOM/BIGDATASE.2018.00183
12. Huang, H., Chen, X., Wang, J.: Blockchain-based multiple groups data sharing with anonymity and traceability. Sci. China Inf. Sci. **63**(3), 1–13 (2020). https://doi.org/10.1007/S11432-018-9781-0/METRICS
13. Cachin, C., Vukolić, M.: Blockchain consensus protocols in the wild (Keynote Talk). DROPS-IDN/8016, vol. 91, pp. 1–16 (2017). https://doi.org/10.4230/LIPICS.DISC.2017.1
14. Bernabe, J.B., Canovas, J.L., Hernandez-Ramos, J.L., Moreno, R.T., Skarmeta, A.: Privacy-preserving solutions for blockchain: review and challenges. IEEE Access **7**, 164908–164940 (2019). https://doi.org/10.1109/ACCESS.2019.2950872

15. Haleem, A., Javaid, M., Singh, R.P., Suman, R., Rab, S.: Blockchain technology applications in healthcare: an overview. Int. J. Intell. Networks **2**, 130–139 (2021). https://doi.org/10.1016/J.IJIN.2021.09.005
16. Wood, G.: Ethereum: A Secure Decentralised Generalised Transaction Ledger (2014)
17. Szabo, N.: Smart Contracts : Building Blocks for Digital Markets (2018)
18. Christidis, K., Devetsikiotis, M.: Blockchains and smart contracts for the Internet of Things. IEEE Access **4**, 2292–2303 (2016). https://doi.org/10.1109/ACCESS.2016.2566339
19. Omolara, A.E., Jantan, A.: Modified honey encryption scheme for encoding natural language message. Int. J. Electric. Comput. Eng. **9**(3), 1871–1878 (2019). https://doi.org/10.11591/IJECE.V9I3.PP1871-1878
20. Zhang, C., Wu, C., Wang, X.: Overview of blockchain consensus mechanism. ACM International Conference Proceeding Series, pp. 7–12 (2020). https://doi.org/10.1145/3404512.3404522
21. Ma, G., Ge, C., Zhou, L.: Achieving reliable timestamp in the bitcoin platform. Peer Peer Netw. Appl. **13**(6), 2251–2259 (2020). https://doi.org/10.1007/S12083-020-00905-6/METRICS
22. Kang, J., Yu, R., Huang, X., Maharjan, S., Zhang, Y., Hossain, E.: Enabling localised Peer-to-Peer electricity trading among plug-in hybrid electric vehicles using consortium blockchains. IEEE Trans. Industr. Inform. **13**(6), 3154–3164 (2017). https://doi.org/10.1109/TII.2017.2709784
23. Tosh, D., Shetty, S., Foytik, P., Kamhoua, C., Njilla, L.: CloudPoS: a proof-of-stake consensus design for blockchain integrated cloud. IEEE International Conference on Cloud Computing, CLOUD, vol. 2018-July, pp. 302–309 (2018). https://doi.org/10.1109/CLOUD.2018.00045

Economic Growth and Social Development

Designing a Big Data Analytic Tool for Predicting Girl Child Learner Drop Out in the Eastern Cape Province of South Africa

Nosipho Mavuso[1]([✉]) [iD], Nobert Jere[1] [iD], and Nelly Sharpley[2] [iD]

[1] Walter Sisulu University, Nelson Mandela Drive, Mthatha, Eastern Cape, South Africa
nmavuso@wsu.ac.za
[2] University of KwaZulu-Natal, Durban, KwaZulu-Natal, South Africa

Abstract. The benefit of education in the socio-political development of a country cannot be underestimated. Research has shown a strong correlation between education and socio-economic factors. In South Africa, approximately, 60% of young South Africans drop out of school, without finishing Grade 12 and obtaining their matric certificate. This can be attributed to various factors ranked by the study findings such as pregnancy, drug and substance abuse, socio-economic factors, and rape. It is thus important to address these challenges early. In essence, it is crucial to determine the factors that expose the girl-child to the risks of dropping out of school. In this paper, we present the design and development of a tool to predict the likelihood that a learner would drop out of school. The tool makes use of the risk factors determined through a qualitative approach, through interviews, focus group discussions and workshops with principals, teachers, and the School Governing Body. Pregnancy was highly ranked as the main contributing factor for learners dropout rate. Using the tool, we predicted accurately the likelihood of a learner being a dropout, by providing 3 levels of ranking, high risk, medium risk, and low risk. In addition, the tool also provided insights into the relationship between the student's living arrangements, the distance they travel to school and the financial standpoint of the parents. Developing analytic tool using data from remote areas enable smart city planners to consider disadvantaged communities. Smart schools may be difficult to achieve if dropout issues are not addressed.

Keywords: Big Data Analytics · Drop Out · Prediction · Girl Child

1 Introduction

Learner dropout has been a topic of interest in South Africa in the past decade. This is primarily due to the increase in both global and national reports of students who drop-out of high school. The challenge of school dropout is not trivial due to the complexity and number of factors involved, many of which have been well documented in the literature.

Dropout harms the life of learners and has increased the pressure on economic development in many countries [1]. Furthermore, reports in the literature have pointed to a possible relationship between learner dropout and criminal behaviour among adolescents. The work in [2] reported a correlation between learner dropout and child abuse.

© ICST Institute for Computer Sciences, Social Informatics and Telecommunications Engineering 2024
Published by Springer Nature Switzerland AG 2024. All Rights Reserved
M. Masinde et al. (Eds.): AFRICATEK 2023, LNICST 520, pp. 73–90, 2024.
https://doi.org/10.1007/978-3-031-63999-9_5

The current challenges facing learners and communities such as poverty, family issues, health challenges, inadequate infrastructure at the schools and the community environment have led to high dropout numbers. As a result, research on dropouts has become a major interest to many stakeholders with government departments trying to reduce and avoid dropout [3]. Several dropout monitoring strategies, ideas and techniques have been proposed. As a result, some monitoring solutions have produced positive results, such as the various features of Learning Management Systems, that provide the identification of students at risk. One of the main challenges has been that dropout is only identified or acted on when a learner is already out of school [4]. In addressing the challenges, technologies and software developed have proposed and developed systems and applications that assist in dropout management [5]. Some developers have applied artificial intelligence, machine learning and big data analytic techniques to attempt to address dropout.

Using big data, a pattern of declining performance over time is a good predictor of student drop-out, and having dependents, being married, or serving in the military lowers the risk of dropping out. One of the technologies used is data mining, whose primary goal is to discover patterns, profiles, and trends through data analysis using advanced data analysis techniques and pattern recognition technologies [6]. The risk of dropping out was higher among older students, female students, and students with prior college education or transfer credits. Tools for data mining are used to discover data, gain a deeper comprehension of it, and predict future behaviour [7]. In a similar vein, [8] utilised data mining to locate educational data on dropouts and identified additional issues, such as privacy concerns, that must be considered in the studies.

According to [9] a list of data mining methods, which were divided into artificial intelligence and statistical method methods, approximately, 79% (22 of 28 studies) used decision tree classifiers. This method is utilised, as stated by [10] because of its adaptability when processing numerical and categorical data, its monotonous transformations of explanatory variables, and the ease with which results can be interpreted. In addition, it provides higher accuracy rates. The ID3 (Decision tree classifier) algorithm is more sensitive than other algorithms when it comes to classifying data from student history registers. Since these data mining approaches are regarded as powerful tools for solving classification problems and are utilised frequently for their simplicity and ease of understanding, neural network classifiers and support vector machines hold the second highest frequency of use [11]. Linear Regression and Logistic Regression are popular methods for classifying data based on its characteristics and are adaptable to the use of categorical and continuous predictor variables.

This paper presents a big data analytic tool that was developed based on the girl-child dropout factors as pointed out by participants from OR Tambo District Municipality in Eastern Cape Province in South Africa. The dropout factors as given by the engaged learners were considered for the development of the dropout analytic tool. There are main factors that are attributed to learner dropout. The paper presents a big data analytic tool that was developed based on the factors that were collected from school-going girls between Grades 8–12. The understanding of different factors affecting learners' dropout provides an informative environment thatassists in future planning.

In the following section, we present the literature review, Sect. 2 showcases the description of the case, and Sect. 3 is the Girl Child School Dropout Model. Section 4 is the methodology. Section 5, the analysis of dropout factors subsequently follows. Lastly, the conclusion and references are given in Sects. 6 and 7.

1.1 What Are the Factors Affecting Dropout?

The phenomenon of school dropout is perceived as a process that is caused by a variety of factors. Most studies have indicated several factors related to learner dropouts globally [12]. The following are the most cited factors generally leading to learner dropouts and before the Covid-19 pandemic crisis; pregnancy, parents' educational status, age at entry to first grade, substance abuse, bullying, family responsibility, school distance, teachers' attitudes, poverty, poor academic performance, failure to cope with school, a lack of social skills to cope with life's challenges, early employment, a lack of parental care and role models, child-headed families, media influence, poor payment of teachers, child labour, early marriage for young girls, and a lack of school/personal effects, to mention a few [13–16]. These factors have a huge bearing on how disadvantaged communities could be developed and as Africa moves towards a smart environment, there is no room to ignore these factors.

These factors seem to differ in ranking per socioeconomic status, country to country and between low-income countries and high-economic countries. Over and above the noted ongoing crisis of learner dropouts worldwide, the Covid-19 pandemic added much to the learner dropout crisis globally, even so, the countries on the periphery were mostly affected due to a lack of resources to confirm the online learning spaces and ensure continuity in learning [17]. A joint UNESCO, UNICEF andWORLD BANK report in 2021 presented the global disruption to education caused by the Covid-19 pandemic as constituting the worst education crisis on record. The magnitude of the shock is still not fully understood, but emerging evidence is deeply concerning about the state of the global education crisis. Schools closed in 19 out of every 20 countries around the world, for a median of 17 weeks [18]. Inadequate facilities, such as a lack of computers, and internet facilities, were the major factors that limited learner engagement. It was also observed that Covid-19 disrupted educational activities and reduced educational opportunities for disadvantaged people [19]. Covid-19 displaced students and teachers and created multiple barriers to teaching and learning. These effects were felt by educational institutions, educators, students, parents and other stakeholders in education [20]. Globally, studies on learner dropouts at the time of the Covid-19 pandemic relate learner dropout to consequences like learning poverty, economic impact, and learners older than the current grade [19]. The variations in the gaps between those who have and have not need to be considered in driving smart schools.

1.2 Technologies/Innovation Challenges at Schools

Technology has been assimilated well in various industries, including service industries such as retail, transport and education, thereby giving prominence to the development of the Fourth Industrial Revolution [21]. However, in education, digital transformation has been lagging behind although technology has been one of the major innovations which can potentially model the educational landscape. The education landscape in second world countries and marginalised communities has been faced with resistance in transformation into digitalisation due to a lack of skills, high cost of infrastructure and restricted application [22]. Regardless, the pandemic has catapulted the transformation of the education sector to digital learning and has forced even marginalised schools to reconsider their position in the digital transformation [22]. Digital transformation in the field of education is focused primarily on the use of computers as well as advancing the learning environment into sharing of materials and data analytics that assist in comprehending the needs of both educators and learners [23]. The incorporation of technology into traditional teaching and learning is, however, challenged by external and internal barriers to the teacher's implementation of technology. External barriers are first-order constraints. These include access constraints, teacher training and support.

Access constraints are challenges to do with an inadequate supply of connectivity, including the equipment. Without adequate computer hardware, software, and internet connectivity, it is impossible to implement technologies in schools. The provision of computers is the most basic stage in the introduction of technology in educational institutions. Many schools are on a drive to provide computer hardware in the form of tablets, laptops, or desktops. However, most schools in marginalised communities have challenges getting funding to ensure a 1:1 computer-learner ratio and they rely on government funding [24]. Where government funding is insufficient, these schools need to search for alternative sources to stock up their computers. Another strategy for ensuring adequate computers in schools is the use of the Bring Your Own device strategy where learners provide their own gadgets [25]. The challenge with this strategy comes with regards to learners who cannot afford these gadgets. In addition, the issue of cost even goes beyond acquiring computers in schools. The running costs of technology include purchasing software, maintenance, replacement parts, insurance, and internet access [26]. Marginalised schools, particularly those in rural areas of most developing countries are affected by a lack of electricity to power the computers, safe storage space and general infrastructure [26]. These can prove costly and result in non-implementation of technology in under-funded institutions.

Another challenge of note in the implementation of technology in the education sector is the alienation of socio-economic groups. [24] reported that in South Africa, although there is a significant increase in participation in technology-driven learning areas, a clear divide is shown in the proportion of white students and that of African descent. This is a direct influence of the colonial era which saw white students having a historical advantage over those of African descent and this has translated into economic status and participation in technology-based subjects or learning areas [27].

Although the provision of Information and Communication Technoogy (ICT)infrastructure is detailed in the policies of many countries, debatably, many states have not prioritised it. Many African governments have comprehended it as a secondary need, especially with regards to marginalised areas where ICT has not been introduced in the first place. In Kenya, the Poverty Reduction Strategy has acknowledged the role of technology in poverty alleviation. However, 'bureaucracy,a lack of professionalism in the business sector, corruption, illiteracy, and poverty' have hampered the roll-out of ICT programmes in different sectors including schools [28].

After the availability of computers, learners should have enough contact time with the computers. Even though many schools are working towards a 1:1 computer-learner ratio, effective learning only occurs if they are given adequate time to access the computers. [29] revealed that the minimum recommended period should be an hour of contact time. In addition to adequate contact time, consistency and regularity should be maintained.

Training is also a huge constraint in the implementation of technology in schools. Teachers must be technologically trained so that they will be able to impart skills to learners. In some instances, teachers will be constrained from fully harnessing the potential of technology in the classroom. The biggest constraint to incorporating technology into teaching and learning is insufficient teacher training [30]. Teacher training cultivates confidence in using teaching and learning technology, surfing the internet during research, or using various software. Additionally, teacher training is not a once-off event, thus frequent training is a necessity since innovation and technology are ever-changing [27]. As a result, schools and responsible authorities should constantly offer capacity-building exercises to boost their teachers' confidence and skills. Even teachers who are appointed who have already existing computer skills need capacity building because of the constant technological changes.

After the provision of computers and training, support barriers follow. Technology being ongoing, various kinds of support are needed both in the initial phases and many times after. In this respect, support comes through technical support and administrative/peer support [27]. With technical support, content creators of educational software/programmes are expected to give continuous support to users. Support can also be rendered through peer groups as the level of expertise increases. On the other hand, a lack of support from content creators will result in the failure of technology to be implemented in schools.

Internal barriers or second-order barriers to implementing technology in the classroom involve the decisions that teachers make to use technology in their teaching [31]. These barriers include attitude, beliefs, and knowledge [27]. The attitude of the teacher on pedagogy and the incoming technology determines the extent of use and incorporation into the curriculum. While well-equipped schools focus on how technology can be incorporated into teaching and learning, ill-resourced and marginalised schools focused on whether technology should be included [30]. These two approaches result in differences in the level of incorporation into teaching and learning. The latter represents schools where traditional teaching methods are upheld at the expense of technology. [26] reported that a lack of know-how on the use of technology is one of the major factors affecting the implementation of technology in rural schools in South Africa.

Second-order challenges are also presented through confidence in skills and knowledge. Most of the learners nowadays belong to a class of 'digital natives' who grew up with technology and are familiar with it [32]. Most teachers are referred to as 'digital immigrants' who were born without digital exposure and were introduced to it at a later stage [32]. Due to this dynamic, most teachers may feel that they are not technologically competent as opposed to the learners whom they are supposed to teach, and this may reduce their confidence levels. This lack of confidence will strip them of control in the classroom, hence they will stick to the traditional methods of teaching, disregarding the role of technology in teaching and learning [27].

1.3 Technologies to Monitor the Girl Child at School

a. Bluetooth-powered messaging service

According to [33] the Centre for Social Concern and Development (CESOCODE), a non-governmental organisation based in Malawi was monitoring the welfare of girls and assisting with necessary interventions during the pandemic, utilising technology as the main intervention tool. The organisation used bluetooth-powered mobile-to-mobile messaging service to monitor the girls during the time they were out of school due to lockdowns. The girls can report any cases of abuse through this service.

b. Social media

CESOCODE has also made use of social media platforms such as Facebook to broadcast podcasts focusing on educating and conscientising girls on issues about domestic violence and health. The podcast is also delivered in Sign Language to cater for girls with hearing disabilities. The girls can report any abuse or challenges they are facing using social media such as WhatsApp and Facebook [33].

c. Loudspeakers

CESOCODE also educates girls in rural areas through messages broadcasted by loudspeakers. A vehicle moves around communities, with someone educating the masses through loudspeakers. They also make use of posters, brochures, and flyers to disseminate messages of hope to the girls [33].

d. Use of helpline services

Telephone helplines originated around the 1950s and their popularity was exacerbated by the increase in the use of the telephone as a mode of communication [34]. The first helplines to be established were by Samaritans and Childline. Helplines offer education and support for medical and psychological conditions to reduce a wide array of challenges in communities. Currently, different kinds of helplines are available, including Human Immunodeficiency Virus (HIV), child protection, girl-child protection, suicide prevention, domestic abuse, sexual abuse, addiction, depression, sexual identity, and bullying [35, 36]. Helplines offer different scopes of assistance to the callers. Some offer counsel and information while others are contact points for reporting social ills. In addition, helplines are available free of charge and currently, calls can be made from any type of phone, whether landline or cell phone. Helplines have also diversified their modes of contact into emails, text messages, video-calling and chat services [37]. Most helplines operate 24 h daily to ensure accessibility. Helplines can be used to ensure the well-being of girls such that they will be in the right state of mind to attend school and be as competitive as boys of their age.

2 Description of the Case

The Eastern Cape Province is one of the most negatively affected provinces in terms of learner dropout rates. The province is dominated by townships to rural areas. There is no doubt that those who live below the poverty datum line are always hit harder by any challenge. The focus is on girl children as they are the ones who are gravely affected with dropping out. While this disruption to education and the expected reduction in global growth have far-reaching effects for all, their impact will be particularly detrimental to the most disadvantaged students and their families, especially in poorer countries [38]. Education across the globe faces great challenges, and developing countries such as South Africa are gravely affected, by socio-economic factors, infrastructure challenges, and a lack of resources. Approximately, 300 000 children have potentially dropped out of primary schools across South Africa in 6 months, including the national lockdown. Then, 126,553 children in KwaZulu-Natal have missed school, 114, 558 in Western Cape, 8153 in Eastern Cape, 55,571 in Gauteng and 800 in Limpopo [39].

Eastern Cape province, the poorest province in South Africa, has recorded approximately 130,000 learner dropouts during the 2020 academic year at all levels. As Covid-19 forced 743 million girls out of school in 185 countries, the rising dropout rates disproportionately affected adolescent girls, as disease outbreaks affect girls and boys differently. This exacerbates gender gaps in education and leads to increased risk of sexual exploitation, early and unintended pregnancy, and child, early and forced marriages [40].

In South Africa, most school dropouts take place in Grades 10 and 11. Approximately, 60% of young South Africans dropout of school without finishing Grade 12 and obtaining their matric certificate, which is the school leaving qualification. There is a huge inequality gap in South Africa, and this can also be identified in the levels of dropout rates [12]. As a result of the country's racist, colonial and apartheid social and economic policies, the levels of dropout differ significantly by race [41]. According to a 2011 General Household Survey, the attainment of matric was so imbalanced, with only 44% of Black and Coloured youth aged 23–24 attaining matric compared to 83% of Indian youth and 88% of White youth [42].

2.1 The OR Tambo District

Learners who are mostly absent at school are at risk of problems associated with drug and alcohol abuse, and personality changes turn to crime to support expensive chemical dependence habits. Worth noting girls also bear a greater negative cost with rises in sexual abuse, teenage pregnancy, and early marriage. The most concerning of them all is the fact that distance learning solutions, whether low- or high-tech, often indirectly discriminate against girls due to power dynamics within families. Besides, when schools re-open, poorer children and girls are less likely to return, with increased dropout rates caused partly by fear, stigmatisation and, in some cases, deliberate exclusion.

This is a result of the difficulty in attempting to conceptualise how each of the complex risk factors, such as family, school, individuals, and community interact during the process of disengagement and dropout [43]. A single risk factor cannot be used when an accurate prediction of dropout cause, risk or impact is made. The OR Tambo district as shown in Fig. 1 is the second district with the highest number of high school dropouts.

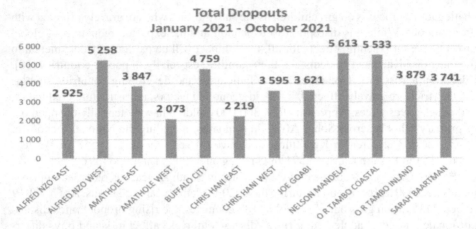

Fig. 1. Eastern Cape District's Dropout Statistics

3   Girl Child School Dropout Model

The big data analytics tool was developed through the data collected in the selected schools for this study. The tool will assist in identifying potential trends in the behaviours of the girl child, thus assisting in the formulation of situation-specific intervention strategies. The analysis of data and the implementation of machine learning algorithms to predict dropouts entails scrutinising patterns, trends, and risk factors among students who are at risk of dropping out of school [44]. The Web-Based Big Data analytics tool is designed for girls in high schools across Eastern Cape province to connect the capabilities of Big Data to predict the likelihood of dropout. The tool can be utilised by various stakeholders in the Department of Basic Education to predict the dropping out of a girl child. Users of the tool in various schools include principals, teachers, and the girllLearners. The tool's predictive capabilities can be utilised as an intervention tool to pinpoint students who are at risk of discontinuing their education. This identification process can be based on a multitude of factors, such as attendance, academic performance, and socio-economic background [45]. A range of analytical techniques such as trend analysis have been applied in dropout prediction, including the examination of historical data by analysing past student records, academic performance, attendance patterns, and demographic information [44]. Once learners who are at risk are identified, schools can thereafter implement proactive interventions. These interventions can take the form of personalised counselling, mentorship programmes, or additional academic support to address specifically the unique challenges faced by each student [45]. The integration of a predictive tool for education within a smart city framework can contribute to the overall development and efficiency of the city. By analyzing student enrollment patterns, demographic changes, and historical data, it is possible to predict future education resource needs. These insights can be utilized by smart cities to optimize the allocation of resources, including classrooms, teachers, and educational materials, based on projected demand. This ensures that educational facilities are efficiently distributed (Fig. 2).

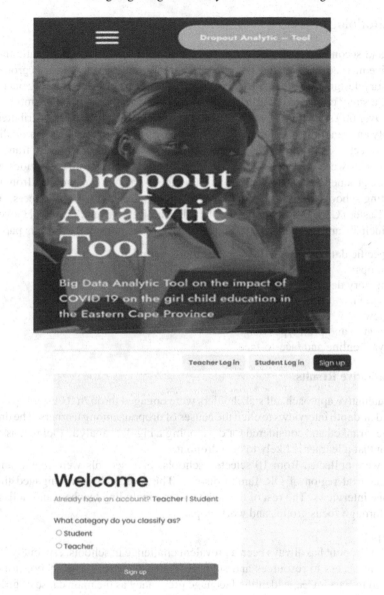

Fig. 2. Drop out Predictive Tool Home Page

4 Methodology

Primary and secondary data were collected. Data were collected using qualitative and quantitative methods. Qualitative data were obtained from interviews, focus groups and participatory design. The collected data were recorded and transcribed to work out related topics. The study collected data on female learners from schools in OR Tambo district in 2021. Over 600 schooling girls participated. The questionnaires were distributed systematically and randomly to students in 10 schools in OR Tambo district. For qualitative data, all collected data from focus groups, workshops and interviews were transcribed and key themes were formulated. The common dropout factors from the various participants were grouped and then a ranking was provided. Various stakeholders from the 10 participating schools were involved. These included parents, teacher, learners, principals, and Eastern Cape District Officials. Only data collected from the School Governing Body, principals and teachers in OR Tambo District were considered for this paper.

- The specific data collection tools and methods included:
- Workshops
- Participatory design
- Focus groups
- Interviews
- Experiential and prototype design
- Surveys – online and face-to-face

4.1 Qualitative Results

For the qualitative approach, all stakeholders were engaged through focus groups, workshops, and in-depth interviews to elicit the causes of dropout among learners. The dropout factors were ranked and considered for developing a big data analytic tool that assists in predicting that a learner is likely to be a dropout.

Data were collected from 10 selected schools. Five schools were inland and five from the coastal region of OR Tambo district. The principals were engaged through one-on-one interviews. The rest of the stakeholders, including teachers and SGBs were engaged through focus groups and workshops.

a) Principals

Learner dropout has always been a prevalent challenge in schools, especially in rural areas, where access to resources and schools itself is difficult. The school principals interviewed in Eastern Cape identified teenage pregnancy as the main cause of girl-child abandonment,.

Below are the views of some of the principals:

"The school is in one of the poorest areas, you find that some of the kids have parents who are not working, in fact, in the whole homestead, no one is working. You find that in some of the children's homesteads, the parents are not around, they have migrated to other areas to try find employment, leaving the children alone to be independent".

"At one time, a learner experienced contractions at school and she had to be rushed to hospital with our cars so after that the school requested that parents be

present in class with their children when they are pregnant so that they are the ones who take care of them when giving birth. This is why some parents decide to keep their pregnant children at home because they cannot be on guard 24/7".

"When boys go to initiation, which is seasonal, you find that some of them go but do not come back, which also ultimately leads to dropping out, and this may be caused by various reasons, although this study is for girls, boys dropping out sometimes leads to girls also dropping out since some of them follow their boyfriends, get married and have children."

Principals pointed out that another important factor is social harm in the communities in which they serve. Students are without their biological parents due to death or distance, which means that they either stay with grandparents or other family members or they stay alone to become victims of crime, rape and are caught in blessor-blessee relationships for their survival. They experiment with drugs, are involved in unprotected sex, fall pregnant, and have no support after giving birth, leading to abandonment.

Ratings of factors provided by the principals:

- Top 3 Ranked: Pregnancy, Drug and Substance Abuse and Child-Headed Homes.
- 3 Medium Ranked: Socio-Economic Factors, Peer Pressure, and Rape.

b) School Governing Body

In this study, the parents revealed that the dropout rate of girls is higher than the dropout rate of boys and the foremost cause for girls to dropout is pregnancy.

Below are the views of some of the SGB:

"Mothers have a big contribution in these girls' pregnancies because if they get plastics of groceries from their daughters' sugar dads, they allow them to do whatever they like".

"Akunkwenkwe akuntombazana, bayanxila qha, and we cannot say anything because siyaboyika xa bekulameko"

Translated as *"Whether it's a boy or a girl, they're just drinking, and we cannot say anything because we fear them when they are in that intoxicated state"*.

Ratings of factors provided by the School Governing Body:

- 3 Top Ranked: Pregnancy, Drug and Substance Abuse, and Repeating Grades.
- 3 Medium Ranked: Socio-Economic Factors, Child-Headed Homes, and Learner Rotation in Schools Due to Covid-19 (Fig. 3).

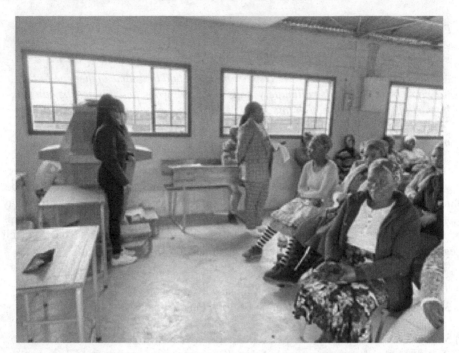

Fig. 3. School Governing Body's Focus Group Discussions

c) Teachers

The teachers were asked to give their opinions on the reasons for the girl children dropping out of school. They pointed to several factors that contribute to girls dropping out of school. The teachers mentioned that the predominant factor is teenage pregnancy, followed by drug and alcohol abuse. They believed that female children have been subjected to drug abuse, particularly dagga as these are readily available. Another noticeable trend was teenage pregnancy caused by teachers themselves.

Below are the views of some of the teachers:

"There are a lot of cases, as men we play a big role towards schoolgirls, for example, a male teacher can sleep with a learner, and when the girl becomes pregnant, the teacher can decide to deny the child, then, the girl decides to do abortion at school, and it will be known that that girl was impregnated by the teacher, thus the girl ends up not going to school".

"Poverty is the main cause of dropout because a learner cannot afford a new uniform, as most of the time, other learners are given school uniform by former learners. As time goes on, the uniform is torn and a student cannot further her studies because she does not have a uniform. Financial instability, not having money to pay rent as most learners are renting when they are doing Grade 12, most students in their home survive on grants; most of the parents cannot afford to pay rent for their learners to be close to school so other learners decide to dropout because of lack of financial support."

"They are also a lot of rape cases around our community in which girls are raped and threatened so most of the girls end up leaving school because of traumatic experiences."

"Pregnancy is one of the factors that cause school dropout, as when girls are pregnant, their parents do not encourage them to go back to school after giving birth."

"The only monitoring system is the register."

Ratings of factors provided by the teachers:

- 3 Top Ranked: Drug and Substance Abuse, Pregnancy, and Socio-Economic Factors.
- 3 Medium Ranked: Rape, Parents Deceased Due to Covid-19, and a Lack of Transport.

5   Analysis of Drop-Out Factors

Intrinsic Factors: related to learners' individual dispositions, behaviours or personal choices that lead to early school leaving. Student Individual: Traits students possess regardless of demographics such as substance abuse, law violations, and pregnancies. *Push out:* school-related factors that are experienced by the learners as exclusion from school. These included both unintentional and conscious efforts by educators or school management to limit the number of learners who write Grade 12 community examinations, which lead to a student dropping out of school.

Extrinsic: barriers that exist at home or in the community that have resulted in a learner dropping out of school

The web-based big data analytics tool was developed for girls in high schools in Eastern Cape province to connect the power of big data to predict the likelihood of dropping out of school. The tool can be used by the various stakeholders in the Department of Basic Education to predict a girl's dropout rate. The users of the tool in the different schools include principals, teachers, and students. The big data analysis tool was developed using the data collected in the schools selected for this study. The tool helps identify potential behavioural trends in girls, thereby helping in formulating situation-specific intervention strategies.

The tool is useful for the education sector, but the information and topics covered are unlimited to the sector. Information on the interconnected socio-economic, environmental, political, and cultural challenges is discussed on the tool's homepage. The learner is asked a series of questions to learn more about the challenges, life circumstances, financial situations and various social issues that apply to a learner (Fig. 4).

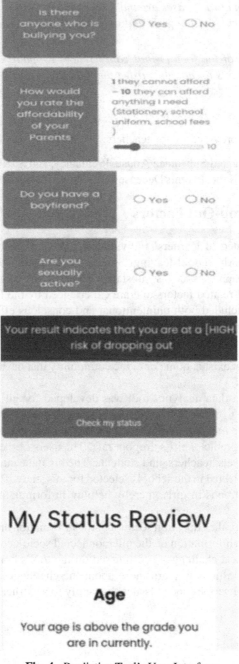

Fig. 4. Predictive Tool's User Interface

Because of personal questions learners are asked, the tool makes provision for privacy controls to protect the learners' rights to privacy. Teachers and principals are unable to see the learners' responses to all the questions asked on the system.

All the questions asked on the tool are rated as per the results from the data collected within the schools and ratings from the stakeholders as well as the literature consulted. After answering all questions asked, the learner can click on the [check status] button, and their results will be displayed (Fig. 5).

> Your result indicates that you are at a [LOW] risk of dropping out

My Status Review

Age

Your age is okay for the grade you are in currently.

Money

Your financial status is good

Sex

You are not sexually active

Fig. 5. Dropout Prediction Status Review

The tool allows teachers/principals to utilise the information for report based purposes. After a teacher signs up on the tool, they have only view permissions of the students' final prediction results. The teacher can only view the level of dropout risk for a learner. The learners' personal details and responses are only visible to them.

6 Conclusion

There are large quantities of data in the education sector, and this study demonstrated this through only one district in the province which contributed towards the dropout prediction tool. The ultimate goal is to connect the capabilities of Big Data to accelerate and enhance the impact of the sector and provide solutions to current and future problems encountered as a result of learner dropout. Through the data analytics capabilities of the tool, there is a lot that has been discovered, mostly through the help of teachers, parents and principals who contributed greatly by sharing their real-life experiences of the education system and rating dropout factors. This tool was developed based on the ratings from all the participants and is key to expanding further studies across other districts and eventually, the entire Eastern Cape Province. The study shows that understanding of the existing digital inequalities is critical towards innovative solutions. Data analytics based on societal factors is relevant in ensuring smart sustainable solutions for South Africa.

References

1. Sarker, Md., Islam, N., Min, W., Hossin, M.A.: Economic effect of school dropout in Bangladesh. Int. J. Inform. Educ. Technol. **9**(2), 136–142 (2019)
2. Mennen, O.K., Weybright, W.C., Aldridge, N.S.: Effects of child abuse on school dropout among students in USA. J. Educ. **5**(2) (2022). https://doi.org/10.53819/81018102t5065
3. Fleisch, B., Shindler, J., Perry, H.: Who is out of school? Evidence from the Community Survey 2007, South Africa (2010)
4. Meinck, F., Cluver, L.D., Boyes, M.E., Ndhlovu, L.D.: Risk and protective factors for physical and emotional abuse victimisation amongst vulnerable children in South Africa. Child Abuse Rev. **24**, 182–197 (2015)
5. Tulasi, B.: Significance of big data and analytics in higher education. Int. J. Comput. Appl. **68**(14), 21–23 (2013)
6. Fatima, S.A., Fatima, S.T., Alwi, S.K.K.: Major causes of female dropouts at different educational levels in Karachi. Global Educ. Stud. Rev. **VI**(I), 293–305 (2021). https://doi.org/10.31703/gesr.2021(vi-i).30
7. Job, M.: An efficient way of applying big data analytics in higher education sector for performance evaluation. Int. J. Comput. Appl. **180**(23), 25 (2018)
8. Yukselturk, E., Ozekes, S., Türel, Y.: Predicting dropout student: an application of data mining methods in an online education program. Eur. J. Open Distan. e-Learn. **17**(1), 119 (2014)
9. Magana, A.J., Silva Coutinho, G.: Modeling and simulation practices for a computational thinking-enabled engineering workforce. Comput. Appl. Eng. Educ. **25**(1), 62–78 (2017)
10. Khan, M., Ibrahim, R., Ghani, I.: Cross domain recommender systems: cross domain recommender systems. ACM Comput. Surv. **50**(3), 1–27 (2017)
11. Verma, A., Kumar, D.: Evaluating and enhancing efficiency of recommendation system using big data analytics. Int. Res. J. Eng. Technol. **4**(3), 1518–1527 (2017)
12. Motala, S., Dieltiens, V., Sayed, Y.: Physical access to schooling in South Africa: mapping dropout, repetition and age-grade progression in two districts. Comp. Educ. **45**, 251–263 (2009)
13. De Ridder, K.A.A., et al.: High school dropout and long-term sickness and disability in young adulthood: a prospective propensity score stratified cohort study (the Young-HUNT study). BMC Public Health **13**(1) (2013). https://doi.org/10.1186/1471-2458-13-941
14. Nabugoomu, J.: School dropout in rural Uganda: stakeholder perceptions on contributing factors and solutions. Educ. J. **8**(5), 185 (2019). https://doi.org/10.11648/j.edu.20190805.13
15. Nabugoomu, J., Seruwagi, G. K., Hanning, R.: Addressing poverty, malnutrition and poor health for adolescent mothers in rural eastern Uganda: recommendations of local level stakeholders. Afric. J. Health Sci. **33**(4) (2020)
16. Nakajima, M., Kijima, Y., Otsuka, K.: Is the learning crisis responsible for school dropout? a longitudinal study of Andhra Pradesh, India. Int. J. Educ. Dev. **62**, 245–253 (2018). https://doi.org/10.1016/j.ijedudev.2018.05.006
17. Ramsdal, G.H., Wynn, R.: How young people who had dropped out of high school experienced their re-enrolment processes. Int. J. Educ. Res. **106** (2021). https://doi.org/10.1016/j.ijer.2021.101732
18. UNESCO. WHAT'S NEXT? lessons on education recovery: findings from a survey of ministries of education amid the COVID-19 Pandemic (2021). https://en.unesco.org/gem-report/taxonomy/term/238
19. Onyema, E.M., et al.: Impact of coronavirus pandemic on education. J. Educ. Pract. (2020). https://doi.org/10.7176/jep/11-13-12

20. Laura, M., Evans, D.K.: Learning Loss and Student Dropouts during the COVID-19 Pandemic: A Review of the Evidence Two Years after Schools Shut Down. CGD Working Paper 609. Center for Global Development, Washington, D (2022). https://www.cgdev.org/publication/learning-loss-and-student-dropouts-during-covid-19-pandemic-review-evidence-two-years
21. Manasia, L., Ianos, M.G., Chicioreanu, T.D.: Pre-service teacher preparedness for fostering education for sustainable development: an empirical analysis of central dimensions of teaching readiness. Sustainability (Switzerland) 12(1), 4–6 (2020)
22. Mhlanga, D.: Industry 4.0: the challenges associated with the digital transformation of education in South Africa. In: Aydin, O. (ed), the impacts of digital transformation, efeacademy, Instabul, pp. 12–25 (2020)
23. Fomunyam, K.G.: Education and the fourth industrial revolution: challenges and possibilities for engineering. Int. J. Mech. Eng. Technol. 10(08), 271–284 (2019)
24. Kayembe, C., Nel, D.: Challenges and opportunities for education in the Fourth Industrial Revolution. Afric. J. Public Affairs 11(3), 79–94 (2019)
25. Afreen, R.: Bring Your Own Device (BYOD) in higher education: opportunities and challenges. Int. J. Emerg. Trends Technol. Comput. Sci. 3, 233–236 (2014)
26. Dzansi, D.Y., Amedzo, K.: Integrating ICT into rural South African schools: possible solutions for challenges. Int. J. Educ. Sci. 6(2), 341–348 (2014)
27. Johnson, A.M., Jacovina, M.E., Russell, D.E., Soto, C.M.: Challenges and solutions when using technologies in the classroom. In: Crossley, S.A., McNamara, D.S. (eds.) Adaptive educational technologies for literacy instruction, pp. 13–29. Taylor & Francis, New York (2016)
28. Hallberg, D., Kulecho, M., Kulecho, A., Okoth, L.: Case studies of Kenyan digital villages with a focus on women and girls. J. Lang. Technol. Entrepren. Africa 3(1), 255–273 (2011)
29. Warschauer, M., Zheng, B., Niiya, M., Cotten, S., Farkas, G.: Balancing the one-to-one equation: Equity and access in three laptop programs. Equity Excell. Educ. 47(1), 46–62 (2014)
30. Ertmer, P.A., Ottenbreit-Leftwich, A., Sadik, O., Sendurur, E., Sendurur, P.: Teacher beliefs and technology integration practices: a critical relationship. Comput. Educ. 59, 423–435 (2012)
31. Ertmer, P.A.: Addressing first-and second-order barriers to change: Strategies for technology integration. Educ. Tech. Res. Dev. 47(4), 47–61 (1999)
32. Gallardo-Echenique, E., Marques-Molas, L., Bullen, M., Strijbos, J.: Let's talk about digital learners in the digital era. Int. Rev. Res. Open Distrib. Learn. (2015). http://www.irrodl.org/index.php/irrodl/article/view/2196/3337. Accessed 23 Oct 2021
33. Carroll, R.: The new normal- how technology is helping CESOCODE prevent child marriages during COVID (2020). https://www.girlsnotbrides.org/articles/the-new-normal-how-technology-is-helping-cesocode-fight-child-marriage-during-covid-19/. Accessed 7 Oct 2021
34. Morgan, K., Chakkalackal, L., Cyhlarova, E.: Lifelines: Evaluation of mental health helplines. Mental health helpline partnership (2012). https://www.mentalhealth.org.uk/sites/default/files/life_lines.pdf. Accessed 14 Oct 2021
35. Arullapan, N., et al.: Quality of counselling and support provided by the South African National AIDS Helpline: content analysis of mystery client interviews. S. Afr. Med. J. 108(7), 596–602 (2018)
36. UNFPA–UNICEF. Adapting to COVID 19 (2020). https://www.unfpa.org/sites/default/files/resource-pdf/Responding_to_COVID-19_Pivoting_the_GPECM_to_the_pandemic.pdf. Accessed 14 Oct 2021
37. Dinh, T., Farrugia, L., O'Neill, B., Vandoninck S., Velicu, A.: Insafe helplines: operations, e¬ffectiveness and emerging issues for internet safety helplines (2016).https://www.betterinternetforkids.eu/documents/167024/507884/Helpline+Fund+Report+-+Final/4cf8f03a-3a48-4365-af76-f03e01cb505d. Accessed 14 Oct 2021

38. De Witte, K., Cabus, S., Thyssen, G., Groot, W.: A critical review of the literature on school dropout. Educ. Res. Rev. **10**, 13–28 (2013)
39. Mhlanga, D., Moloi, T.: COVID-19 and the digital transformation of education: what are we learning on 4IR in South Africa? Educ.Sci. **10**, 180 (2020). https://doi.org/10.3390/educsci10 070180
40. Hutchinson, G.: How will Plan International support girls, young women and vulnerable groups? s.l.: s.n (2020)
41. Moses, E., van der Berg, S., Rich, E.: A society divided: how unequal education quality limits social mobility in South Africa. RESEP: University of Stellenbosch.: Synthesis report for the Programme to Support Pro-poor Policy Development (PSPPD) (2017)
42. Hartnack, A.: Background document and review of key South African and international literature on school dropout. Sustainable Livelihoods Foundation, Cape Town (2017)
43. Hallgarten, J.: Four lessons from evaluations of the education response to Ebola, s.l.: Education Development Trust (2020)
44. Kawchale, N., Satao, R.: Predictive analytics in education context. Int. J. Mod. Trends Sci. Technol. **02**(11), 77–82 (2016)
45. Biasi, V., De Vincenzo, C., Fagioli, S., Mosca, M., Patrizi, N.: Evaluation of predictive factors in the drop-out phenomenon: interaction of latent personal factors and social-environmental context. J. Educ. Soc. Res. **9**(4), 92–103 (2019). https://doi.org/10.2478/jesr-2019-0059

Health and Well-Being

A Machine Learning Approach to Mental Disorder Prediction: Handling the Missing Data Challenge

Tsholofelo Mokheleli[1]([✉]) [iD], Tebogo Bokaba[1] [iD], Tinofirei Museba[1] [iD], and Nompumelelo Ntshingila[2] [iD]

[1] Department of Applied Information Systems, University of Johannesburg, Johannesburg, South Africa
{tsholofelom,tbokaba,tmuseba}@uj.ac.za
[2] Department of Nursing Science, University of Johannesburg, Johannesburg, South Africa
mpumin@uj.ac.za

Abstract. In recent years, the application of Machine Learning (ML) to predict mental disorders has gained significant attention due to its potential for early prediction. This study highlights the challenges of ML in mental disorders prediction, such as missing data in mental health datasets, by comparing four data imputation methods: Mode, Multivariate Imputation by Chained Equations, Hot Deck, and K-Nearest Neighbor (K-NN) to enhance predictive accuracy; and utilizing four ML classifiers and three ensemble methods: Bagging, Boosting, and Stacking, with Mode and K-NN imputation datasets to show consistent performance. The study ultimately contributes to early mental disorder diagnosis and intervention in alignment with the United Nations Sustainable Development Goal 3 (SDG 3) for global health and well-being, by highlighting ML and data imputation's potential in mental health analysis and paving the way for further advancements in the field.

Keywords: Data Imputation · Machine Learning · Mental Disorders Prediction · Missing Values

1 Introduction

There is a growing interest in utilizing Machine Learning (ML) to predict mental disorders [1]. This surge in interest is primarily driven by the potential of ML to assist in the early identification of mental disorders [2]. ML is a subfield of artificial intelligence that involves the development of algorithms and models that can analyze and learn from data, enabling computers to make predictions or decisions without being explicitly programmed [3]. ML algorithms have showcased impressive abilities in analyzing extensive datasets encompassing medical records, physiological measurements, and patient-reported symptoms. This capability allows for predicting the likelihood of developing mental disorders and assessing the effectiveness of different treatment options [4]. Mental disorders are conditions that disrupt the thoughts, emotions, behaviors, and

M. Masinde et al. (Eds.): AFRICATEK 2023, LNICST 520, pp. 93–106, 2024.
https://doi.org/10.1007/978-3-031-63999-9_6

mental well-being of an individual, leading to distress and daily life challenges [5]. Accurately predicting mental disorders holds substantial significance, as it can lead to timely interventions, personalized treatment strategies, and an overall enhancement in the quality of life for individuals affected by these conditions [6, 7]. With the advancement of technology and data-driven approaches, the potential for harnessing predictive models to improve mental health care continues to grow progressively promising.

However, while using ML for predicting mental disorders is undoubtedly a promising avenue, it also presents challenges, particularly in the context of the unique characteristics of mental disorder datasets. Among these challenges, missing values emerge as a critical concern. Missing values introduce data inconsistencies and incompleteness, which can delay the accuracy and reliability of predictive models in this domain [8].

Mental health datasets often have missing data due to incomplete patient responses, data collection errors, data capturing, or privacy concerns. Ignoring missing data may compromise the accuracy and reliability of analyses, potentially resulting in biased outcomes. Handling missing data is thus crucial for accurate insights from ML models. Data imputation methods can be used to estimate missing data. This study used ML algorithms to address missing data, including a comparative evaluation of four data imputation methods: Mode, Multivariate Imputation by Chained Equations (MICE), Hot Deck, and K-Nearest Neighbor (K-NN).

The study aimed to shed light on the significance of mental disorder prediction and dealing with missing data in the dataset. The study's main contributions lie in comparing data imputation methods to reduce the impact of missing data on the accuracy of a mental disorder prediction model, and to enhance mental health care through data-driven approaches such as applying ML algorithms and ensemble learning methods. Therefore, the study aligns with the United Nations Sustainable Development Goal 3 (SDG 3), which strives to ensure good health and well-being for all [9].

2 Related Work

This section aims to comprehensively examine the existing literature to gain insight into the challenges posed by missing data when employing ML for predicting mental disorders. Several studies have contributed valuable insights into utilizing ML for mental disorder prediction and addressing the complexities introduced by missing data.

Henry et al. [10] focused on predicting mental health treatment for information technology (tech) employees. Their study aimed to predict the necessity of mental health treatment among these employees using the Open Sourcing Mental Illness (OSMI) dataset. To handle the missing data in the dataset, the authors removed instances that had missing value rates exceeding 85%. The study used ensemble methods such as Bagging, Light Gradient-Boosting Machine (GBM), and Stacking to develop the predictive models. It also used Binary Particle Swarm Optimization (BPSO) for feature selection. The study found that ensemble methods do not consistently yield superior predictions.

Li [11] focused on applying ML to predict mental disorders and interpret feature importance. The study used Random Forest (RF), K-NN, and Decision Tree (DT) algorithms. The authors addressed the issue of missing data by deleting observations that exceeded half of the dataset. The RF model and Grid Search Optimization (GSO) yielded the best predictive performance.

Mitravinda et al. [12] explored mental health patterns and risk factors within the tech industry, employing the OSMI dataset. The strategy utilized XGBoost and Gradient Boosting classifiers and yielded notable predictive accuracies. The strategy entailed the removal of columns featuring over 50% missing data.

Using ML algorithms, Bajaj et al. [13] investigated non-invasive mental health prediction. The study aimed to identify the most effective predictive model among various algorithms, including Logistic Regression (LR), DT, K-NN, Adaboost, and RF. The authors used two datasets, one comprising mental health patient questionnaires and the other containing information from MRI scans of Alzheimer's patients. The authors deleted the missing data instead of data imputation. The study underscored the importance of using data that includes demographic, behavioral, and psychological factors that have the potential to further enhance prediction accuracy.

Olatunde et al. [14] formulated a classification model for mental disorders employing a variety of algorithms, such as LR, Support Vector Machine (SVM), Naïve Bayes (NB), and DT. Despite facing substantial missing data in the dataset, they managed data cleaning by discarding columns with 1 000 or more missing data and rows containing at least 11 missing data. Imputation methods were applied to categorical features, filling missing data with the most frequent value, or replacing them with a new "missing."

Duncan et al. [15] investigated the connection between mental health and academic performance in Canadian secondary school students. The missing data for all variables were addressed by employing multiple imputations using R packages and the MICE technique. This approach preserved the hierarchical structure of the data by imputing values at the individual level while considering schools as a random intercept higher-order clustering factor.

Luo [16] investigated challenges linked to missing data within clinical datasets. This study revolved around the Data Analytics Challenge of Missing Data Imputation (DACMI), which offers a shared clinical dataset and ground truth for developing and evaluating missing data imputation techniques for clinical data. The study focused on imputing missing data in 13 commonly measured blood laboratory tests. It randomly removed one recorded result per laboratory test per patient admission and used these as the ground truth for evaluation. This rigorous evaluation methodology ensured the accuracy and reliability of the imputation techniques. The ML algorithms used in the study were LightGBM, XGBoost, and MICE imputation techniques.

The significant gaps identified in the literature reviewed are related to the insufficient exploration of data imputation techniques for handling missing data within mental health datasets. Many studies have leaned towards removing rows or columns with missing data [10–14], a practice that can lead to data loss and introduce potential bias into the models. Despite the numerous investigations into predictive modeling for mental health results, a recurring pattern emerges where the resolution for missing data tends to involve removal or deletion rather than embracing more comprehensive data imputation strategies. Considering the identified gaps, this study used and compared various data imputation methods to assess their impact on enhancing predictive accuracy and overall performance in models for predicting mental disorders. While some studies primarily utilized single-year data from the OSMI dataset, this study took a more comprehensive approach by combining six different OSMI datasets to create a more extensive dataset.

3   Methodology

This section presents the dataset overview, data preprocessing and experimental setup. It also discusses the data imputation techniques applied, ML algorithms and ensemble methods, and evaluation metrics.

3.1   Data Collection

The dataset utilized in this study was sourced from Open Sourcing Mental Illness (OSMI), a nonprofit organization focused on promoting mental wellness within the workplace and open-source communities [17]. The OSMI website administers a survey that captures the life experiences of individuals employed in technology-oriented companies, encompassing their mental health history and consultation practices. The OSMI dataset enjoys widespread recognition within the mental health domain. This study took a unique approach by combining datasets from 2016 to 2021 to enrich the scope of data analysis. Unlike previous studies that worked with constrained data subsets [11, 18], this investigation harnessed the broader dataset to train and test ML algorithms models with improved effectiveness.

Table 1 presents a summary of the dataset, along with the features and instances in each dataset used to make up the final dataset used in the study. Table 2 shows a statistical analysis of the missing data within the dataset and the percentages of the missing data.

Table 1. Summary of the Dataset.

No.	Year	Features	Instances
1	2016	63	1433
2	2017	123	756
3	2018	123	417
4	2019	82	352
5	2020	120	180
6	2021	124	131

3.2   Data Preprocessing

The data preprocessing stage is a preparatory phase in data analysis where raw data is cleaned, transformed, and organized to ensure its quality and suitability for further analysis. During this stage, data cleaning and preparation tasks are carried out.

The process began with removing irrelevant columns from the dataset spanning 2016 to 2021. This entailed the selection and retention of important columns which were renamed for simplicity and the assurance of data quality. Textual data was transformed into numerical form using label encoding. The resulting dataset consisted of 3 269 rows and 25 columns, making it ready for ML analysis. The selection criteria for retaining columns were based on their consistent presence across all yearly datasets from 2016 to 2021.

Table 2. Overview of Data Completeness and Missing Data, Including Percentages.

Variables	Missing	Non-null	Missing in %	Non-null in %
Self Employed	0	3 269	0.0	100
Company Role	1 429	1 840	43.7	56.3
Mental Importance	546	2 723	16.7	83.3
Discuss MH	1 410	1 859	43.1	56.9
Coworkers	428	2 841	13.1	86.9
Work Interfere	2 723	546	83.3	16.7
Past Mental Health	23	3 246	0.7	99.3
Gender	28	3 241	0.9	99.1
Mental Health Diagnosed	1 080	2189	33	67

3.2.1 Data Imputation

The study employed four distinct data imputation techniques: Mode, MICE, Hot Deck, and K-NN. These techniques were chosen for their ability to effectively handle missing data by offering various advantages and trade-offs, thereby ensuring a comprehensive exploration of imputation methods.

Mode is a straightforward method to address missing data within a dataset. It involves substituting absent values with the mode, the most frequently occurring value in the corresponding variable [19, 20]. This technique suits categorical or nominal data with distinct categories or labels.

MICE stands out as a more advanced approach for handling missing data, as it employs an iterative process to impute missing data across a dataset by generating multiple complete datasets, each incorporating imputed values [21, 22]. This iterative procedure is particularly beneficial because it focuses on individual variables during each cycle while incorporating regression models with other variables as predictors, allowing for a more comprehensive and precise imputation process.

Hot Deck is a valuable method for handling missing data and operates by replacing missing data in datasets with values from similar or "neighboring" observations. This approach leverages the concept that when two observations share similarities in specific aspects, their missing data can be effectively attributed using the available data from the other observation, contributing to enhanced data completeness and accuracy [19, 23].

K-NN, an effective data imputation technique, capitalizes on the principle of data point similarity to address missing data. It is especially advantageous when dealing with numerical and continuous variables. K-NN imputation operates by identifying the 'k' nearest complete data points to the one with missing data and subsequently estimating the missing value by drawing insights from the values of these neighboring data points, promoting precise and context-aware imputation [24].

3.3 Experimental Setup

The experiments were performed on Google Research Colab, also referred to as Colab, which is a cloud-based platform that provides a user-friendly interface for executing Jupyter notebooks [25]. Colab offers an extensive range of pre-installed libraries and frameworks frequently utilized in tasks involving data analysis, ML, and Deep Learning. This platform was chosen for the study due to its suitability and convenience.

The experiments began with data preprocessing, including dataset concatenation and label encoding to convert text to numbers (see Fig. 1). Inconsistencies and ambiguous categories were resolved by observation; for instance, ages below 16 were removed and treated as missing data. The four data imputation techniques outlined above were applied to create clean datasets for baseline model construction. Baseline models employed four classifiers and five evaluation metrics, detailed in the subsequent section. For the construction and testing of the baseline models, and the ensemble models, the data was split into an 80% training set and a 20% testing set. This split was crucial to provide ample data for the training phase while ensuring a robust evaluation of the models on unseen data during the testing phase. K-fold cross-validation was employed to assess how well the ML model will generalize and perform on different folds of data.

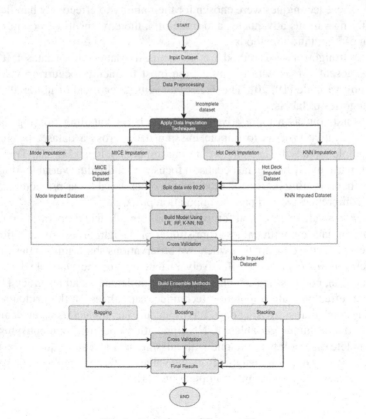

Fig. 1. Experimental Process Flow

3.4 ML Algorithms and Ensemble Methods

This section discusses the ML algorithms employed in the study, encompassing various approaches. The initial baseline model featured four classifiers: LR, RF, K-NN, and NB.

LR is a statistical method used in binary classification and regression tasks. It models the probability of an instance belonging to a particular class based on its independent variables [26]. LR is widely recognized for its user-friendly nature.

RF is a supervised learning method that constructs a "forest" using multiple decision trees trained through the "Bagging" technique. Bagging is based on the concept that aggregating multiple learning models enhances the overall predictive capability [27].

K-NN is a flexible ML algorithm for classification and regression. It predicts by considering the k closest data points and uses majority class (classification) or average value (regression) among them [26].

NB is a powerful, simple classification algorithm. It uses Bayes' theorem to calculate class probabilities based on observed features, using feature mean and standard deviation estimates for each class [28].

The study employed three prominent ensemble methods to enhance the predictive capabilities of the models: Bagging, Boosting, and Stacking.

Bagging and Boosting were selected due to their proven effectiveness in the literature for improving model accuracy. Stacking was introduced as an innovative approach not previously explored in the reviewed literature to enhance model robustness by combining multiple learners for superior predictions. Bagging, short for Bootstrap Aggregating, involves training multiple instances of a base model on different subsets of the training data and combining their predictions to reduce variance and improve overall model stability [29].

Boosting focuses on iterative training models, assigning more weight to instances misclassified in previous iterations. This adaptive learning process helps create a strong, accurate model by giving higher importance to challenging data points [30].

Stacking combines the strengths of various base models by training a meta-model that learns from their collective predictions [31]. These ensemble techniques provide opportunities for improving model performance and offer valuable insights into how different algorithms complement each other to tackle complex predictive tasks effectively.

3.5 Evaluation Metrics

A diverse set of evaluation metrics is essential to assess the performance of ML models in predicting mental disorder outcomes. This study employed a comprehensive suite of metrics, including accuracy, precision, recall, f1 score, and the Area Under the Receiver Operating Characteristic Curve (AUC-ROC). Multiple metrics are imperative, particularly when addressing mental disorders, as they provide a more holistic assessment beyond accuracy. The formulas for all the metrics are shown in Eq. 1–5. The formulas involve these keywords: True Positive (TP) for correctly identifying a positive outcome, False Positive (FP) for incorrectly identifying a positive outcome that is not there, True Negative (TN) for correctly identifying a negative outcome, and False Negative (FN) for incorrectly identifying a negative outcome that exists [32, 33].

$$Accuracy = \frac{Number\ of\ correctly\ predicted\ instances}{Total\ number\ of\ instances} \qquad (1)$$

$$Precision = \frac{True\ Positives}{(True\ Positives + False\ Positives)} \qquad (2)$$

$$Recall = \frac{True\ Positives}{(True\ Positives + False\ Negatives)} \qquad (3)$$

$$F1score = 2 * \frac{(Precision * Recall)}{(Precision + Recall)} \qquad (4)$$

$$AUC - ROC = sum(\frac{(TPR[i] + TPR[i+1]) * (FPR[i+1] - FPR[i])}{2}) \qquad (5)$$

where true positive rate (TPR) and false positive rate (FPR) are calculated:

$$TPR = \frac{TP}{(TP + FN)} \qquad (6)$$

$$FPR = \frac{FP}{(FP + TN)} \qquad (7)$$

4   Experimental Results and Discussion

This section showcases the experimental results obtained through the utilization of data imputation techniques and ML algorithms previously detailed in the methodology section. The 80:20 data split discussed in Sect. 3.3 was used during the generation of the results presented in Sects. 4.1 and 4.2.

4.1   Initial Models

Four models were constructed using four classifiers from the imputed datasets. The results of the top-performing models are presented in Tables 3 and 4. The best data imputation methods were determined based on cumulative metrics scores and cross-validation results, including mean cross-validation accuracy and standard deviation in cross-validation accuracy.

Mode imputation exhibited mean cross-validation accuracy ranging from 74% to 92%, with LR achieving 89%, RF 92%, K-NN 74%, and NB 88%, all having a standard deviation in cross-validation accuracy of no more than 0.02. Precision ranged from 74% to 93%, while Recall ranged from 90% to 96%. F1 scores consistently exceeded 82%, as shown in Table 3.

K-NN imputation showed results close to Mode, with LR at 89%, RF at 92%, K-NN at 73%, and NB at 89%, maintaining a standard deviation in cross-validation accuracy of no more than 0.02. K-NN imputation yielded favorable Precision results from 72% to 93%. Recall also demonstrated a strong performance, from 90% to 97%. The F1 Score also showed robust results, with the lowest score being 82% (Table 4).

Mode and K-NN emerged as the top data imputation methods, demonstrating consistent performance across metrics and cross-validation.

Table 3. Model Performance with Mode-Imputed Data.

	Classifiers			
Metrics	LR	RF	K-NN	NB
Accuracy	0.89	0.92	0.73	0.89
Precision	0.89	0.92	0.74	0.93
Recall	0.96	0.96	0.93	0.90
F1 Score	0.92	0.94	0.82	0.91
AUC-ROC	0.86	0.90	0.64	0.88
Cross-validation Acc (%)	89	92	74	88

Table 4. Model Performance with K-NN-Imputed Data.

	Classifiers			
Metrics	LR	RF	K-NN	NB
Accuracy	0.89	0.92	0.72	0.89
Precision	0.88	0.92	0.72	0.93
Recall	0.96	0.97	0.94	0.90
F1 Score	0.92	0.94	0.82	0.92
AUC-ROC	0.85	0.90	0.62	0.88
Cross-validation Acc (%)	89	92	73	89

Overall, among the models, the best classifiers can also be identified. RF and NB consistently demonstrated strong performance across various imputation methods and metrics. While the models performed well, there is room for improvement by incorporating ensemble methods to enhance their overall performance.

4.2 Ensemble Methods

Three ensemble methods in ML were discussed in the methodology section. The ensemble methods utilized the Mode imputation dataset as it exhibited encouraging results considering the cumulative score of the metrics. In the Bagging analysis, LR and RF were employed as base models. RF had a high mean cross-validation accuracy (0.92) and low standard deviation (0.01), making it a strong candidate for Bagging. LR also had a relatively high mean accuracy (0.89) and a low standard deviation (0.01).

Boosting aims to improve model performance by focusing on misclassified instances. RF and LR were again chosen as base models. Of the possible combinations of classifiers that were tested, RF and LR were the ones that performed the best.

Stacking focuses on the diversity of base classifiers that complement each other. All four classifiers offered diversity, and LR was used as the meta-learner to combine the predictions of the diverse base models.

Table 5 shows the results of the ensemble methods. The methods achieved similar accuracy, precision, and F1 score results. However, Boosting with a recall of 0.97 slightly outperformed Bagging and Stacking with recalls of 0.96. Stacking also slightly outperformed Boosting and Bagging regarding AUC ROC, with 0.90 compared to 0.89 for the latter. Stacking may be considered the best ensemble method as it embraces diversity, and as AUC-ROC is a critical metric for assessing the overall discriminative power of a model, is especially effective in binary classification tasks. The cross-validation results demonstrate that Stacking consistently performed well across all folds of the dataset, achieving an impressive mean cross-validation accuracy of 92%. In comparison, Bagging achieved a slightly lower accuracy of 90%, while Boosting attained 85%. All three ensemble methods exhibited a low standard deviation of 0.01 in cross-validation accuracy, indicating their stability and reliability.

Table 5. Ensemble Method Results Using Mode-Imputed Data

	Ensemble Method		
Metrics	Bagging	Boosting	Stacking
Accuracy	0.92	0.92	0.92
Precision	0.92	0.92	0.92
Recall	0.96	0.97	0.96
F1 Score	0.94	0.94	0.94
AUC-ROC	0.89	0.89	0.90
Cross-validation Acc (%)	90	85	92

4.3 Comparative Analysis

In comparing the performance of initial models and ensemble methods for handling missing data in mental disorder datasets, the study observed that Mode and K-NN imputation methods consistently demonstrated strong performance, with RF and NB as the standout classifiers across various imputation techniques and metrics. The initial models showed that Mode imputation consistently outperformed K-NN imputation in terms of mean cross-validation accuracy, precision for LR, RF and NB classifiers, and had comparable Recall scores. Mode imputation can be considered the best-performing method among the two for handling missing data in mental disorder datasets.

However, while these initial models showed promise, the introduction of ensemble methods further enhanced their overall performance. Among the ensemble methods, Stacking exhibited the most balanced performance, achieving comparable accuracy, precision, and F1 score results to Bagging and Boosting. Stacking excelled in terms of AUC-ROC, a critical metric for assessing discriminative power in binary classification. Stacking's consistently high cross-validation accuracy of 92% and low standard deviation indicated its stability and reliability, suggesting its potential as an effective approach to handling missing data in mental disorder datasets.

5 Contributions of the Study

This study has significantly addressed the escalating worldwide challenges associated with mental disorders. It aimed to bridge a void in the current body of literature by employing ML algorithms and data imputation techniques to impute missing data and predict and analyze the occurrence of mental disorders. The study has not only made significant advancements in theoretical contributions but has also generated implications, both theoretical and practical, that are relevant to the field.

Theoretical Contributions: The study contributes to understanding how data imputation techniques can effectively be used in mental disorders prediction using ML. It also adds to the growing research examining how ML can be applied to mental disorder prediction.

Theoretical Implications: The study's results could impact how mental healthcare data are analyzed, highlighting the significance of data imputation techniques. This paper could inspire further research to improve ML algorithms specifically designed for mental disorder prediction purposes.

Practical Implications: The ML data imputation compared and discussed has the potential to enhance the accuracy of predictive models for mental disorders, which can be valuable for early diagnosis and treatment. The findings could also impact the development of systems that promote improved decision-making based on data.

6 Limitation and Future Work

A limitation of the study was the presence of class imbalance within the dataset. The unequal distribution of data across different classes can pose challenges for ML models, potentially leading to biased predictions. As a result of class imbalance, the predictive accuracy of the models may not have fully realized their potential. Incorporating hyperparameter tuning can be a critical consideration for future research in this domain.

Future work should prioritize addressing class imbalance as a foundational step in model improvement. Techniques like oversampling, undersampling, or advanced resampling methods can help rebalance the dataset. Implementing hyperparameter tuning and feature selection processes can further boost model performance, especially in mental disorder prediction, where accuracy is crucial. Future work can significantly enhance predictive models for mental health outcomes by systematically addressing these limitations and refining modeling approaches.

7 Conclusion

By addressing the critical issues of missing data in mental health datasets and employing various data imputations and ensemble methods, this study has made significant strides in aligning with the United Nations SDG 3, namely, to improve global health and well-being. It has laid a strong foundation for developing predictive models for mental disorders. The study contributes to early diagnosis and intervention and opens the door to more advanced algorithms and evaluation metrics that can substantially enhance the accuracy and reliability of these predictive models.

This study marks an important milestone in leveraging the power of ML within the realm of mental health. It offers promising avenues for the early detection and management of mental disorders, aligning with the broader goals of SDG 3. Furthermore, it underscores the potential of ML and data imputation techniques in mental health analysis while highlighting future research and improvement areas. As cutting-edge technologies are embraced, and approaches are refined, the potential for making even greater strides in the crucial mental health analysis and care field is evident.

References

1. Garriga, R., et al.: Machine learning model to predict mental health crises from electronic health records. Nat. Med. **28**(6), 1240–1248 (2022). https://doi.org/10.1038/s41591-022-01811-5
2. Awal, G.K., Rao, K.: Can machine learning predict an employee's mental health? Commun. Comput. Inform. Sci. **1417**, 235–247 (2021). https://doi.org/10.1007/978-3-030-88378-2_19
3. Ercan, U.K., Özdemir, G.D., Özdemir, M.A., Güren, O.: Plasma medicine: the era of artificial intelligence. Plasma Processes Polym. (2023). https://doi.org/10.1002/ppap.202300066
4. Vahdat, M., Oneto, L., Anguita, D., Funk, M., Rauterberg, M.: Can machine learning explain human learning? Neurocomputing **192**, 14–28 (2016). https://doi.org/10.1016/j.neucom.2015.11.100
5. Galderisi, S., Heinz, A., Kastrup, M., Beezhold, J., Sartorius, N.: Toward a new definition of mental health. World Psych. **14**(2), 231–233 (2015). https://doi.org/10.1002/wps.20231
6. Allahyari, E., Roustaei, N.: Applying artificial neural-network model to predict psychiatric symptoms. Biomedicine (Taipei) **12**(1) (2022). https://doi.org/10.37796/2211-8039.1149
7. Yi, Y., Park, Y.-H.: Structural equation model of the relationship between functional ability, mental health, and quality of life in older adults living alone. PLoS ONE **17**(8), e0269003 (2022). https://doi.org/10.1371/journal.pone.0269003
8. Ridzuan, F., Wan Zainon, W.M.N.: A review on data cleansing methods for big data. Procedia Comput. Sci. **161**, 731–738 (2019). https://doi.org/10.1016/j.procs.2019.11.177

9. Salvo, D., et al.: Physical activity promotion and the United Nations Sustainable Development Goals: building synergies to maximize impact. J. Phys. Act. Health **18**(10), 1163–1180 (2021). https://doi.org/10.1123/jpah.2021-0413
10. Henry, M., Isa, S.M.: Mental health treatment prediction for tech employee with the implementation of ensemble methods. J. Theor. Appl. Inf. Technol. **100**(8), 2675–2685 (2022)
11. Li, Y.: Application of machine learning to predict mental health disorders and interpret feature importance. In: 2023 3rd International Symposium on Computer Technology and Information Science (ISCTIS), pp. 257–261. IEEE (2023). https://doi.org/10.1109/ISCTIS58954.2023.10213032
12. Mitravinda, K.M., Nair, D.S., Srinivasa, G.: Mental health in tech: Analysis of workplace risk factors and impact of COVID-19. SN Comput. Sci. **4**(2) (2023). https://doi.org/10.1007/s42979-022-01613-z
13. Bajaj, V., Bathija, R., Megnani, C., Sawara, J., Ansari, N.: Non-invasive mental health prediction using machine learning: an exploration of algorithms and accuracy. In: 2023 7th International Conference on Intelligent Computing and Control Systems (ICICCS), pp. 313–321. IEEE (2023). https://doi.org/10.1109/ICICCS56967.2023.10142504
14. Olatunde, O., Falola, B.: Classification of mental health disorders. Tech. Rep. (2021). https://doi.org/10.13140/RG.2.2.34918.60483
15. Duncan, M.J., Patte, K.A., Leatherdale, S.T.: Mental health associations with academic performance and education behaviors in Canadian secondary school students. Can. J. Sch. Psychol. **36**(4), 335–357 (2021). https://doi.org/10.1177/0829573521997311
16. Luo, Y.: Evaluating the state of the art in missing data imputation for clinical data. Brief Bioinform. **23**(1) (2022). https://doi.org/10.1093/bib/bbab489
17. OSMI. About OSMI. Open Sourcing Mental Health (2023). https://osmihelp.org/about/about-osmi.html. Accessed 8 Sep 2023
18. Tate, A.E., McCabe, R.C., Larsson, H., Lundström, S., Lichtenstein, P., Kuja Halkola, R.: Predicting mental health problems in adolescence using machine learning techniques. PLoS One **15**(4) (2020). https://doi.org/10.1371/journal.pone.0230389
19. Xu, X., Xia, L., Zhang, Q., Wu, S., Wu, M., Liu, H.: The ability of different imputation methods for missing values in mental measurement questionnaires. BMC Med. Res. Methodol. **20**(1), 42 (2020). https://doi.org/10.1186/s12874-020-00932-0
20. Makaba, T., Dogo, E.: A comparison of strategies for missing values in data on machine learning classification algorithms. In: 2019 International Multidisciplinary Information Technology and Engineering Conference (IMITEC), pp. 1–7. IEEE (2019). https://doi.org/10.1109/IMITEC45504.2019.9015889
21. Alruhaymi, A.Z., Kim, C.J.: Why can multiple imputations and how (MICE) algorithm work? Open J. Stat. **11**(05), 759–777 (2021). https://doi.org/10.4236/ojs.2021.115045
22. Ganapathy, S., Bhaskarapillai, B., Dandge, S.: The effect of multiple imputations by chained equations on the factors associated with immunization coverage in India. Int. J. Health Sci. Res. **11**(6), 249–262 (2021). https://doi.org/10.52403/ijhsr.20210638
23. Myers, T.A.: Goodbye, listwise deletion: presenting Hot Deck imputation as an easy and effective tool for handling missing data. Commun. Methods Meas. **5**(4), 297–310 (2011). https://doi.org/10.1080/19312458.2011.624490
24. Liao, S.G., et al.: Missing value imputation in high-dimensional phenomic data: imputable or not, and how?. BMC Bioinform. **15**(1) (2014). https://doi.org/10.1186/s12859-014-0346-6
25. Google Colab Team. Google Colaboratory. Google (2023). https://colab.google/. Accessed 16 June 2023
26. Reddy, U.S., Thota, A.V., Dharun, A.: Machine learning techniques for stress prediction in working employees. In: 2018 IEEE International Conference on Computational Intelligence and Computing Research, ICCIC 2018, Institute of Electrical and Electronics Engineers Inc. (2018). https://doi.org/10.1109/ICCIC.2018.8782395

27. Mohamed, E.S., Naqishbandi, T.A., Bukhari, S.A.C., Rauf, I., Sawrikar, V., Hussain, A.: A hybrid mental health prediction model using Support Vector Machine, Multilayer Perceptron, and Random Forest algorithms. Healthcare Anal. **3**, 100185 (2023). https://doi.org/10.1016/j.health.2023.100185

28. Ali, L., et al.: A feature-driven decision support system for heart failure prediction based on $\chi 2$ Statistical Model and Gaussian Naive Bayes. Comput. Math. Methods Med. **2019**, 1–8 (2019). https://doi.org/10.1155/2019/6314328

29. Breiman, L.: Bagging predictors. Mach. Learn. **24**(2), 123–140 (1996). https://doi.org/10.1007/BF00058655

30. Wang, G., Sun, J., Ma, J., Xu, K., Gu, J.: Sentiment classification: the contribution of ensemble learning. Decis. Support. Syst. **57**, 77–93 (2014). https://doi.org/10.1016/j.dss.2013.08.002

31. Aboneh, T., Rorissa, A., Srinivasagan, R.: Stacking-based ensemble learning method for multi-spectral image classification. Technol. (Basel) **10**(1), 17 (2022). https://doi.org/10.3390/technologies10010017

32. Ruuska, S., Hämäläinen, W., Kajava, S., Mughal, M., Matilainen, P., Mononen, J.: Evaluation of the confusion matrix method in the validation of an automated system for measuring feeding behaviour of cattle. Behav. Proc. **148**, 56–62 (2018). https://doi.org/10.1016/j.beproc.2018.01.004

33. Chicco, D., Tötsch, N., Jurman, G.: The Matthews correlation coefficient (MCC) is more reliable than balanced accuracy, bookmaker informedness, and markedness in two-class confusion matrix evaluation. BioData Min **14**(1), 13 (2021). https://doi.org/10.1186/s13040-021-00244-z

Towards a Smart Healthcare System for Non-Communicable Diseases (NCDs) Management: A Bibliometric Analysis

Kudakwashe Maguraushe(✉) ⓘ and Patrick Ndayizigamiye ⓘ

Department of Applied Information Systems, University of Johannesburg,
Bunting Road Campus, Auckland Park, Johannesburg 2092, South Africa
{kmaguraushe,ndayizigamiyep}@uj.ac.za

Abstract. The World Health Organization has chastised the persistence and gradual progression of non-communicable diseases (NCDs) and their impact on human nature, which necessitates an urgent review of measures to combat them. This study employed a bibliometric analysis to comprehensively review and synthesise the body of knowledge on smart healthcare systems for NCD management. The study identified major developments, knowledge gaps, and major contributors to the research field. Biblioshiny and VOSviewer software were used to retrieve data from the Scopus database, and performance analysis and science mapping were used to analyse the data. The search string used was (("Smart Healthcare" OR "Smart Healthcare System" OR "Intelligent Healthcare" OR "Healthcare IoT") AND ("Non-Communicable Disease" OR "NCDs" OR "Chronic Disease" OR "Chronic Illness") AND ("Management" OR "Disease Management" OR "Healthcare Management" OR "Patient Management")). The results revealed that the number of articles on smart healthcare systems for NCD management increased exponentially between 2007 and 2023, signifying a rising need for technology improvements in combating NCDs. Keywords that emerged include machine learning, remote sensing, Internet of Things, wearable devices, and mobile health. These terms are increasingly being used within healthcare and reflect a multidisciplinary approach to the management of NCDs. The study recommends that given the substantial co-authorship, more interdisciplinary research can be used to explore underrepresented topics or approaches.

Keyword: Smart Healthcare · Non-Communicable Diseases (NCDs) · Internet of Things (IoT) · Artificial Intelligence (AI)

1 Introduction and Background

According to the World Health Organization (WHO), non-communicable diseases (NCDs) are chronic conditions that persist over an extended period and generally exhibit a gradual progression [1, 2]. There are four main categories of NCDs: malignancies (lung cancer and colorectal cancer), diabetes mellitus (DM), chronic respiratory conditions

M. Masinde et al. (Eds.): AFRICATEK 2023, LNICST 520, pp. 107–125, 2024.
https://doi.org/10.1007/978-3-031-63999-9_7

(asthma and chronic obstructive pulmonary disease), and cardio-vascular conditions (stroke, heart attacks and hypertension) [3]. NCDs are among the top causes of mortality [4]. In fact, seven out of 10 deaths worldwide are caused by NCDs [5, 6]. This is further amplified by global statistics that point to NCDs being the cause of 74% of deaths worldwide and being a major cause of disability and loss of productivity [2]. By 2030, it is expected that 52 million people will die from NCDs, and low - and middle-income countries will account for 80% of these deaths [7]. In addition, these countries are increasingly carrying the burden associated with the economic and health expenses related to NCDs [8]. This necessitates an urgent review of measures intended to combat NCDs.

Although NCDs cannot always be prevented, several actions may lower the chances of contracting them. Therefore, it is imperative to take preventative measures as a way of reducing the impact of NCDs [8]. The majority (80%) of risk factors for early cardiovascular disease, stroke, and diabetes can be controlled by the dissemination of knowledge (awareness) on risk factors [9, 10]. According to Chen et al., these risk factors include smoking, abusing alcohol, eating poorly, a lack of exercise, being overweight or obese, and having elevated blood pressure, high blood sugar levels, and high cholesterol levels [9]. If NCDs can be identified and predicted in their early stages, healthcare interventions can be implemented to minimize their adverse effects on patients [10]. An example of tools that can be used to predict the potential of contracting NCDS includes wearable sensors for health monitoring, activity tracking, disorder prediction, treatment evaluation, home rehabilitation, and safety monitoring, to name a few [11]. In addition, the use of mobile health (mHealth) is considered one of the solutions to eradicating the surge of NCDs [12]. According to Hsu, Alavi and Dong, mHealth entails the use of smartphones, patient monitoring programs, and other wireless equipment as part of healthcare interventions to treat a variety of medical and public health disorders. mHealth can also be used for self-management through smart healthcare [13]. Self-management through smart healthcare comprises a collection of tools that a person employs daily to control a chronic condition like NCDs and encourage recovery [14].

Traditional healthcare systems are challenged by scarce resources and rising service demand and smart healthcare systems are poised to be a viable response to these problems [15]. By utilizing cutting-edge technologies and creative strategies, smart healthcare seeks to improve healthcare in terms of intelligence (data gathering), effectiveness, and sustainability [16]. By utilizing the Internet of Things (IoT), artificial intelligence (AI), cloud computing, and big data, smart healthcare can transform the healthcare system to make it more personalized, effective, and convenient [17].

Therefore, the purpose of this study was to employ a bibliometric analysis approach to comprehensively review and synthesise the body of knowledge on smart healthcare systems for the management of NCDs and to identify major developments, knowledge gaps, and major contributors to the research field. Thus, the objectives of this study were:

i. To determine the key themes in the literature that relate to the application of smart healthcare systems for the management of NCDs.
ii. To identify the most influential journals and authors related to research on smart healthcare systems for the management of NCDs.

iii. To evaluate, using citation analysis, the significance of important publications and authors related to research on smart healthcare systems for the management of NCDs.
iv. To identify gaps within the current body of knowledge related to research on smart healthcare systems in NCD management and propose future studies.
v. To determine the geographical dispersion of research endeavours in the application of smart healthcare systems to manage NCDs.

2 Methodology

Bibliometric analysis is a quantitative tool for analyzing research trends [18]. It was used in this study to assess the output of publications, research trends, and publishing trends on smart healthcare systems for NCD management. Biblioshiny and VOSviewer software were used to retrieve data from the Scopus database on the 12th of September 2023. The period under study was 2007 to 2023. Performance analysis (publication trends, top contributing authors, top contributing journals, top contributing institutions and top contributing countries) and science mapping (relationships, co-occurrences, network analysis) were used in the bibliometric analysis [19]. The search string used to search for articles from the Scopus database was: ALL (("Smart Healthcare" OR "Smart Healthcare System" OR "Intelligent Healthcare" OR "Healthcare IoT") AND ("Non-Communicable Disease" OR "NCDs" OR "Chron-ic Disease" OR "Chronic Illness") AND ("Management" OR "Disease Management" OR "Healthcare Management" OR "Patient Management")).

3 Results

A total of 1235 original documents (journal articles, conference papers, review articles, book chapters, books, editorials, notes, retracted, letters and surveys) were retrieved from the Scopus online database for the period 2007 to 2023. The documents revealed 691 sources, 6 432 keywords and 3251 author's keywords. A total of 4522 authors contributed to the documents. The collaboration index was 4.54, indicating a high degree of collaboration among the documents as depicted in Table 1.

Table 1. Basic information on the selected articles

Database: Scopus	
Timespan: 2007 to 2023	
Annual growth rate: 36.34%	
Authors: 4522	
Single-authored documents: 56	
Average of co-authors per document: 4.54	
International collaboration (in percentage): 34.98%	
Distribution by document type: Journals (613), conference articles (237), review articles (193), book chapters (161), books (16), editorials (5), notes (5), retracted (3), letter (1), and survey (1)	

The retrieved documents were published in 495 diverse sources. The top 20 sources are depicted in Table 2. The journal IEEE Access had the highest total citations (TC) (n = 2300) with 41 publications (NP = 41) on smart healthcare systems for NCDs management. The journal also had the highest h-index and g-index (see Table 2).

Table 2. Source local impact

Element	h_index	g_index	m_index	TC	NP
IEEE Access	21	41	3,00	2300	41
Journal of Medical Systems	10	13	1,00	839	13
Sensors	10	15	3,33	245	26
Sensors (Switzerland)	8	9	0,80	1118	9
Journal of Ambient Intelligence and Humanized Computing	7	12	0,64	252	12
Future Generation Computer Systems	6	6	0,60	505	6
IEEE Internet of Things Journal	6	7	1,20	299	7
International Journal of Environmental Research and Public Health	6	10	1,50	118	18
Journal of Biomedical Informatics	6	7	0,67	281	7
Lecture Notes in Computer Science (including subseries Lecture Notes in AI and Bioinformatics)	6	10	0,35	113	19
Soft computing	6	7	0,75	111	7
Wireless Personal Communications	6	10	0,75	217	10
Cluster Computing	5	6	0,56	162	6
Healthcare (Switzerland)	5	7	1,67	66	15
International Journal of Medical Informatics	5	5	1,00	85	5
Journal of Healthcare Engineering	5	7	1,67	101	7
Journal of Medical Internet Research	5	8	1,25	118	8
Journal of Network and Computer Applications	5	6	0,83	527	6
Wireless Communications and Mobile Computing	5	7	0,63	71	7
Computational Intelligence and Neuroscience	4	9	1,33	109	9

The authors Chung K and Wu J had 11 publications each, with the former having a superior h-index and the g-index, and 324 total citations (TC). In contrast, Wu J had 7 and 10 for the h-index and g-index respectively and 110 total citations. Zaidan BB had the highest TC with nine publications, resulting in an h-index of 7. Table 3 depicts the top 20 authors with the highest impact.

Table 3. Author's local impact

Element	h_index	g_index	m_index	TC	NP
Chung K	8	11	0,89	324	11
Albahri AS	7	7	1,17	512	7
Albahri OS	7	7	1,17	512	7
Wu J	7	10	2,33	110	11
Zaidan AA	7	7	1,17	512	7
Zaidan BB	7	9	1,17	516	9
Alsalem MA	6	6	1,00	376	6
Fogliatto FS	6	7	1,50	193	7
Tortorella GL	6	7	1,50	193	7
Gou F	5	8	1,67	71	8
Kumar A	5	9	0,83	200	9
Tang H	5	6	1,67	147	6
Zhu J	5	6	0,50	45	8
Bhatt V	4	5	1,00	26	5
Chakraborty S	4	5	1,00	29	6
Clark CCT	4	6	1,00	60	21
Elhoseny M	4	4	0,80	130	4
Gupta A	4	7	0,80	56	7
Jara AJ	4	4	0,27	178	4
Kumar R	4	7	0,80	94	7

Figure 1 shows the country's rate of production in terms of publications on smart healthcare systems for NCD management. The period for this exponential growth spans from 2007 to 2023. Although all the top countries (India, China, USA, United Kingdom, Iran, and South Korea) experienced an exponential growth rate, India's rate of growth in terms of production surpassed 800 articles. China also experienced considerable growth in terms of production. This is probably the reason why China and India had the highest number of total citations (3187 and 1532 respectively). Table 4 depicts the most cited countries.

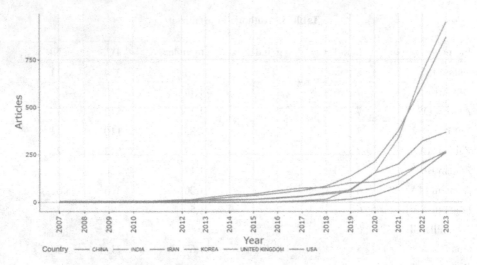

Fig. 1. Country production

Table 4. Most cited countries

Country	TC	Average article citations
China	3187	18,3
India	1532	9,6
USA	1440	28,2
South Korea	1084	17,2
Canada	1071	51
Australia	950	45,2
Malaysia	802	33,4
Iran	793	16,5
Italy	581	23,2
United Kingdom	557	15,5
Saudi Arabia	491	18,9
Egypt	428	32,9
Spain	380	18,1
Brazil	368	28,3
New Zealand	297	74,2
Croatia	293	146,5
Thailand	195	195

(*continued*)

Table 4. (*continued*)

Country	TC	Average article citations
Bangladesh	192	24
Germany	168	12
Iraq	154	30,8

Table 5 depicts the most globally cited articles. The most cited article is titled *Wearable Sensors for Remote Health Monitoring* and was authored by Majumder, S., Mondal, T., and Deen, M.J. in 2017. The article was published in the journal *Sensors* and received a record 720 citations. Amongst the top 20 publishers, *IEEE Access* published the highest number of articles related to smart healthcare in the context of NCDs with 4 articles (20%).

Table 5. Top 20 most globally cited articles

Author(S)	Publisher	Article Title	TC	TC/Year
Majumder et al. (2017) [1]	Sensors	Wearable Sensors for Remote Health Monitoring	720	102,86
Baker et al. (2017) [20]	IEEE Access	Internet of Things for Smart Healthcare: Technologies, Challenges, and Opportunities	678	96,86
Yin et al. (2016) [21]	Journal of Industrial Information Integration	The Internet of Things in Healthcare: An Overview	534	66,75
Chen et al. (2016) [22]	Mobile Networks and Applications	Smart Clothing: Connecting Humans with Clouds and Big Data for Sustainable Health Monitoring	314	39,25
Nizetic et al. (2020) [23]	Journal of Cleaner Production	Internet of Things (IoT): Opportunities, Issues, and Challenges Towards a Smart and Sustainable Future	293	73,25
Liu et al. (2019) [24]	IEEE Access	A Novel Cloud-Based Framework for the Elderly Healthcare Services Using Digital Twin	279	55,80

(*continued*)

Table 5. (*continued*)

Author(S)	Publisher	Article Title	TC	TC/Year
Qi et al. (2017) [25]	Pervasive and Mobile Computing	Advanced Internet of Things for Personalised Healthcare Systems: A survey	279	39,86
Tian et al. (2019) [26]	Global Health Journal	Smart Healthcare: Making Medical Care More Intelligent	278	55,60
Ghamari et al. (2016) [27]	Sensors	A Survey on Wireless Body Area Networks for Healthcare Systems in Residential Environments	228	28,50
Nweke et al. (2019) [28]	Information Fusion	Data Fusion and Multiple Classifier Systems for Human Activity Detection and Health Monitoring: Review and Open Research Directions	225	45,00
He et al. (2021) [29]	International Journal of Information Management	Information Technology Solutions, Challenges, and Suggestions for Tackling the COVID-19 Pandemic	215	71,67
Chen et al. (2018) [30]	Future Generation Computer Systems	Edge Cognitive Computing Based Smart Healthcare System	206	34,33
Aceto et al. (2018) [31]	Journal of Network and Computer Applications	The Role of Information and Communication Technologies in Healthcare: Taxonomies, Perspectives and Challenges	206	34,33
Chen et al. (2022) [32]	Chemical Reviews	Electronic Textiles for Wearable Point-of-Care Systems	201	100,50
Dey et al. (2017) [33]	IEEE Transactions on Consumer Electronics	Developing Residential Wireless Sensor Networks for ECG Healthcare Monitoring	201	28,71
Pal et al. (2018) [34]	IEEE Access	Internet-of-Things and Smart Homes for Elderly Healthcare: An End User Perspective	195	32,50

(*continued*)

Table 5. (*continued*)

Author(S)	Publisher	Article Title	TC	TC/Year
Baig et al. (2017) [35]	Journal of Medical Systems	A Systematic Review of Wearable Patient Monitoring Systems – Current Challenges and Opportunities for Clinical Adoption	186	26,57
Lan et al. (2018) [36]	Journal of Medical Systems	A Survey of Data Mining and Deep Learning in Bioinformatics	174	29,00
Muhammed et al. (2018) [37]	IEEE Access	UbeHealth: A Personalized Ubiquitous Cloud and Edge-Enabled Networked Healthcare System for Smart Cities	174	29,00
Selvaraj and Sundaravaradhan (2020) [38]	SN Applied Sciences	Challenges and Opportunities in IoT Healthcare Systems: A Systematic Review	173	43,25

A total of 6432 keywords were included in the Keywords Plus list. Figure 2 shows a Treemap chart of the 50 most frequently used terms based on "Keywords Plus". The size of the rectangular areas depicts how prominent a keyword is in research related to smart healthcare and NCDs. Healthcare, Internet of Things, Human, Humans, and Diseases are the five most prominent terms.

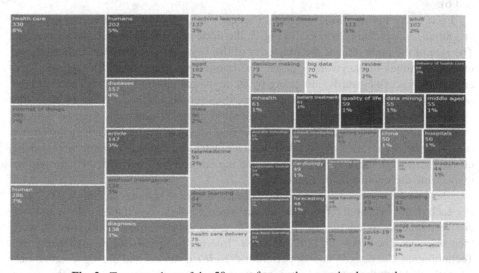

Fig. 2. Treemap chart of the 50 most frequently occurring keywords.

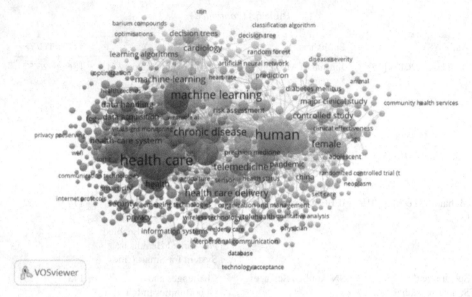

Fig. 3. The co-occurrence analysis

VOSviewer was used to compute the co-occurrence analysis. For each of the 721 keywords, the total strength of the co-occurrence links with other keywords was calculated and the keywords with the greatest total link strength were selected. Human, Healthcare, Humans, Internet of Things and Machine Learning were the keywords that showed the highest total link strength, with at least 170 occurrences and 2553 link strength. This is depicted in Fig. 3.

For the co-occurrence analysis, the following applies [19] (also applies to Figs. 4, 5 and 6):

Each entity in a network, such as an article, author, country, institution, keyword, or journal, is depicted by a node. In Fig. 3, the node specifically represents a keyword. The size of the node reflects the frequency of the keyword's occurrence, indicating the number of times the keyword appears. The connection between nodes represents the co-occurrence of keywords, indicating when keywords appear together. The thickness of the connection indicates the frequency of these co-occurrences. A larger node signifies a higher occurrence of the keyword, while a thicker connection between nodes indicates a higher frequency of co-occurrences between keywords. Each thematic cluster is represented by a varied colour. Within each cluster, the nodes and connections can be utilised to analyse the coverage of topics and the relationships between them, providing insight into the manifestation of themes.

The co-citation of various references used was also investigated using VOSviewer. For each of the 116 cited references, the total strength of the co-citation links with other cited references was calculated. The cited references with the greatest link strength were then selected. The article by [20] and titled "Internet of Things for Smart Healthcare: Technologies, Challenges, and Opportunities" in *IEEE Access* had the highest total link strength of 84, with strong associations on co-citations. The study stresses the use of

IoT-based systems in the form of wearables for monitoring blood pressure, vital signs, and oxygen levels within blood. The high number of citations in this article signifies the relevance of technological interventions in mitigating NCDs within healthcare. Figure 4 depicts the co-citations analysis.

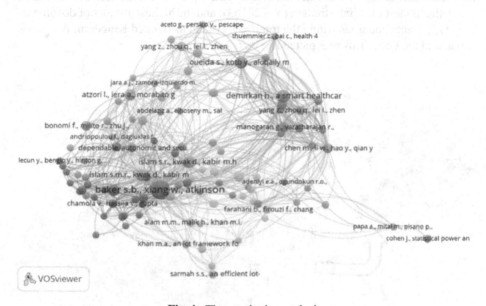

Fig. 4. The co-citation analysis

VOSviewer was also used for the bibliometric coupling of sources. For each of the 43 sources selected, the total strength of the bibliometric coupling links with other authors was calculated and the sources with the greatest link strength were selected. True to what has been confirmed so far in this study, *IEEE Access* has the highest number of documents (n = 41), the highest number of citations (n = 2300) and the strongest total

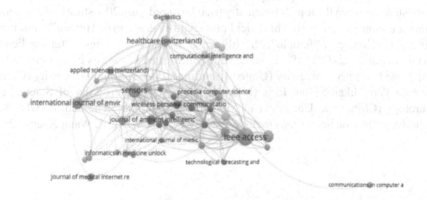

Fig. 5. Bibliometric coupling of sources

link strength (n = 243). Other sources within the top five were *Sensors, Healthcare (Switzerland), Electronics (Switzerland)* and *Diagnostics,* as summarised in Fig. 5.

Using the criterion of at least five sources per country, a total of 60 countries were loaded from a possible 113 countries, and the total strength of the bibliometric coupling links with other countries was calculated. India had the highest value in terms of links (n = 59), the highest total link strength (n = 20163), and the highest number of documents (n = 312). Other countries within the top five included the United Kingdom, Australia, China, and the USA. This is depicted in Fig. 6.

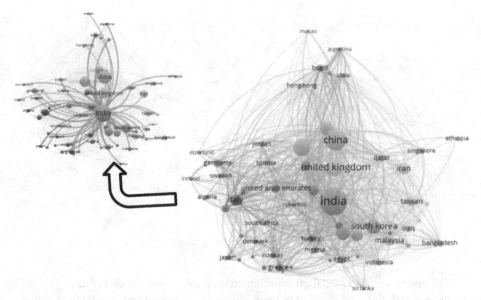

Fig. 6. Bibliometric coupling of countries.

A three-field plot analysis was performed using Biblioshiny to classify authors, their affiliations, and the most frequently used keywords and this is depicted in Fig. 7. The relationships between the top 20 frequently used keywords, top 20 institutions and top 20 authors are summarised by the three-field plot (Sankey diagram). "Human", "humans", "artificial intelligence", "female", "healthcare", "Internet of Things", "telemedicine", "chronic diseases" and "aged" are some of the most used keywords by top institutions that include Coventry University (United Kingdom), Central South University (China), Universiti Pendidikan Sultan Idris (Malaysia), Huazhong University of Science and Technology (China) and University of Melbourne (Australia). The authors who were very active within the institutions include Wu J., Chen M., Wang Y., Wang X. and Zhang Y.

ID   AU_UN   CR_SO

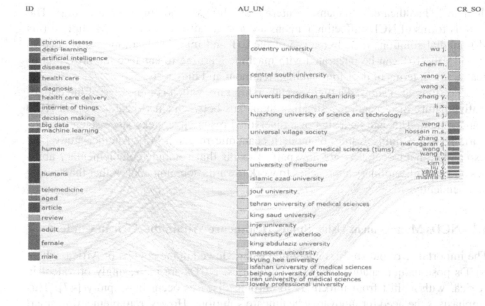

Fig. 7. The Three-field plot for keywords, affiliations, and authors

4 Discussion

The number of articles on smart healthcare systems for NCD management increased exponentially between 2007 to 2023, as is evidenced from this study. This can signify a rising need for technology improvements to combat NCDs. China has witnessed an upsurge in a variety of NCDs and various stakeholders have taken a strong stance and effort to control them [39]. Research by [40] posits that NCDs have been China's biggest, yet neglected, health challenge. This is why China, according to Wu *et al.*, has been increasing its budget yearly to help fight the challenge of NCDs [41]. It is not surprising, therefore, that China reports a high number of authors who publish research related to smart healthcare systems and NCD management.

An analysis of the publications on smart healthcare systems for NCD management reflects *IEEE Access* as the most significant publisher in terms of the number of citations and publications. The *IEEE Access* journal is a reputable, multi-disciplinary source for innovative research in smart healthcare systems, based on its scope on its website [42].

The article by [1], titled *"Wearable Sensors for Remote Health Monitoring"* is the most cited article, based on the results depicted in this study. The article described a simple yet cost-effective system prioritising the healthcare welfare of the elderly. It gained much visibility and audience because of its emphasis on remote healthcare monitoring using IoT-based systems [43, 44]. According to Rejeb *et al.*, IoT systems have advanced, opening up new possibilities and solutions for healthcare services, including remote patient monitoring and treatment [43].

This study also identified the top search terms and popular subjects related to smart healthcare systems for NCD management. The top five most used keywords were "human," "healthcare," "humans," "Internet of Things," and "machine learning." The various forms of NCDs affecting humans are now a cause for concern. Multiple forms of remedial solutions include the use of the IoT and machine learning. As alluded to by [44], the IoT can be integrated with machine learning to enhance the provision of healthcare in terms of decision-making, treatment and diagnosis.

The study also showed a high co-authorship rate, which is indicative of the collaborative nature of research investigating the nexus between smart healthcare and NCD management. This can be a sign of a diversified research strategy since scientific networking is a defining feature of modern academic research [45]. Another study [46] also added that researchers are now part of teams that combine complementary abilities and multidisciplinary approaches to work towards common goals rather than acting independently.

4.1 NCDs Management Using Smart Healthcare Within the African Context

The importance of our study is magnified when viewed in the context of Africa, where NCDs pose unique challenges and opportunities. NCDs are increasingly prevalent in Africa, with a shift from infectious to chronic diseases occurring rapidly [47]. This emphasises the need for innovative healthcare solutions. However, implementing smart healthcare systems in Africa faces obstacles such as inadequate infrastructure, economic challenges, and the glaring problem of the digital divide [48]. Despite these challenges, the continent is expanding mobile network coverage and Internet accessibility, and this offers unprecedented prospects for digital health interventions [49]. Recent initiatives like the Digital Transformation Strategy for Africa (2020–2030) by the African Union demonstrate a commitment to harness digital technologies in healthcare [50]. To effectively utilise smart healthcare technologies for managing NCDs in Africa, it is essential to develop strategies that consider local healthcare systems, cultural factors, and technological infrastructure [51]. These strategies should focus on improving accessibility and efficiency in healthcare delivery while ultimately striving to enhance health outcomes within the African setting.

4.2 Theoretical Contributions

The present study makes several noteworthy theoretical contributions to the field of smart healthcare systems and the management of NCDs:

- Through the execution of a comprehensive bibliometric analysis, this study expands the comprehension of the development and status of smart healthcare technologies within the context of NCD management.
- The findings shed light on the interdisciplinary nature of research in smart healthcare, demonstrating how collaborations across diverse fields can enhance the examination and application of technologies in healthcare.
- The study enriches the existing body of theory by showcasing the integration of emerging technologies such as the IoT, machine learning, and wearable devices in healthcare, presenting a fresh perspective on technology-driven solutions for healthcare.

4.3 Theoretical Implications

The theoretical implications of this study are threefold:

- The findings of this study have the potential to guide future research agendas by identifying gaps and trends in the literature, particularly about the application of smart technologies in the management of NCDs.
- The bibliometric approach employed in this study can serve as a model for future research in similar domains, promoting the adoption of data-driven methodologies to comprehend intricate healthcare challenges.
- The research contributes to the theoretical understanding of how emerging technologies can be effectively incorporated into healthcare systems, especially in the management of NCDs.

4.4 Practical Implications

The practical implications of this study hold great significance for various stakeholders:

- The study offers valuable insights into the effective implementation of smart technologies in healthcare settings, emphasising the necessity for policies that support the integration of these technologies in the management of NCDs.
- The findings can inform the development of novel technologies and research initiatives, with a focus on areas that are presently underrepresented or possess substantial potential for enhancing the management of NCDs.
- The study's global perspective on smart healthcare systems provides valuable information for international health organisations and initiatives aiming to combat NCDs through technological advancements.

4.5 Limitations

The bibliometric approach employed in this study, although comprehensive, is subject to the following limitations:

- The use of Scopus as the exclusive database may have resulted in the confinement of the literature surveyed.
- Furthermore, the search strategy, which relied on keywords, and although extensive, may not have encompassed all critical studies, particularly those using diverse terminologies or emerging technologies that have not yet gained widespread recognition in the field.

4.6 Recommendations

Based on the findings of this study, we propose the following recommendations:

- There should be encouragement for more profound interdisciplinary research endeavours, which would allow for the exploration of areas that have been underrepresented and the integration of diverse areas of expertise.
- Emphasis on policy: Policymakers should strive to achieve a balance in the research landscape, with particular attention given to regions and countries that have not been adequately represented in smart healthcare research.

- The scope of impactful research should be broadened beyond dominant journals such as *IEEE Access*, encompassing a wider array of publications. This expansion would foster a research environment that is more inclusive and comprehensive.

5 Conclusion

This article offers a well-organised and perceptive bibliometric analysis that adds to the body of knowledge presently available on smart healthcare systems for NCD management. The various forms of NCDs affecting humans are now a cause for concern. The results reflect the global stance of many countries where a large portion of their budgets is also invested in combating NCDs. This could also perhaps be the reason why many authors, many institutions and many countries have increased their focus and output in formulating various ways of managing NCDs. The study points to the increase in the number of articles on smart healthcare systems for NCD management, which are receiving convincing citations. Fundamentally, technologies like the IoT, machine learning, remote sensing, wearable devices, and mobile health are increasingly being used within healthcare and reflect a multidisciplinary approach to the management of NCDs. The field of smart healthcare systems for NCD management is characterised by its high co-authorship.

References

1. Majumder, S., Mondal, T., Deen, M.J.: Wearable sensors for remote health monitoring. Sensors **17**(130), 1–45 (2017). https://doi.org/10.3390/s17010130
2. WHO, Non-communicable Diseases Progress Monitor 2022, October 2022. https://www. who.int/publications/i/item/9789240047761
3. Chamroonsawasdi, K., Chottanapund, S., Tunyasitthisundhorn, P., Nawaphan, P., Ruksujarit, T., Phasuksathaporn, P.: Development and validation of a questionnaire to assess knowledge, threat and coping appraisal, and intention to practice healthy behaviors related to non-communicable diseases in the Thai population. Behavioural Sci. Dm, 1–10 (2017). https:// doi.org/10.3390/bs7020020
4. Shrikhande, S.S., et al.: Climate change and health?': knowledge and perceptions among key stakeholders in Puducherry, India. Int. J. Environ. Res. Public Health **20**(6) (2023). https:// doi.org/10.3390/ijerph20064703
5. Singh Thakur, J., Nangia, R., Singh, S.: Progress and challenges in achieving noncommunicable diseases targets for the sustainable development goals. FASEB BioAdvances **3**(8), 563–568 (2021). https://doi.org/10.1096/fba.2020-00117
6. Goel, R.K., Vishnoi, S.: Strengthening and sustaining health-related outcomes through digital health interventions. J. Eng. Sci. Technol. Rev. **12**(2), 10–17 (2023). https://doi.org/10.25103/jestr.162.02
7. Ndinda, C., Ndhlovu, T.P., Juma, P., Asiki, G., Kyobutungi, C.: The evolution of non-communicable diseases policies in post-apartheid South Africa. BMC Public Health **18**(Suppl 1) (2018). https://doi.org/10.1186/s12889-018-5832-8
8. Chen, L., et al.: Non-communicable disease-related sustainable development goals for 66 belt and road initiative countries. Int. J. Heal. Policy Manag. **12**(1), 1–13 (2023). https://doi.org/10.34172/ijhpm.2022.6172

9. Kristoffersson, A., Lindén, M.: Wearable sensors for monitoring and preventing noncommunicable diseases: a systematic review. Information (Switzerland) **11**(11), 1–31 (2020). https://doi.org/10.3390/info11110521

10. Davagdorj, K., Bae, J.W., Pham, V.H., Theera-Umpon, N., Ryu, K.H.: Explainable artificial intelligence based framework for non-communicable diseases prediction. IEEE Access **9**, 123672–123688 (2021). https://doi.org/10.1109/ACCESS.2021.3110336

11. Ferdousi, R., Hossain, M.A., El Saddik, A.: Early-stage risk prediction of non-communicable disease using machine learning in health CPS. IEEE Access **9**, 96823–96837 (2021). https://doi.org/10.1109/ACCESS.2021.3094063

12. Sumarsono, S., Sakkinah, I.S., Permanasari, A.E., Pranggono, B.: Development of a mobile health infrastructure for non-communicable diseases using design science research method: a case study. J. Ambient Intell. Humans. Comput. **14**(9), 12563–12574 (2022). https://doi.org/10.1007/s12652-022-04322-w

13. Hsu, C.H., Alavi, A., Dong, M.: Editorial: mHealth for non-communicable diseases. Front. Public Health **10**(July), 1–3 (2022). https://doi.org/10.3389/fpubh.2022.918982

14. Wu, Y., et al.: Associations between e-health literacy and chronic disease self-management in older Chinese patients with chronic non-communicable diseases: a mediation analysis. BMC Public Health **22**(1), 1 (2022). https://doi.org/10.1186/s12889-022-14695-4

15. Mishra, P., Singh, G.: Internet of medical things healthcare for sustainable smart cities: current status and future prospects. Appl. Sci. **13**(15) (2023). https://doi.org/10.3390/app13158869

16. Mbunge, E., Batani, J., Gaobotse, G., Muchemwa, B.: Virtual healthcare services and digital health technologies deployed during coronavirus disease 2019 (COVID-19) pandemic in South Africa: a systematic review. Glob. Heal. J. **6**(2), 102–113 (2022). https://doi.org/10.1016/j.glohj.2022.03.001

17. Yang, C.H., Chen, Y.C., Hsu, W., Chen, Y.H.: Evaluation of smart long-term care information strategy portfolio decision model: the national healthcare environment in Taiwan. Ann. Oper. Res. **326**(1), 505–536 (2023). https://doi.org/10.1007/s10479-023-05358-7

18. Rashid, S., Rehman, S.U., Ashiq, M., Khattak, A.: A scientometric analysis of forty-three years of research in social support in education (1977–2020). Educ. Sci. **11**(4), 1–18 (2021). https://doi.org/10.3390/educsci11040149

19. Donthu, N., Kumar, S., Mukherjee, D., Pandey, N., Lim, W.M.: How to conduct a bibliometric analysis: an overview and guidelines. J. Bus. Res. **133**(March), 285–296 (2021). https://doi.org/10.1016/j.jbusres.2021.04.070

20. Baker, S.B., Xiang, W.E.I., Atkinson, I.A.N.: Internet of things for smart healthcare: technologies, challenges, and opportunities. IEEE Access **5**, 26521–26544 (2017)

21. Yin, Y., Zeng, Y., Chen, X., Fan, Y.: The Internet of things in healthcare: an overview. J. Ind. Inf. Integr. **1**, 3–13 (2016). https://doi.org/10.1016/j.jii.2016.03.004

22. Chen, M., Ma, Y., Song, J., Lai, C., Hu, B.: Smart clothing: connecting human with clouds and big data for sustainable health monitoring. Mob. Netw. Appl. **21**, 825–845 (2016). https://doi.org/10.1007/s11036-016-0745-1

23. Nizetic, S., Solic, P., Lopez-de-Ipi-na, D., Gonzalez-de-Artaza, Patrono, L.: Internet of Things (IoT): opportunities, issues and challenges towards a smart and sustainable future. J. Clean. Prod. **274**, 1–32 (2020). https://doi.org/10.1016/j.jclepro.2020.122877

24. Liu, Y., et al.: A novel cloud-based framework for the elderly healthcare services using digital twin. IEEE Access **7**, 49088–49101 (2019). https://doi.org/10.1109/ACCESS.2019.2909828

25. Qi, J., Yang, P., Min, G., Amft, O., Dong, F., Xu, L.: Advanced internet of things for personalised healthcare systems: a survey. Pervasive Mob. Comput. **41**, 132–149 (2017). https://doi.org/10.1016/j.pmcj.2017.06.018

26. Tian, S., et al.: Smart healthcare: making medical care more intelligent. Glob. Heal. J. **3**(3), 62–65 (2019). https://doi.org/10.1016/j.glohj.2019.07.001

27. Ghamari, M., Janko, B., Sherratt, R.S., Harwin, W., Piechockic, R., Soltanpur, C.: A survey on wireless body area networks for eHealthcare systems in residential environments. Sensors **16**, 1–33 (2016). https://doi.org/10.3390/s16060831

28. Nweke, F.H., Ying, T., Mujtaba, G., Al-garadi, M.A.: Data fusion and multiple classifier systems for human activity detection and health monitoring: review and open research directions. Inf. Fusion **46**, 147–170 (2019). https://doi.org/10.1016/j.inffus.2018.06.002

29. He, W., Justin, Z., Li, W.: Information technology solutions, challenges, and suggestions for tackling the COVID-19 pandemic. Int. J. Inf. Manage. **57**, 1–8 (2021). https://doi.org/10.1016/j.ijinfomgt.2020.102287

30. Chen, M., Li, W., Hao, Y., Qian, Y., Humar, I.: Edge cognitive computing based smart healthcare system. Futur. Gener. Comput. Syst. **86**, 403–411 (2018). https://doi.org/10.1016/j.future.2018.03.054

31. Aceto, G., Persico, V., Pescapé, A.: The role of information and communication technologies in healthcare: taxonomies, perspectives and challenges. J. Netw. Comput. Appl. **107**, 125–154 (2018). https://doi.org/10.1016/j.jnca.2018.02.008

32. Chen, G., Xiao, X., Zhao, X., Tat, T., Bick, M., Chen, J.: Electronic textiles for wearable point-of-care systems. Chem. Rev. **122**, 3259–3291 (2022). https://doi.org/10.1021/acs.chemrev.1c00502

33. Dey, N., Ashour, A.S., Shi, F., Member, S., Fong, S.J., Sherratt, R.S.: Developing residential wireless sensor networks for ECG healthcare monitoring. IEEE Trans. Consum. Electron. **63**(4), 442–449 (2017)

34. Pal, D., Funilkul, S., Charoenkitkarn, N., Kanthamanon, P.: Internet-of-things and smart homes for elderly healthcare: an end user perspective. IEEE Access **6**, 10483–10496 (2018). https://doi.org/10.1109/ACCESS.2018.2808472

35. Baig, M.M., Gholamhosseini, H., Moqeem, A.A., Mirza, F., Lindén, M.: A systematic review of wearable patient monitoring systems – current challenges and opportunities for clinical adoption. J. Med. Syst. **41**(115), 1–9 (2017). https://doi.org/10.1007/s10916-017-0760-1

36. Lan, K., et al.: A survey of data mining and deep learning in bioinformatics. J. Med. Syst. **42**(139), 1–20 (2018)

37. Muhammed, T., Mehmood, R., Katib, I.: UbeHealth: a personalized ubiquitous cloud and edge-enabled networked healthcare system for smart cities. IEEE Access **6**, 32258–32285 (2018). https://doi.org/10.1109/ACCESS.2018.2846609

38. Selvaraj, S., Sundaravaradhan, S.: Challenges and opportunities in IoT healthcare systems: a systematic review. SN Appl. Sci. **2**(1), 1–8 (2020). https://doi.org/10.1007/s42452-019-1925-y

39. Peng, W., et al.: Trends in major non-communicable diseases and related risk factors in China 2002–2019: an analysis of nationally representative survey data. Lancet Reg. Heal. - West. Pacific, 100809 (2023). https://doi.org/10.1016/j.lanwpc.2023.100809

40. Tang, S., Ehiri, J., Long, Q.: China 's biggest, most neglected health challenge: non-communicable diseases. Infect. Dis. Poverty **2**(7), 1–6 (2013)

41. Wu, F., et al.: Non-communicable diseases control in China and Japan. Global. Health **13**(1), 1–11 (2017). https://doi.org/10.1186/s12992-017-0315-8

42. IEEE Access, IEEE Access: A Multidisciplinary Open Access Journal. IEEE Access (2023). https://ieeeaccess.ieee.org/about-ieee-access/learn-more-about-ieee-access/#AScope CoveringallIEEEFieldsofInterest. Accessed 30 September 2023

43. Rejeb, A., et al.: The Internet of Things (IoT) in healthcare: taking stock and moving forward. Internet of Things (Netherlands) **22**, 100721, February 2023. https://doi.org/10.1016/j.iot.2023.100721

44. Kumar, M., et al.: Healthcare Internet of Things (H-IoT): current trends, future prospects, applications, challenges, and security issues. Electron. **12**(9), (2023). https://doi.org/10.3390/electronics12092050

45. de P. F. E Fonseca, B., Sampaio, R.B., de A. Fonseca, M.V., Zicker, F.: Co-authorship network analysis in health research: method and potential use. Heal. Res. Policy Syst. **14**(1), 1–10 (2016). https://doi.org/10.1186/s12961-016-0104-5
46. Thelwall, M., et al.: Why are coauthored academic articles more cited: higher quality or larger audience? J. Assoc. Inf. Sci. Technol. **74**(7), 791–810 (2023). https://doi.org/10.1002/asi.24755
47. Nyirenda, M.J.: Non-communicable diseases in Sub-Saharan Africa: understanding the drivers of the epidemic to inform intervention strategies. Int. Health **8**(3), 157–158 (2016). https://doi.org/10.1093/inhealth/ihw021
48. Iyawa, G.E., Herselman, M., Botha, A.: Digital health innovation ecosystems: from systematic literature review to conceptual framework. Proc. Comput. Sci. **100**, 244–252 (2016). https://doi.org/10.1016/j.procs.2016.09.149
49. Cachalia, F., Klaaren, J.: Digitalisation in the health sector: a south African public law perspective. Potchefstroom Electron. Law J. **25** (2022). https://doi.org/10.17159/1727-3781/2022/v25i0a12979
50. African Union: The Digital Transformation Strategy for Africa (2020–2030). Sci. Technol. Prog. Countermeasures (Chinese)**36**(16), 100–107 (2019)
51. Achieng, M.S., Ogundaini, O.O.: Digital health and self-management of chronic diseases in Sub-Saharan Africa: a scoping review. SA J. Inf. Manag. **24**(1) (2022). https://doi.org/10.4102/sajim.v24i1.1550

A Systematic Review on the Use of AI-Powered Cloud Computing for Healthcare Resilience

Kudakwashe Maguraushe(✉) ⓘ, Patrick Ndayizigamiye ⓘ, and Tebogo Bokaba ⓘ

Department of Applied Information Systems, University of Johannesburg,
Bunting Road Campus, Auckland Park, Johannesburg 2092, South Africa
{kmaguraushe,ndayizigamiyep,tbokaba}@uj.ac.za

Abstract. This study investigated the role of Artificial Intelligence-powered cloud computing systems in fostering healthcare resilience, using a systematic review of its range of applications and their groundbreaking implications. In-depth applications in diagnostics, care delivery, mental health care, and healthcare supply chains demonstrate how these digital technologies greatly strengthen healthcare services. The results highlight AI's decisive influence on healthcare supply chains, emphasizing its critical role in maximizing performance, efficiency, and resource use. The study sheds light on the significance of digitalization in enhancing the operational effectiveness and resilience of healthcare supply chains. The study provides recommendations based on the insights, with an emphasis on enhancing research collaborations, addressing contextual factors impacting the adoption of digital technologies, and guaranteeing interoperability and standardization in health Internet of Things devices. The implementation of cloud computing systems powered by AI in the healthcare industry is intended to be optimized by these suggestions. The study provides a foundational point of reference, providing an in-depth examination and recommended strategies for leveraging AI-powered cloud computing to improve healthcare resilience, pointing stakeholders in the direction of a robust and sustainable healthcare future.

Keywords: cloud-based · artificial intelligence · healthcare resilience · systematic review

1 Introduction

The term "healthcare" describes the comprehensive approach to maintaining and improving human health, which includes both physical and mental well-being [1]. This continuous process involves preventing illness, diagnosing conditions, and providing treatment [2]. On the other hand, "smart healthcare" is used to refer to the use of sensor-equipped devices that utilize cloud computing technologies. These devices enhance healthcare services by collecting real-time medical data and seamlessly transfer it to cloud networks for efficient processing and analysis [3]. As suggested by [4], cloud computing enables network utilization of pooled computational resources on-demand, which is particularly beneficial in the healthcare sector. By maintaining healthcare records on cloud

M. Masinde et al. (Eds.): AFRICATEK 2023, LNICST 520, pp. 126–141, 2024.
https://doi.org/10.1007/978-3-031-63999-9_8

platforms, significant improvements can be achieved in security features and efficiency, ultimately lowering the overhead costs associated with cloud computing, as noted in [5]. The transition to cloud-based systems minimizes potential dangers from outsiders and reduces the risk of cyberattacks, making it the most widely used method for storing and maintaining healthcare data in the modern day. However, the widespread adoption of cloud storage sometimes raises concerns about patient privacy and security [5]. Furthermore, this technological advancement extends to the realm of machine learning which is a subset of artificial intelligence (AI) that analyzes data and enables machines to learn using sophisticated mathematical functions [6]. The integration of AI with cloud-based healthcare data not only enhances data analysis capabilities but also proves to be financially beneficial for organizations, as they spend less by storing data in the cloud while ensuring that the records are secure.

The term resilience generally refers to the capacity to recover from an adverse situation and adapt to previous challenges, whether it be for an individual or a group [7]. Healthcare resilience is a complex concept that includes the capacity of healthcare organizations to endure, react to, and recover from disasters [8]. It is a dynamic characteristic of the healthcare system, influenced by its environment and the strategies it uses to maintain resilience [9]. Resilience is also vital in evaluating the preparedness of healthcare infrastructure for disasters, with an emphasis on returning to normal operation after a disaster [10].

The integration of AI in healthcare management is increasingly recognized as a pivotal enhancement, offering substantial improvements in the diagnosis and prognosis of serious medical disorders [2]. AI, a major disruptive emerging technology, holds the potential to revolutionize healthcare [4], making it more resilient in the face of challenges. This resilience is crucial as it ensures the healthcare system's ability to adapt, recover, and effectively respond to crises, such as pandemics or natural disasters. By utilizing AI's capabilities, which involve a blend of methodologies, algorithms, and approaches, machines are empowered to mimic human intelligence [11]. This development aims at creating autonomous, intelligent systems, contributing significantly to healthcare resilience. An example of this is AI-powered healthcare resilience solutions which complement telehealthcare. Telehealthcare, through its remote patient monitoring services, has begun to close the distance between healthcare providers and their patients [12]. These AI-driven solutions are further advanced by incorporating technologies like the Internet of Things (IoT), which enhances the healthcare system's ability to respond dynamically to varying patient needs and environmental factors. Such integration of AI not only advances medical practices but also fortifies the healthcare system against future challenges, underlining the importance of resilience in this sector.

The adoption and use of AI-powered cloud computing in the domain of healthcare resilience is a growing area of research. In their studies, [13] and [14] proposed frameworks that leverage the capabilities of AI for healthcare applications, with a particular emphasis on reliability, compatibility, and security. The framework proposed by [13] encompasses a cloud-based architecture for mobile and interconnected healthcare, whereas the one proposed by [14] employs AI-enabled smart contracts and a public blockchain network for decentralized healthcare. A study conducted by [15] examined the use of edge and fog computing to address the limitations of cloud-based systems in healthcare, particularly in terms of response time, accessibility, security, and confidentiality. In the study conducted by [16], a framework for cyber resilience is proposed for the next-generation IoT healthcare, which incorporates machine learning and blockchain for the purposes of security and access control [16]. Together, these studies highlight the possibility of AI-empowered cloud computing in bolstering the resilience of healthcare systems.

The primary purpose of this study was to conduct a systematic review of the current state of AI-powered cloud computing applications in healthcare, with a specific focus on their role in enhancing healthcare resilience. The study aimed to evaluate how these technologies contribute to the robustness and adaptability of healthcare systems, particularly in the face of various challenges such as pandemics, natural disasters, and the rapidly evolving nature of healthcare demands. The study was guided by the following research questions: (1) What is the role of AI-powered cloud computing in enabling resilience in healthcare systems? (2) What insights can be drawn for the future use of AI-powered cloud computing systems to enhance healthcare systems resilience?

2 Methodology

2.1 Method

This study employed a systematic review methodology, adhering to the guidelines outlined in the Preferred Reporting Items for Systematic Reviews and Meta-Analysis (PRISMA) statement [17]. A systematic review aims to aggregate data that meets specific criteria to address distinct research questions [17]. PRISMA is instrumental in identifying, selecting, appraising, and synthesizing studies [18]. It guides readers through an article's selection process. This study followed the PRISMA step- by-step guide as outlined by [17–19] as follows:

a. Information Sources: Lists all the databases and other resources consulted in the search for pertinent research studies.
b. Search Strategy: Outlines the search methods, including filters and limitations, applied across the databases (including the search string).
c. Eligibility Criteria: Defines the inclusion and exclusion criteria that guide the selection process.
d. Data Collection Process: Describes the methods used for extracting data from the selected research articles.
e. Data Items: Details the information extracted from the selected research articles including funding sources and PICOS (participants, interventions, comparisons, outcomes, and study design), and discusses the inferences and generalizations made from the selected articles.

2.2 Information Sources and Search Strategy

The following search string was run in the Title, Abstract and Keywords sections of the Scopus database (the query was run on 21 September 2023):

Title, Abstract and Keywords = ("Artificial Intelligence" OR "Machine Learning") AND ("Cloud Computing" OR "Cloud Services" OR "Cloud-based Solutions") AND ("Healthcare Resilience" OR "Resilient Healthcare")).

2.3 Eligibility Criteria

The inclusion and exclusion criteria are summarized in Table 1.

Table 1. Inclusion and exclusion criteria for article search

Inclusion	Exclusion
Journal articles and papers from conference proceedings	Books, book chapters, review articles and dissertations
Focused on the following subject areas: social sciences, engineering, business, management, accounting, computer science, medicine, mathematics, health professions and environmental sciences	Any other subject areas
Language used is English	Articles in other languages
Articles published between 2018 to 2023	Articles published before 2018
Articles which are finalized or in the final stages	Unpublished research with "in press" status, that is currently being worked on
Articles focusing on artificial intelligence/machine learning, cloud computing/cloud services/cloud-based solutions, healthcare resilience/resilient healthcare	Articles that do not interrogate the relationship between artificial intelligence or machine learning with cloud computing or cloud services or cloud-based solutions and healthcare resilience or resilient healthcare

2.4 Data Collection

The data collection process entails describing the procedure for extracting data from reports (such as using independently completed forms or piloted forms) or any other procedures used by the investigator/s for gathering and validating data. In this study, the authors extracted key information (title, author/s, year of publication, objective/purpose of the study, method(s)/tools used, key findings and recommendation(s)) from the eligible articles and papers using a data extraction form. Table 2 depicts key data items considered in the extraction of data which were used in the form.

Table 2. Data items

No.	Data item	Description
1	Title	Title of the paper
2	Year	Publication year of the paper
3	Author/s	Author/s of the paper

(*continued*)

Table 2. (*continued*)

No.	Data item	Description
4	Abstract	Summary of the paper
5	Keywords	Words used to specify the content of the paper
6	Type of publication	Is it a journal article/conference paper etc.?
7	Channel of publication	Medium in which the paper was published
8	Country	Country in which the paper was published

3 Results

Based on the search criteria specified in Table 1, a total of 13 articles were identified from the Scopus online database as relevant to the research questions guiding this investigation. Since Scopus was the only database used, there were no duplicate articles. After an initial screening based on titles, five articles were excluded, leaving eight for further examination. Subsequently, upon reviewing the abstracts, one more article was removed, leaving seven for in-depth analysis. Following a thorough review of the full texts, two further articles were deemed unsuitable. Consequently, five articles were ultimately selected for detailed analysis. Figure 1 summarizes this selection procedure.

The subsequent sub sections present more details about the selected five papers including the year and country of publication, type of research, and keywords used in the selected publications,

3.1 Year of Publication

Figure 2 shows the categorization of the articles based on their year of publication (from 2018 to 2023). Of the five selected articles, one (20%) was published in 2021, one (20%) was published in 2022, and three (60%) were published in 2023. No articles were published in 2018, 2019 or 2020. This shows that there is an increase in the number of publications on research that focuses on AI-powered cloud computing applications in healthcare.

3.2 Country of Publication

The selected articles in Fig. 3 are categorized by the countries of the institutions where the first authors are affiliated. An author's affiliation, typically a university or research institution, is listed next to their name, providing insight into the country they belong to. According to this analysis, two of the chosen articles (40%) had a first author from an Australian institution; India also had two articles (40%) with a first author from its institutions; and Brazil had one instance (20%) where the first author was affiliated with an institution in that country. This indicates that, based on our research criteria, only three countries have published articles focusing on AI-powered cloud computing applications in healthcare.

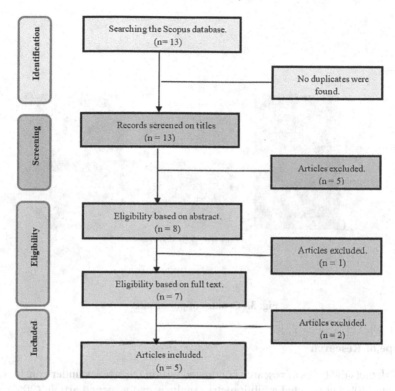

Fig. 1. Selection procedure followed in this study.

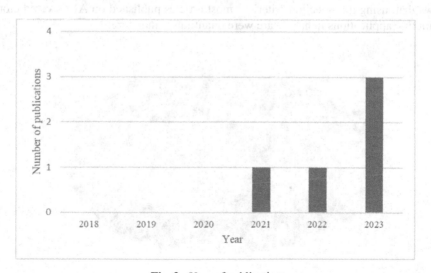

Fig. 2. Year of publication

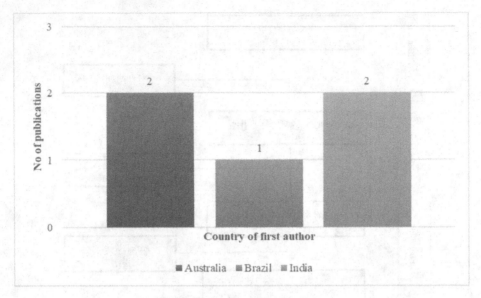

Fig. 3. Country of publication

3.3 Type of Research

Figure 4 depicts the types of research conducted within the articles under consideration. One article (20%) conducted a bibliometric analysis and a second article (20%), comprised a systematic review (20%). Three articles (60%) used quantitative research. This shows that, using the selection criterion, most articles published on AI-powered cloud computing applications in healthcare were quantitative in nature.

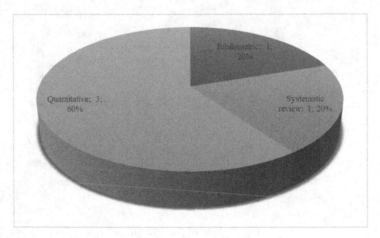

Fig. 4. Type of research

3.4 Keywords Used

Table 3 shows the top 10 keywords used in the selected articles (as presented in their abstracts) and the frequency of their usage. The keyword "Healthcare" was most used in four publications, referring to healthcare business or healthcare supply chain [20], healthcare supply chain and healthcare 4.0 [21], healthcare [22], or healthcare 4.0 [23]. The term "Resilience" appeared in three publications, denoted as resilience [21, 22], or resilient healthcare or resilience abilities [23]. Two publications mentioned "Artificial intelligence" [19, 24], while an equal number referred to "Big data analytics" [19, 24]. Including this information about the keywords employed and their frequency within the five selected articles facilitates the identification of publications related to AI-powered cloud computing applications in healthcare.

Table 3. Keywords used.

No.	Keyword	Frequency	No.	Keyword	Frequency
1	Healthcare	4	6	Supply chain management	2
2	Resilience	3	7	Internet of Things	1
3	Artificial intelligence	2	8	Digital health technology	1
4	Big data analytics	2	9	Natural disaster	1
5	Industry	2	10	3D printing	1

Table 4 depicts the summary of the selected articles. The authors, the purpose or objective of the article, the methodology used, the key findings or results, and the recommendations of each article are provided.

4 Discussion

The discussion of the findings delineated above is based on the two research questions that guided the study:

What is the role of AI-powered cloud technologies in enabling resilience in healthcare systems?

The integration of AI and cloud computing in the healthcare industry is a transformative advancement that allows for advanced data management and real-time decision-making. This integration has the potential to improve healthcare services, especially in medical decision-making, data security, and health monitoring. It has been noted that AI is revolutionizing healthcare by utilizing large, interconnected datasets to accelerate breakthroughs and provide decision support [23]. The use of cloud computing in healthcare integration, specifically within e-health solutions, has been examined with a focus on enhancing data accessibility and reducing wait times [21].

The use of AI-powered cloud computing in healthcare has been demonstrated in various real-world situations, showing its practical application. During the COVID-19 pandemic, studies [24] indicate that these technologies allowed for remote diagnosis and

Table 4. Summary of the selected articles

Author(s)	Objective/ Purpose of the Study	Method(s)/ Tools Used	Key Findings/ Results	Recommendation(s)
Marques da Rosa et al. (2021) [23]	Explored the effects of digital healthcare systems on resilient systems' monitoring, anticipatory, response, and learning capacities	A quantitative study comprising a survey of 109 resilient healthcare providers and healthcare professionals from both developing and developed nations	Identified four digital healthcare technologies that have a significant impact on the four resilience abilities: digital platforms for collaborative exchange of information and patient data, digital non-invasive care, interlinked emergency medical support, and virtual consultations and development of care strategies in real-time	Prioritising various technologies and applications can direct financial and human resources towards a resilient healthcare deployment
Sood et al. (2022) [24]	In the context of COVID-19, the objective was to give a scientometric analysis of the literature pertaining to impact of Industry 4.0 technologies healthcare services	A bibliometric study of key reference and indexed databases (Web of Science, Scopus, and Google Scholar). CiteSpace was used as a mapping tool to detect and represent the metrics of publications. The period under publication was 2019–2021 focusing on all journals within the Computer Science and Engineering subject area. 4763 records were retrieved	Deep learning, machine learning, diagnostic imagine, artificial intelligence, predictive analysis, big data, deep neural network, image segmentation and computerised tomography were some of the highly frequently used keywords that emerged as a result of a search on the impact of artificial intelligence and industry 4.0 in healthcare, especially in the context of the COVID-19 pandemic	Scholars, decision-makers, and academic institutes should continually expand their research collaborations and emphasize the use of cutting-edge technologies in the healthcare industry, including 5G, deep learning, machine learning, 4D printing, and the Internet of Things

(continued)

Table 4. (*continued*)

Author(s)	Objective/ Purpose of the Study	Method(s)/ Tools Used	Key Findings/ Results	Recommendation(s)
Lokmic-Tomkins et al. (2023) [22]	Examined the ways in which digital health technology can be depended upon to provide high-quality healthcare interventions amid natural disasters and support the corresponding preparatory and recovery endeavours	Employed a qualitative literature review, followed by more in-depth narrative analyses to assemble case studies. There were no time or geographic restrictions. English-language publications were selected using PubMed/MEDLINE, Web of Science, Scopus, and CINAHL databases. The search string used was ("digital health technolog*") OR ("digital health") AND ("natural disasters") AND ("healthcare")."	Digital health technologies and related interventions are increasingly seen as a solution to building climate-resilient healthcare systems. There is a global consensus effort to address the growing pressures from climate-driven environmental changes on the community's health and the healthcare systems. In addition, it can be concluded that the management of preparedness, response, and recovery in the context of natural disasters is increasingly being done using digital health technology	A large global movement and methodological approach known as "citizen science" that involves active public engagement in the creation of scientific knowledge is fundamental Digital healthcare systems that are climate-resilient should be able to foresee, respond to, deal with, and recover from climate-related disasters The need to create national or worldwide frameworks for healthcare systems to respond to climatic disasters
Bag et al. (2023) [21]	Investigated the origins of a big data analytics and artificial intelligence (BDA-AI) technology-based collaborative platform for enhancing absorptive capacity in omnichannel healthcare procedures. Also explores the impact of the collaborative BDA-AI platform's supercharged absorptive ability on omnichannel healthcare processes and organizational performance	Data was gathered using a structured questionnaire from supply-chain healthcare executives based in South Africa. The respondents were surveyed online using Google survey forms. Data was gathered from 279 respondents for a year (January 2020–January 2021) during phases 1 and 2 of the study	Results show that managerial aspects will help healthcare organizations establish a collaborative platform driven by BDA-AI technology to assimilate, transfer, and utilize crucial knowledge from enormous datasets. It will enable healthcare supply chains to function innovatively for the benefit of healthcare organizations	Future studies to examine the moderating impact of competitiveness and knowledge traits are needed. Also needed is research on how absorptive capacity develops over time in the context of artificial intelligence

(*continued*)

Table 4. (*continued*)

Author(s)	Objective/ Purpose of the Study	Method(s)/ Tools Used	Key Findings/ Results	Recommendation(s)
Tortorella et al. (2023) [20]	Aimed to determine how Industry 4.0 adoption and resilience development are affected by the contextual factors of healthcare supply chains. Additionally, examined how resilient people do better on Industry 4.0 across a variety of contextual variables	Examined 179 organizations from health supply chains in Brazil and India. Multiple data approaches were used to analyze the responses	When the contextual variables are considered separately, large health supply chain agents are more likely to acquire resilience skills and use Industry 4.0 technology. However, the combined analysis of Industry 4.0 and resilience revealed numerous strong relationships among small organizations	Findings justify health supply chain managers boosting resilience through digitization. Organizations in the health supply chain can choose their environment to customize programmes for digitization and resilience

monitoring of patients, ensuring that healthcare services continued without interruption. They also played a crucial role in storing, collaborating on, and accessing data, especially during the pandemic. The potential of AI in healthcare extends to diagnosis, treatment recommendations, patient engagement, and administrative tasks [21]. Cloud computing has been particularly important in facilitating collaboration, communication, and essential online services during the pandemic [24]. These studies collectively emphasize how AI-powered cloud computing significantly improves the efficiency and effectiveness of healthcare operations.

This study found that the future of AI in the healthcare sector is characterized by rapid advancements, and it has already made significant progress in the sector. The incorporation of IoT devices for continuous monitoring of patients and the development of advanced machine learning algorithms to enhance the accuracy of diagnostics are poised to bring about a transformative impact on the delivery of healthcare services [24]. These revolutionary developments not only boost patient outcomes but also optimize healthcare operations, leading to enhanced efficiency and cost-effectiveness [20]. The significance of AI in reshaping the future of healthcare is emphasized, with particular attention given to the importance of privacy, data sharing, and genetic information.

What insights can be drawn for the future use of AI-powered cloud computing systems to enhance healthcare systems resilience?

This study noted that incorporating AI-enabled cloud computing in the healthcare sector necessitates careful examination of policy implications. It is crucial to establish uniformity in data formats and ensure interoperability among diverse healthcare systems to facilitate a seamless exchange of information. Implementing regulatory frameworks becomes crucial to govern the ethical use of AI, guaranteeing responsible and advantageous application of these technologies. Policy creators should likewise think about the broader communal consequences, such as the potential for job displacement and the necessity for new skill sets among healthcare professionals.

The educational and training requirements are vital due to the dynamic nature of healthcare technology [23]. Consequently, there arises a demand for educational curricula that encompass the fundamental principles of AI and cloud computing, data analytics, as well as cybersecurity. To sufficiently prepare the healthcare workforce for this new era of digital healthcare, it is imperative to develop training programs that equip healthcare professionals with the necessary skills to effectively utilize these technologies.

The contribution of digital healthcare technologies like AI-powered cloud-based systems to the resilience of healthcare services is enormous [22]. In terms of practice, determining the impact that digital healthcare technologies have on improving the resilience of healthcare services may assist managers in establishing the rules for a digital transformation. The findings of [22] may encourage more aggressive investments in the adoption of digital technologies, prioritizing those with greater resilience-related potential. The usage of digital healthcare technology to provide resilient services may increase across the hospital if their advantages are well understood. That could assist in persuading significant internal and external stakeholders of the value of systematically implementing healthcare. As articulated by [24] in their bibliometric analysis research on the influence of AI in healthcare, social distancing, cloud computing, machine learning, telehealth, medical computing, medical imagine, IoT, mhealth telemedicine, and

3D printing are some of the key hotspots that have been identified since 2020. They are considered instrumental for sustainable future healthcare solutions.

An analysis was also done on the use of AI, combined with big data, on the healthcare supply chain for empowering absorptive capacity and its impact on healthcare processes and performance [21]. The study noted that, since organizational knowledge is tied to context, circumstance, and business practices that occur throughout everyday contacts, healthcare supply chain managers need to concentrate on the preconditions for developing effective absorptive capacity. Every stage of the information acquisition process is intricate, yet knowledge from outside sources is valuable, but it must be transformed and applied in new contexts. As discovered in the study by [21], the use of AI and big data analytics opens the possibility of more rapid medicine production and dissemination. Virtual aids for nursing were also perceived to be useful as they can be used with individualized treatment.

4.1 Theoretical Contribution

This research provides a substantial theoretical contribution by synthesizing the existing knowledge on the integration of AI and cloud computing in the healthcare sector. It adds to the knowledge of the role of AI-powered cloud computing in healthcare resilience and what important considerations should be taken note of for its future application in enabling healthcare resilience. This contribution is crucial in comprehending the role of emerging technologies in augmenting healthcare delivery and management.

4.2 Theoretical Implications

This research emphasizes the necessity to reevaluate conventional healthcare theories considering technological progress. The study proposes that future theoretical models in healthcare management should incorporate the intricacies of AI and cloud computing to remain pertinent. Furthermore, it challenges prevailing theories of healthcare resilience by introducing a technology-driven perspective, which could incite additional academic discussion and research in this field.

4.3 Practical Implications

The study's findings have several practical implications. Firstly, healthcare providers might explore utilizing cloud computing powered by AI to optimize data management and predictive analytics, potentially improving the quality of patient care. In addition, policymakers can employ the insights identified to establish regulations and frameworks that promote the ethical and efficient utilization of AI in healthcare. Moreover, valuable details for technology developers and practitioners are provided, equipping them with insight into the specific demands and restrictions in healthcare, thereby empowering the development of more targeted and efficient solutions.

4.4 Limitations of the Study

It is acknowledged that the results of this study are derived from previous research and may not encompass all the latest advancements in AI and cloud computing because these technologies are evolving rapidly. Secondly, the applicability of these findings may be restricted since healthcare systems across the globe have different capabilities and resources for incorporating such technologies.

4.5 Recommendations

This study recommends that subsequent research should concentrate on conducting empirical investigations to authenticate the theoretical discoveries expounded in this study. It is also recommended that healthcare systems should allocate resources towards training initiatives that enable healthcare professionals to acquire the essential proficiencies required to assimilate AI and cloud computing technologies. Lastly, policymakers should prioritize the development of comprehensive policies that foster unity between sophisticated healthcare systems and those that lack sufficient resources.

5 Conclusion

This systematic review examined the role of AI-powered cloud computing in the context of healthcare resilience. It sheds light on important considerations that need to be noted moving forward towards the use of AI-powered cloud computing in the context of healthcare resilience. The results indicate that AI-powered cloud computing greatly enhances data management, predictive analytics, and decision-making in healthcare. However, there are challenges such as concerns about data privacy. The study emphasizes the importance of interdisciplinary collaboration and policy development to ensure the ethical use of technology in healthcare. It also provides practical implications for various stakeholders in the field. Overall, the analysis drawn from this study establishes a foundation for understanding the role of AI-powered cloud computing in enhancing healthcare resilience and offers insights for future research and implementation in this rapidly evolving area.

References

1. Fischer, M.: Fit for the future? a new approach in the debate about what makes healthcare systems really sustainable. Sustain. **7**(1), 294–312 (2015). https://doi.org/10.3390/su7010294
2. Mohapatra, S., Swarnkar, T.: Artificial intelligence for smart healthcare management: brief study. In: Mishra, D., Buyya, R., Mohapatra, P., Patnaik, S. (eds.) Intelligent and Cloud Computing. Smart Innovation, Systems and Technologies, vol. 153. Springer, Singapore (2021). https://doi.org/10.1007/978-981-15-6202-0_37
3. Taj, I., Jhanjhi, N.Z.: Towards industrial revolution 5.0 and explainable artificial intelligence: challenges and opportunities. Int. J. Comput. Digit. Syst. **12**(1), 285–310 (2022). https://doi.org/10.12785/ijcds/120124

4. Yadav, S., Kaushik, A., Sharma, S.: Simplify the difficult: artificial intelligence and cloud computing in healthcare. In: Verma, J.K., Saxena, D., González-Prida, V. (eds.) IoT and Cloud Computing for Societal Good. EAI/Springer Innovations in Communication and Computing. Springer, Cham (2022). https://doi.org/10.1007/978-3-030-73885-3_7

5. Chennam, K.K., Uma Maheshwari, V., Aluvalu, R.: Maintaining IoT healthcare records using cloud storage. In: Nath Sur, S., Balas, V.E., Bhoi, A.K., Nayyar, A. (eds.) IoT and IoE Driven Smart Cities. EAI/Springer Innovations in Communication and Computing. Springer, Cham (2022). https://doi.org/10.1007/978-3-030-82715-1_10

6. Khan, M., Pasha Khan, S.: Perspectives of healthcare sector with artificial intelligence. In: Shukla, R., Agrawal, J., Sharma, S., Chaudhari, N., Shukla, K. (eds.) Social Networking and Computational Intelligence. Lecture Notes in Networks and Systems, vol. 100. Springer, Singapore (2020). https://doi.org/10.1007/978-981-15-2071-6_12

7. Ambrose, J.W., Layne, D.M., Nemeth, L.S., Nichols, M.: A systematic concept analysis of healthcare team resilience in times of pandemic disasters. Nurs. Forum 57(4), 671–680 (2022). https://doi.org/10.1111/nuf.12723

8. Zhong, S., Clark, M., Hou, X.: Proposing and developing the definition and conceptual framework for healthcare resilience to cope with disasters. Emergencias (2015). http://eprints.qut.edu.au/68257/

9. Rohova, M., Koeva, S.: Health system resilience: review of the concept and a framework for its understanding. J. IMAB 27(4), 4060–4067 (2021). https://www.journal-imab-bg.org/issues-2021/issue4/vol27issue4p4060-4067.html

10. Wulff, K., Donato, D., Lurie, N.: What is health resilience and how can we build it? Annu. Rev. Public Health 36, 361–374 (2015). https://doi.org/10.1146/annurev-publhealth-031914-122829

11. Epstein, R.M., Krasner, M.S.: Physician resilience: what it means, why it matters, and how to promote it. Acad. Med. 88(3), 301–303 (2013). https://doi.org/10.1097/ACM.0b013e318280cff0

12. Kumar, M., et al.: Healthcare Internet of Things (H-IoT): current trends, future prospects, applications, challenges, and security issues. Electron 12(9) (2023). https://doi.org/10.3390/electronics12092050

13. Sodhro, A.H., Zahid, N.: AI-enabled framework for fog computing driven e-healthcare applications. Sensors 21(23) (2021). https://doi.org/10.3390/s21238039

14. Puri, V., Kataria, A., Sharma, V.: Artificial intelligence-powered decentralized framework for internet of things in healthcare 4.0. Trans. Emerg. Telecommun. Technol., December 2020, 1–18 (2021). https://doi.org/10.1002/ett.4245

15. Greco, L., Percannella, G., Ritrovato, P., Tortorella, F., Vento, M.: Trends in IoT based solutions for health care: moving AI to the edge. Patt. Recognit. Lett. 135, 346–353 (2020)

16. Vasiliki, K., Sarigiannidis, P., Argyriou, V., Lagkas, T., Vitsas, V.: A cyber resilience framework for NG-IoT healthcare using machine learning and Blockchain. IEEE Int. Conf. Commun., 1–6 (2021). https://doi.org/10.1109/ICC42927.2021.9500496

17. Moher, D., Liberati, A., Tetzlaff, J., Altman, D.G.: Preferred reporting items for systematic reviews and meta-analyses: the PRISMA statement. J. Clin. Epid. 62, 1006–1012 (2009)

18. Page, M.J., et al.: The PRISMA 2020 statement: an updated guideline for reporting systematic reviews. J. Clin. Epidemiol. 134, 178–189 (2021)

19. Knobloch, K., Yoon, U., Vogt, P.M.: Preferred reporting items for systematic reviews and meta-analyses (PRISMA) statement and publication Bias. J. Cranio-Maxillofacial Surg. 39(2), 91–92 [21]

20. Tortorella, G., et al.: Resilience development and digitalization of the healthcare supply chain: an exploratory study in emerging economies. Int. J. Logist. Manag. 34(1), 130–163 (2023). https://doi.org/10.1108/IJLM-09-2021-0438

21. Bag, S., Dhamija, P., Singh, R.K., Rahman, M.S., Sreedharan, V.R.: Big data analytics and artificial intelligence technologies based collaborative platform empowering absorptive capacity in health care supply chain: an empirical study. J. Bus. Res. **154**, 113315 (2023). https://doi.org/10.1016/j.jbusres.2022.113315

22. Lokmic-Tomkins, Z., Bhandari, D., Bain, C., Borda, A., Kariotis, T.C., Reser, D.: Lessons learned from natural disasters around digital health technologies and delivering quality healthcare. Int. J. Environ. Res. Public Health **20**(5), 1–28 (2023). https://doi.org/10.3390/ijerph200 54542

23. Marques da Rosa, V., Saurin, T.A., Tortorella, G.L., Fogliatto, F.S., Tonetto, L.M., Samson, D.: Digital technologies: an exploratory study of their role in the resilience of healthcare services. Appl. Ergon. **97**, 103517 (2021). https://doi.org/10.1016/j.apergo.2021.103517

24. Sood, S.K., Rawat, K.S., Kumar, D.: A visual review of artificial intelligence and industry 4.0 in healthcare. Comput. Electr. Eng. **101**, 107948 (2022). https://doi.org/10.1016/j.compel eceng.2022.107948

Sustainability and Environmental Management

Predicting Malaria Outbreak Using Indigenous Knowledge and Fuzzy Cognitive Maps: A Case Study of Vhembe District in South Africa

Paulina Phoobane[1]($\boxtimes$) (iD), Tafadzwanashe Mabhaudhi[2], and Joel Botai[2]

[1] Walter Sisulu University, Mthatha, South Africa
mpmakoetlane@gmail.com
[2] University of KwaZulu Natal, Pietermaritzburg, South Africa
Mabhaudhi@ukzn.ac.za, j.botai@cgiar.org

Abstract. Malaria, a vector-borne disease, remains a major public health problem in many countries, particularly in Sub-Saharan Africa, where health resources are limited. Early warning of malaria outbreaks is crucial for effective control and mitigation of the devastating impacts of malaria. Tapping into the vital role indigenous knowledge (IK) plays in combating infectious diseases and the success of an artificial intelligence technique called fuzzy cognitive map (FCM) in modelling infectious diseases, this paper aims to predict malaria outbreaks using IK and FCM. The concepts used to develop the FCM were the IK indicators participants in Vhembe in South Africa used to ppredict malaria outbreaks. These IK indicators were collected through unstructured interviews. The developed malaria outbreak prediction FCM model was used to conduct simulations and make predictions of malaria outbreaks. As an initial stride for constructing such a tool, this paper demonstrates how the artificial intelligence technique, FCM, can represent IK indicators and predict malaria outbreaks. This promotes the recognition of IK in the effort to control and mitigate malaria outbreaks. Modelling IK using artificial intelligence opens the opportunity to incorporate IK with modern prediction models to develop robust early warning systems based on multiple knowledge systems.

Keywords: Fuzzy cognitive maps · malaria outbreak prediction · indigenous knowledge · malaria indigenous knowledge indicators · Vhembe district · South Africa

1 Introduction

Malaria remains a significant public health concern in many parts of the world, particularly in sub-Saharan Africa [1]. The global tally of malaria cases reached 247 million in 2021 compared to 245 million in 2020 and 232 million in 2019 [1]. On the other hand, Africa, with an estimated 234 million cases in 2021, accounted for 95% of global cases and 96% of malaria deaths, of which 80% were children under 5 years. Even though there

M. Masinde et al. (Eds.): AFRICATEK 2023, LNICST 520, pp. 145–164, 2024.
https://doi.org/10.1007/978-3-031-63999-9_9

are preventive and treatment initiatives to combat malaria, such as RTS, S/AS01 (RTS, S) malaria vaccine, and medicine that includes chemoprophylaxis, malaria continues to claim many people's lives [1].

Various techniques, spanning from machine learning to statistical approaches, have been employed to forecast the occurrence of malaria outbreaks [2–7]. Several studies that have crafted forecasts for malaria prediction and other infectious diseases such as dengue have relied exclusively on modern science approaches [5, 8–10]. However, these approaches have predominately not been in the context of Africa. Even though most have high prediction accuracy, they do not incorporate local knowledge in the prediction. Smylie et al. (2004) [11] argue that early warning systems are more effective if they are relevant and understandable to their intended communities.

A unique approach rooted in Indigenous Knowledge (IK) and Fuzzy Cognitive Map (FCM) methodologies holds promise for enhancing malaria prediction capabilities [12]. Using IK, we tap into the wisdom of local communities, promoting community engagement and ownership in disease surveillance efforts. This article explores a case study conducted in the Vhembe district of South Africa, where the integration of IK and FCM has demonstrated its potential for predicting malaria outbreaks.

2   Related Literature

2.1   Malaria Outbreaks

Malaria is a vector-borne disease spread by the bite of the infected female Anopheles mosquito [13]. Transmission is more intense in places where the mosquito lifespan is longer and where it bites humans rather than other animals [1]. The African vector species' long lifespan and strong human-biting habit are the main reasons most of the world's malaria cases are in Africa [14]. Transmission of malaria also depends on climatic conditions such as temperature and rainfall [15]. Climatic conditions create a conducive environment for malaria to thrive because climate changes impact disease agents' survival, reproduction, or distribution and the means of their transmission environment [16, 17]. Socio-economic factors also affect the severity of malaria and its transmission, including construction activities, education, population intensity and human migration [18, 19]. Indeed, malaria transmission is influenced by a combination of factors contributing to the prevalence and distribution of this vector-borne disease.

In South Africa, Vhembe is one of Limpopo districts prone to malaria outbreaks. Of 129 682 malaria incidences reported in Limpopo province from January 1998 to June 2019, 60% of these incidences were from Vhembe. Vhembe experienced the highest and lowest malaria incidences in 2017 and 2016, respectively, see Fig. 1 below. High incidences of malaria continue to be reported in Vhembe district [20]. On the other hand, Fig. 2 shows malaria incidences in Vhembe according to different months of the year. It can be observed that from 1998 to 2019, June, July, and August were the months with the least number of malaria incidences. The months that recorded high malaria incidences were January, February, March, and April. It can be noted that Vhembe experienced the highest malaria incidences in summer and autumn. The consistent pattern of high malaria incidences in the Vhembe district, particularly during the summer and autumn months, highlights the ongoing need for effective malaria prevention and control measures in this region.

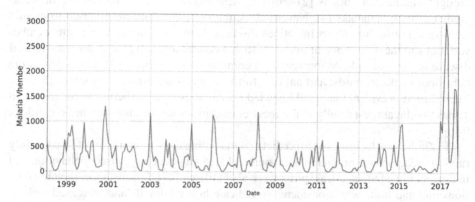

Fig. 1. Malaria incidence trajectories from the year 1998 to 2019 in Vhembe district.

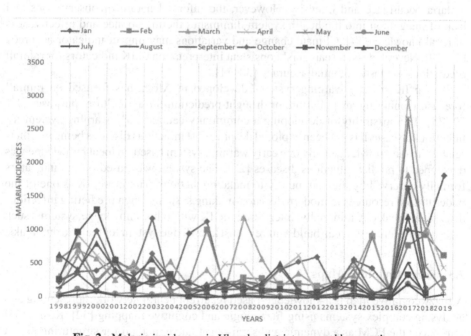

Fig. 2. Malaria incidences in Vhembe district grouped by months.

2.2 Overview of Indigenous Knowledge and Malaria Prediction in African Communities

There is substantial literature on the use of IK to predict weather variations such as drought, rainfall, and floods [21–26] very few studies focusing on the use of IK to predict disease outbreaks [4]. Nevertheless, the same methods can be used to predict weather variations to predict infectious diseases. If the community can relate weather variations to the occurrence of diseases, such a community can predict weather-related disease occurrences [4]. Moreover, local communities use local indicators such as the behaviour of plants, birds, and animals to forecast disease outbreaks such as malaria. Therefore, it is evident that local knowledge can be used in predicting weather-related disease outbreaks, especially if the local communities can predict weather conditions using IK.

In Zimbabwe, IK was used to predict malaria outbreaks. Communities utilized mainly rainfall predictions to predict malaria outbreaks. Plant phenology, insect behaviour, and indicators linked to ancestral spirits were also utilized [27]. For instance, the abundant flowering and fruits were considered to indicate heavy rainfalls and increased malaria risk. The "roaring of mountains" and specific behaviours of ostriches are also considered malaria outbreak indicators. Plant phenology was the most used indicator, predicting malaria occurrence and intensity. However, the informal nature of observations and lack of integration into the health system diminishes the importance and effectiveness of local knowledge [4]. Climate change and variations may impact indicator accuracy [28, 29]. Nevertheless, researchers' consistent interpretation of IK indicators for rainfall predictions suggests potential accuracy [30, 31].

Using IK in early warning systems developed in Africa has focused on rainfall forecast, monitoring air pollution, or drought prediction for agricultural purposes [12, 22, 25]. The possibility of developing a community-centred early warning system for infectious diseases has not been explored despite most infectious diseases being weather-related. To our knowledge, only one early warning system based on local knowledge was developed to predict infectious diseases [27]. The system was based on the indicators formally observed by the community to make predictions. Therefore, IK is one of the underutilized resources in modern decision-making systems when predicting infectious disease outbreaks. Additionally, integrating the IK with other knowledge systems, such as artificial intelligence, can build a more robust knowledge system for malaria outbreaks.

2.3 Fuzzy Cognitive Maps

A fuzzy cognitive map is a knowledge-based recurrent neural network representing and analysing complex systems using fuzzy logic and cognitive mapping [32]. Kosko [33] introduced the FCM as a dynamic and semi-quantitative method for structuring expert knowledge. Its origins can be traced back to cognitive mapping, as Axelrod pioneered in 1976 [34]. FCM, a method based on graph knowledge, functions similarly to traditional cognitive maps. Both consist of concepts and their causal relationships. However, FCM distinguishes itself by representing concepts as fuzzy sets and defining relationships through fuzzy connections [35]. Including fuzzy feedback within FCM enables the extraction and modelling of causal knowledge [36]. By utilizing FCMs, individuals' perceptions can be transformed into conceptual representations and integrated into the system. The FCMs facilitate the creation of a broader perspective by incorporating the collective knowledge and insights of the community [37].

A FCM model is represented as a fuzzy directed graph where the nodes (denoted by C) representing concepts or neurons are interconnected to each other by signed, weighted links representing causal effects [38]. The causal effects are crucial in the systems as they indicate which concept influences the other and to what degree (positive, negative or zero causality). The causal effect is represented as the numeric weight in the range of [−1, 1] and is commonly depicted as an adjacency matrix [38, 39]. On the other hand, each concept is characterised by the fuzzy value P (activation value), which represents the probability of the concept occurrence [32]. The bigger the value of P, the greater its impact on the FCM. The activation value is restricted to $P \in [0, 1]$ (Orang et al., 2022). Zero indicates full absence, an increase from zero to 1 indicates an increase in presence, while 1 indicates full presence, as illustrated by Eq. 1 [39].

$$C(p) = \begin{cases} 1, full\_presence \\ \quad . \\ \quad . \qquad increasing\_presence \\ \quad . \\ 0, full\_absence \end{cases} \qquad (1)$$

The value of each concept, C(P), is influenced by the values of the other connected concepts with their corresponding causal weights and their previous value [39]. An initial activation state of a concept is denoted with C0. A new activation vector of concepts is computed at each step t of the simulation by successive multiplications of the state vector by the weight matrix [40], as depicted in Eq. 2 below.

$$C_i^{(t+1)} = f\left(C_i^t + \sum_{\substack{i \neq j \\ j=1}}^{N} C_j^t W_{ij}\right) \qquad (2)$$

where C_i^t and C_i^{t+1} are the values of the concept Ci at simulation step t and step t + 1, respectively. C_j^t is the value of the concept j at simulation step t. W_{ij} is the weight of the interconnection from concept Ci to concept Cj. The inference procedure calculates new concept values during the simulation and continues until the system reaches either a steady state (equilibrium state), limited cycle or chaotic behaviour [39]. The FCM is said to have converged if it reached equilibrium [39]. On the other hand, function F acts as a threshold, transfer, or activation function to clamp the activation value in the interval [0,1]. The activation functions most extensively used include [38, 39, 41]:

$$\text{bivalent function}: f(x) = \begin{cases} 1, x > 0 \\ 0, x \leq 0 \end{cases} \qquad (3)$$

$$\text{saturation function}: f(x) = \begin{cases} 0, & x < 0 \\ x, 0 < x < 1 \\ 1, & x \geq 1 \end{cases} \qquad (4)$$

$$\text{The trivalent function} : f(x) = \begin{cases} -1, & x < 0 \\ 0, & x = 0 \\ 1, & x > 1 \end{cases} \tag{5}$$

$$\text{The hyperbolic function} : f(x) = \frac{e^{2x} - 1}{e^{2x} - 1} \tag{6}$$

$$\text{The sigmoid function} : f(x) = \frac{1}{1 + e^{\lambda(x-h)}} \tag{7}$$

FCMs have been widely employed in diverse domains to construct monitoring and prediction models [32, 37, 42]. Notably, FCMs have demonstrated their efficacy in predicting infectious diseases such as COVID-19 [38] and pulmonary infections [32], as well as forecasting drought occurrences [12, 43]. Moreover, [37] employed FCMs to monitor levels of environmental pollution from the mines. Furthermore, there has been a growing trend in applying FCMs for modelling IK in recent years. Indeed, IK has the potential to tackle challenges such as malaria outbreaks. The primary goal of constructing an FCM model for a problem is to predict the outcome by interacting with relevant concepts.

3   Methodology of Fuzzy Cognitive Map for Prediction of Malaria Outbreak

3.1   Data Collection

A cohort of 134 participants, purposively and snow sampled and possessing indigenous knowledge, participated in questionnaires to identify the indigenous knowledge indicators utilized in predicting malaria outbreaks. The participants hailed from various villages in the Vhembe district of South Africa. Moreover, these participants provided insights into their perceptions regarding the influence of one indicator on another.

3.2   Identification and Analysis of Concepts for Malaria Prediction

The IK indicators for malaria outbreak prediction were restructured to form the FCM concepts. The concepts were classified into Astronomical and meteorological, Behaviours of Birds, Behaviours of Trees/Plants, Insect behaviour, Myth, Religious Beliefs and others and knowledge of the seasons. The interpretation of IK indicators is also based on the year's four seasons of South Africa.

As illustrated in Table 1 below, there were 35 concepts in total: 20, 5, 3, and 7 for summer, autumn, winter, and spring, respectively. The concepts grouped by seasons and labelled from C1 to Cn where n is the total number of concepts in each season.

Table 1. Concepts for malaria prediction according to seasons.

	Concepts			
	Summer	Autumn	Winter	Spring
Astronomical and meteorological	C1: summer floods C2: summer heavy rainfalls C3: Tilted moon C4: Moon surrounded by clouds C5: Sun surrounded by the clouds C6: Clustered stars along the horizon C7: Moon surrounded by a ring of stars	C1: Autumn lots of rainfalls		C1: Spring rains
Behaviours of Birds	C8: Many birds C9: swallows		C1: sight of unusual birds (less/no malaria)	C2: Sight of many birds
Behaviours of Trees/Plants	C10: Black spots on mangos C11: many mangoes/jackals/marula falling from the tree C12: Tree leaves turning yellow (no malaria)		C2: Fig trees not shedding leaves (no/less malaria)	C3: heavy mangos flowering C4: Quinine Tree ("Munadzi") dripping C5: "mofafa grass" having many ticks
Insect behaviour	C13: Ants gathering food C14: the sight of butterflies, crows/millipedes	C2: Ants gathering food/store them underground C3: cattle frequently running with tails raised up	C3: the sight of many insects/locusts (no/less malaria)	C6: Ants gathering food
Animal Behaviour	C15: the sight of many sardines in dams C16: Croaking frogs C17: Cattle running with tails raised up			C7: many cattle Egrets around cattle

(continued)

Table 1. (*continued*)

	Concepts			
	Summer	Autumn	Winter	Spring
Myth, Religious Beliefs and others	C18: Severe malaria outbreak after a period of 5 – 7 years C19: Dirty water in containers/small pools	C4: Dirty water in tins/small pools		
Knowledge of Seasons	C20: Summer high temperature	C5: Autumn high temperature		

4 Results

4.1 Representing the Concepts and Finding the Causal Effects of Concepts

FCM served as the instrument for gathering, confirming, and authenticating IK indicators used for malaria outbreak predictions in the Vhembe district. The concepts (IK indicators and malaria incidence) identified during the understanding and analysis of IK indicators for malaria prediction were uniquely structured by their respective position n state vector (C1, C2, …Cn). Each indicator represents a concept or node in an FCM.

The causal effects were represented statistically to determine the weights among the concepts. The participants individually stated their perceptions of the causal effects of IK indicators on malaria outbreak and IK indicators to other IK indicators. Tables 2, 3, 4 and 5 below show the statistics representation of the responses in terms of the percentage, mode and mean for each interacting concept for summer, autumn, winter and spring concepts, respectively. The mode and the mean of the responses under each concept were used to aggregate the participants' perceptions. The concepts were categorised according to the four seasons. The weights between concepts and malaria outbreak were declared as values in a range interval $[-1, 1]$. The following linguistic variables were used to express the causal effect {$1 \leq$ Strong positive < 0.5, $0.5 \leq$ Positive < 0, $0 =$ None, $0 \leq$ negative < -0.5, $-0.5 \leq$ strong negative < -1}.

Table 2. Causal Effects of **IK indicators** (concepts) **to malaria outbreak** in **summer**.

IK indicators to malaria outbreak	Causal Effects for Summer Concepts						
	Strong positive	Positive	None	Negative	Strong negative	mode -1 to 1	Mean -1 to 1
Summer floods	64%	36%				1	0.8
Summer Heavy rainfalls	64%	36%				1	0.8
Summer tilted moon		64%	36%			0.5	0.3
Summer moon surrounded by clouds	36%	64%				0.5	0.7
Summer sun surrounded by the clouds	18%	64%	18%			0.5	0.5
Summer clustered stars along the horizon		64%	36%			0.5	0.3
Summer moon surrounded by a ring of stars		64%	36%			0	0.3
Summer many birds		64%	36%			0.5	0.3
Summer many swallows	9%	73%	18%			0.5	0.5
Black spots on mangos	27	55%	18%			0	0.5
Too many mangoes/jackals/marula falling from the tree	18%	64%	18%			0.5	0.5
Summer yellow tree leaves			36%	64%		-0.5	−0.3
Ants gathering food		45%	55%			0	0.2
The sight of butterflies/crows/millipedes	18%	64%	18%			0.5	0.5
Croaking frogs	9%	64%	27%			0.5	0.4
The sight of many sardines in dams	27%	55%	18%			0.5	0.5
Cattle frequently running with tails raised up		55%	45%			0.5	0.3
Severe malaria outbreak after 5 –7 years		45%	55%			0	0.2
Dirty water in containers/small pools	64%	36%				0.5	0.8
Summer high temperature	36%	55%	9%			0.5	0.6

Table 3. Causal Effects of **IK indicators** (concepts) to **malaria outbreak** in **autumn**.

IK indicators to malaria outbreak	Causal effects in autumn					mode -1 to 1	Mean -1 to 1
	Strong positive	Positive	None (0)	Negative	Strong negative		
Autumn heavy rains	45%	55%				1	0.7
Ants gathering food		45%	55%			0	0.2
Cattle frequently running with tails raised up		45%	55%			0	0.2
Dirty water in containers/small pools	64%	36%				0.5	0.8
Autumn high temperature	36%	55%	9%			0.5	0.6

Table 4. Causal Effects of **IK indicators** (concepts) on **malaria outbreak** in **winter**.

IK indicators to malaria outbreak	Causal effects in winter					Mode −1 to1	Mean −1 to 1
	Strong Positive (1)	Positive (0.5)	none	Negative (−0.5)	Strong negative (−1)		
The sight of unusual birds				100%		−0.5	−0.5
The fig "Muhuyu" trees not shedding leaves				82%	18%	−0.5	−0.6
The sight of many insects/locusts				73%	27%	−0.5	−0.6

4.2 Constructing Adjacency Matrices and Developing a Fuzzy Cognitive Map

The representation of the aggregated responses of participants using the mean over mode depicted a good aggregate of causal effects; hence, the mean aggregate was preferred as the best statistic to represent the causal effects for the concepts. The causal effects of other concepts to each other (IK indicators to other IK indicators except malaria incidences) were created in the same fashion as done above for causal effects of IK indicators to malaria incidences.

Table 5. Causal Effects of **IK indicators** (concepts) on **malaria outbreak** in **spring**.

IK indicators to malaria outbreak	Causal effects in spring						
	Strong Positive (1)	Positive (0.5)	None (0)	Negative (−0.5)	Strong negative (−1)	Mode (−1 to1)	Mean (−1 to 1)
Spring rains	36%	45%	18%			1	0.6
The sight of many birds	9%	55%	36%			0.5	0.3
Heavy mangos flowering		82%	18%			0.5	0.4
Quinine Tree dripping		55%	45%			0.5	0.2
The "mofafa grass" having many ticks	18%	55%	27%			0.5	0.4
Ants gathering food		27%	73%			0	0.1
Many cattle Egrets around cattle	9%	55%	36%			0.5	0.3

The FCM was modelled using a software called FCM Expert [39]. The weighted n x n adjacency matrices, denoted by W, were created to statistically represent the causal effects among the concepts and malaria outbreak distinguished by the four weather seasons. Table 5 above illustrates a 6 X 6 weighted matrix for autumn.

In the weighted matrices, the names of all the concepts were written as row headings and concept symbols like C1, C2, ..., Cn., were written as column headings where each cell contains a value, i.e., weight (Wij). The value of Wij indicates how strongly concept Ci (row i) influences concept Cj (column j). The sign of Wij indicates whether the relationship between concepts Ci and Cj is direct or inverse (Hoyos, Aguilar and Toro, 2022). The positive sign (+) was used to indicate a positive causality between concepts, whereas the negative sign (- sign) indicated a negative causality (Napoles et al., 2028). For example, from the matrix representing autumn knowledge (Table 7), w1,6 has a positive value (+0.7), and it, therefore, means the increase in autumn rains (C1) results in an increase in malaria incidences (C6).

Table 6. Summary of mode and mean of concepts (IK indicators) casual effects to malaria for different seasons.

Summer concept	mode	mean	Autumn Concept	mode	mean	winter Concept	mode	mean	spring concept	mode	mean
Summer floods	1	0.8	Autumn heavy rains	1	0.7	The sight of unusual birds	−0.5	−0.5	Spring rains	1	0.6
Summer heavy rainfalls	1	0.8	Ants gathering food	0	0.2	The fig "Muhuyu" trees not shedding leaves	−0.5	−0.6	The sight of many birds	0.5	0.3
Summer tilted moon	0.5	0.3	Cattle frequently running with tails raised up	0	0.2	The sight of many insects/locusts	−0.5	−0.6	Heavy mangos flowering	0.5	0.4
Summer moon surrounded by clouds	0.5	0.7	Dirty water in containers/small pools	0.5	0.8				Quinine Tree ("Munadzi") dripping	0.5	0.2
Summer sun surrounded by the clouds	0.5	0.5	Autumn high temperature	0.5	0.6				The "mofafa grass" having many ticks	1	0.4
Summer clustered stars along the horizon	0.5	0.3							Ants gathering food	0	0.1
Summer moon surrounded by a ring of stars	0	0.3							Many cattle Egrets around cattle	0.5	0.3
Summer many birds	0.5	0.3									
Summer many swallows	0.5	0.5									

(continued)

Table 6. (continued)

	Summer	Autumn		winter		spring
Black spots on mangos	0	0.5				
Too many mangoes/jackals/marula falling from the tree	0.5	0.5				
Summer yellow tree leaves	-0.5	-0.3				
Ants gathering food	0	0.2				
the sight of butterflies/crows/millipedes	0.5	0.5				
Croaking frogs	0.5	0.4				
sight of many sardines in dams	0.5	0.5				
Cattle frequently running with tails raised up	0.5	0.3				
Severe malaria outbreak after 5–7 years	0	0.2				
Dirty water in containers/small pools	0.5	0.8				
Summer high temperature	0.5	0.6				

Table 7. Adjacency matrix for autumn.

Concepts	symbol	C1	C2	C3	C4	C5	C6
Autumn rains	C1	0	0	0	0.8	0	0.7
Ants gathering food	C2	0.3	0	0	0	0	0.2
cattle frequently running with tails raised up	C3	0.3	0	0	0	0	0.2
Dirty water in containers/small pools	C4	0	0	0	0	0	0.8
Autumn high temperature	C5	0	0	0	-0.2	0	0.6
Malaria outbreak (no to low, low to moderate, moderate to high, high to extreme, extremely high)	C6	0	0	0	0	0	0

Table 8. Analysis of the importance of nodes/concepts in the FCM for autumn.

Concepts	Concept type	Indegree	Outdegree	Centrality
Autumn heavy rainfalls	ordinary	0.6	1.5	2.1
Ants gathering food	driver	0	0.5	0.5
Cattle running with their tails raised up	driver	0	0.5	0.5
Dirty water in the containers/small pools	ordinary	0.8	0.8	1.6
Autumn high temperature	driver	0	0.4	
Malaria outbreak (severe, moderate, low, none)	receiver	1.9	0	1.9

On the other hand, W12,21 (–0.3) is a negative value indicating an inverse relationship; an increase in the yellow tree leaves (C12) results in a decrease in malaria incidences (C3). Yellow tree leaves in summer mean drought, hence less malaria incidences. The diagonal of the matrix is zero since it is assumed that the concept does not have a causal effect on itself, and thus, Wii = 0. The concepts with no relationship were also given the value of zero.

From the autumn concepts in Table 1, the relationships were graphically represented as shown in Fig. 3.

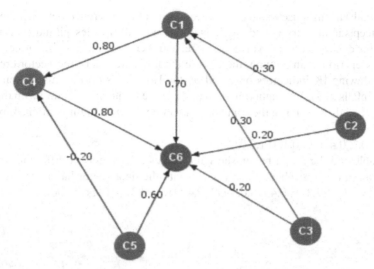

Fig. 3. FCM for autumn (Key: C1 = Autumn heavy rainfalls, C2 = Ants gathering food, C3 = Cattle frequently running with their tails raised up, C4 = Dirty water in the containers/small pools, C5 = Autumn high temperature C6 = Malaria outbreak (none-low, low-moderate, moderate-high, high-extreme).

The FCM indices such as significance of in-degree (sum of weights of the incoming links to a concept), outdegree (sum of weights of outgoing links from a concept) and centrality of the concepts (sum of weights of the outgoing and ingoing links) [44] were calculated using the mental modeler software. Table 6 illustrates the FCM indices for autumn concepts.

The high centrality of the concept indicates that the weights and connections are higher; thus, the concept is more central to the system [40]. Concept centrality emphasizes the importance of the concepts in the FCM [36]. Centrality is computed as the sum of the corresponding indegree and outdegree causal weight [44]. The concepts with high centrality for autumn are heavy rainfalls and dirty water in the containers/small pools. These IK indicators are crucial for malaria outbreak prediction in autumn in Vhembe (Table 7).

5 Applying Malaria Outbreak Prediction FCM for Scenario Analysis

For simulation, the IK experts were asked to report the IK indicators observed in the autumn. The observed IK indicators were captured using a mobile app. The autumn seasonal adjacency matrix was chosen for simulation. In each scenario, there is an initial vector Vi, representing the values of the observed IK indicators in autumn. If a certain IK indicator is not observed, it takes a value of zero in the initial vector; otherwise, it takes a value between 0 and 1. The final vector, Vf, represents the last state achieved through the inference procedure. This research study used the fixed-point attractor of

0.001 (default) as the steady state. This means when the difference between the values of the concepts in the current and previous iteration is 0.001 or less, it indicates that the values of the concepts do not evolve anymore, and therefore, the system has converged.

For a scenario run in autumn, these were the initial values of the vector created as per the following IK indicators observed by the IK experts during this season (heavy autumn rainfalls (0.3), ants gathering food (0.4), cattle frequently running with their tails raised up (0.0), dirty water in the containers/small pools (0.1), autumn high temperature (0.1)):

Vi = {0.3, 0.4, 0.0, 0.1, 0.1,0.0}.

The table and the graph below show the values of concepts at different iterations. The equilibrium was reached at iteration 11 with the final vector having the following values: Vf = {0,499, 0.5, 0.4998,0,4959, 0.4998, 0.4837} (Figs. 4 and 5).

Step	C1	C2	C3	C4	C5	C6
0	0.3	0.4	0.0	0.1	0.1	0.0
1	0.3186	0.4502	0.2689	0.2769	0.31	0.0666
2	0.3702	0.4751	0.3865	0.3406	0.4061	0.1397
3	0.4152	0.4876	0.4435	0.3802	0.4532	0.2099
4	0.4474	0.4938	0.4718	0.4118	0.4766	0.274
5	0.4686	0.4969	0.4859	0.4375	0.4883	0.3299
6	0.4817	0.4984	0.4929	0.4575	0.4942	0.3764
7	0.4896	0.4992	0.4965	0.472	0.4971	0.4131
8	0.4941	0.4996	0.4982	0.4821	0.4985	0.4407
9	0.4967	0.4998	0.4991	0.4889	0.4993	0.4606
10	0.4982	0.4999	0.4996	0.4932	0.4996	0.4744
11	0.499	0.5	0.4998	0.4959	0.4998	0.4837

Fig. 4. Inference process showing the number of iterations.

The output of the simulation run provides the predicted value of the output concept, malaria outbreak. This value is in the closet set of [0,1], representing the grade of the expected malaria outbreak. The output concept, malaria outbreak, is extracted from the final vector from the inference process (Table 8).

Where x is the value of the malaria concept from the final vector, Vf. The output value will be between 0 and 1, where 0 indicates that the malaria concept is not present (0%) and 1 (100%) malaria concept is fully present. From 0 to 1 will indicate various grades of malaria concept presences.

From the results obtained in the simulation, the malaria outbreak concept shows a value of 0.4837 from the final vector, and using the above formula, it gives 0% of malaria outbreak severity. This result was further expressed into a human-readable format using linguistic variables: $0 \leq$ no to low malaria $<20\%$, $20\% \leq$ *lowtomoderate* $< 40\%$, $40 \leq$ moderate to high $< 65\%$, $65\% \leq$ high to extreme malaria $\leq 80\%$, $80\% <$ extremely high malaria. From the above simulation, no to low malaria incidences could be expected in Vhembe based on observed IK indicators in autumn.

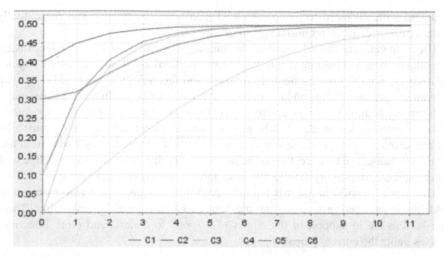

Fig. 5. Inference process for malaria prediction.

6 Conclusion

This research paper uses indigenous knowledge and fuzzy cognitive maps to predict malaria outbreaks. By leveraging the wisdom of local communities and combining it with the power of artificial intelligence through FCMs, the research contributes to developing early warning systems for malaria. The study focuses on the Vhembe district in South Africa and investigates IK indicators used by the community to forecast malaria outbreaks. Through a meticulous data collection, analysis, and modelling process, the paper constructs FCMs that capture the causal relationships between these indicators and malaria outbreaks for different seasons.

The research highlights the significance of community-centered approaches in disease surveillance and prediction. The IK indicators, often rooted in local observations of natural phenomena, offer valuable insights that can enhance the accuracy and relevance of early warning systems. By representing IK indicators as concepts within FCMs, the study establishes a predictive model that integrates traditional knowledge with modern computational methods.

The results of the simulations using FCMs demonstrate how the interconnectedness of these IK indicators can be used to predict the likelihood of malaria outbreaks. The analysis of FCM indices, such as centrality and in/outdegree, emphasizes the importance of specific concepts in influencing the overall system behaviour. This provides a foundation for scenario analysis and prediction under different conditions.

While the paper presents a promising initial stride towards incorporating IK and FCMs for malaria outbreak prediction, it also opens avenues for further research. Using FCMs to model IK can be extended to other regions affected by malaria or other weather-related diseases. Moreover, the paper underscores the potential of combining multiple knowledge systems—traditional and modern—to create robust early warning systems. As the field of AI and disease prediction continues to evolve, embracing local wisdom in tandem with advanced technologies could lead to more effective and contextually relevant disease control and mitigation strategies.

The policymakers should acknowledge and respect indigenous knowledge, fostering collaboration to integrate it into healthcare, particularly in disease-prone regions like malaria. Secondly, investments in research and technology should bridge the gap between indigenous wisdom and modern science, using tools like fuzzy cognitive maps. Furthermore, community engagement in disease surveillance is crucial, empowering locals to contribute knowledge. Lastly, governments and international bodies must allocate resources for initiatives preserving indigenous knowledge through education and cultural exchanges. In essence, the policy would harmonize indigenous knowledge with modern science, improving disease response and preserving cultural heritage.

This work contributes towards building empirical evidence on malaria prediction in Africa domain and broadening the previous research on malaria prediction. These contributions are in support of the efforts to respond to malaria and other infectious diseases under the current global changes.

References

1. World Health Organization: World malaria report (2022). https://www.who.int/teams/global-malaria-programme. Accessed 31 August 2023
2. Githeko, A.K., Ogallo, L., Lemnge, M., Okia, M., Ototo, E.N.: Development and validation of climate and ecosystem-based early malaria epidemic prediction models in East Africa. Malar J. **13**(1) (2014). https://doi.org/10.1186/1475-2875-13-329
3. Kim, Y., et al.: Malaria predictions based on seasonal climate forecasts in South Africa: a time series distributed lag nonlinear model. Sci. Rep. **9**(1), 1 (2019). https://doi.org/10.1038/s41598-019-53838-3
4. Macherera, M., Chimbari, M.J., Mukaratirwa, S.: Indigenous environmental indicators for malaria: a district study in Zimbabwe. Acta Trop. **175**, 50–59 (2017). https://doi.org/10.1016/j.actatropica.2016.08.021
5. Phoobane, P., Masinde, M., Botai, J.: Prediction model for Malaria: an ensemble of machine learning and hydrological drought indices. In: Yang, X.S., Sherratt, S., Dey, N., Joshi, A. (eds.) Proceedings of Sixth International Congress on Information and Communication Technology. Lecture Notes in Networks and Systems, vol. 216. Springer, Singapore (2022). https://doi.org/10.1007/978-981-16-1781-2_51
6. Masinde, M.: Africa's malaria epidemic predictor: application of machine learning on malaria incidence and climate data. In: Proceedings of the 2020 the 4th International Conference on Compute and Data Analysis, pp. 29–37 (2020)
7. Rahman, A., Roytman, L., Goldberg, M., Kogan, F.: Comparative analysis on applicability of satellite and meteorological data for prediction of malaria in endemic area in Bangladesh. J. Trop Med. **2010** (2010). https://doi.org/10.1155/2010/914094
8. Modu, B., Polovina, N., Lan, Y., Konur, S., Taufiq Asyhari, A., Peng, Y.: Towards a predictive analytics-based intelligent malaria outbreak warning system. Appl. Sci. (Switzerland), **7**(8), 1–20 (2017). https://doi.org/10.3390/app7080836
9. Sarkar, B.K., Sana, S.S.: An e-healthcare system for disease prediction using hybrid data mining technique. J. Model. Manag. **14**(3), 628–661 (2019). https://doi.org/10.1108/JM2-05-2018-0069
10. Sharma, V., Kumar, A., Panat, L., Karajkhede, G.: Malaria outbreak prediction model using machine learning. Int. J. Adv. Res. Comput. Eng. Technol. **4**(12), 4415–4419 (2015)

11. Smylie, J., Martin, C.M., Kaplan-Myrth, N., Steele, L., Tait, C., Hogg, W.: Knowledge translation and indigenous knowledge. Int. J. Circumpolar Health **63**(Suppl 2), 139–143 (2004). https://doi.org/10.3402/ijch.v63i0.17877
12. Masinde, M., Mwagha, M., Tadesse, T.: Downscaling Africa's drought forecasts through integration of indigenous and scientific drought forecasts using fuzzy cognitive maps. Geosciences (Switzerland) **8**(4) (2018). https://doi.org/10.3390/geosciences8040135
13. WHO: World Malaria Report 2019, Geneva (2019)
14. World Health Organisation, guideline for malaria vector control, Geneva (2019)
15. Thomson, M.C., Muñoz, Á.G., Cousin, R., Shumake-Guillemot, J.: Climate drivers of vector-borne diseases in Africa and their relevance to control programmes. Infect. Dis. Poverty **7**(1), 1–22 (2018). https://doi.org/10.1186/s40249-018-0460-1
16. Kurane, I.: The effect of global warming on infectious diseases. Osong Publ. Health Res. Perspect. **1**(1), 4–9 (2010). https://doi.org/10.1016/j.phrp.2010.12.004
17. Wu, X., Lu, Y., Zhou, S., Chen, L., Xu, B.: Impact of climate change on human infectious diseases: empirical evidence and human adaptation. Environ. Int. **86**, 14–23 (2016). https://doi.org/10.1016/j.envint.2015.09.007
18. Amuakwa-Mensah, F., Marbuah, G., Mubanga, M.: Climate variability and infectious diseases nexus: evidence from Sweden. Infect. Dis. Model **2**(2), 203–217 (2017). https://doi.org/10.1016/j.idm.2017.03.003
19. Cella, W., et al.: Do climate changes alter the distribution and transmission of malaria? evidence assessment and recommendations for future studies. Rev. Soc. Bras. Med. Trop. **52** (2019). https://doi.org/10.1590/0037-8682-0308-2019
20. Gwarinda, H.B., Tessema, S.K., Raman, J., Greenhouse, B., Birkholtz, L.M.: Parasite genetic diversity reflects continued residual malaria transmission in Vhembe District, a hotspot in the Limpopo Province of South Africa. Malar J. **20**(1), December 2021. https://doi.org/10.1186/s12936-021-03635-z
21. Kanemba, A., Nindi, S.J., Kijazi, A.L., Chang'a, L.B., Liwenga, E.T.: The use of indigenous knowledge in weather and climate prediction in Mahenge and Ismani wards, Tanzania. J. Geogr. Reg. Plann. **6**(7), 274–279 (2013). https://doi.org/10.5897/jgrp2013.0386
22. Masinde, M.: An effective drought early warning system for sub-Saharan Africa: integrating modern and indigenous approaches. In: ACM International Conference Proceeding Series, vol. 28, pp. 60–69, September 2014. https://doi.org/10.1145/2664591.2664629
23. Armatas, C.A., Venn, T.J., McBride, B.B., Watson, A.E., Carver, S.J.: Opportunities to utilize traditional phenological knowledge to support adaptive management of social-ecological systems vulnerable to changes in climate and fire regimes. Ecol. Soc. **21**(1) (2016). https://doi.org/10.5751/ES-07905-210116
24. Jiri, O., Mafongoya, P.L., Mubaya, C., Mafongoya, O.: Seasonal climate prediction and adaptation using indigenous knowledge systems in agriculture systems in Southern Africa: a review. J. Agric. Sci. **8**(5), 156 (2016). https://doi.org/10.5539/jas.v8n5p156
25. Akanbi, A.K., Masinde, M.: Towards the development of a rule-based drought early warning expert systems using indigenous knowledge. In: 2018 International Conference on Advances in Big Data, Computing and Data Communication Systems, icABCD 2018 (2018). https://doi.org/10.1109/ICABCD.2018.8465465
26. Mbewe, M., Phiri, A., Siyambango, N.: Indigenous knowledge systems for local weather predictions: a case of Mukonchi chiefdom in Zambia. Environ. Nat. Resour. Res. **9**(2), 16 (2019). https://doi.org/10.5539/enrr.v9n2p16
27. Macherera, M., Chimbari, M.J.: A review of studies on community based early warning systems. Jamba: J. Disast. Risk Stud. **8**(1), 1–10 (2016). https://doi.org/10.4102/jamba.v8i1.206

28. Son, H.N., Chi, D.T.L., Kingsbury, A.: Indigenous knowledge and climate change adaptation of ethnic minorities in the mountainous regions of Vietnam: a case study of the Yao people in Bac Kan Province. Agric. Syst. 176, July 2019. https://doi.org/10.1016/j.agsy.2019.102683

29. Kom, Z., Nethengwe, N.S., Mpandeli, N.S., Chikoore, H.: Determinants of small-scale farmers' choice and adaptive strategies in response to climatic shocks in Vhembe District, South Africa. GeoJournal 87(2), 677–700 (2020). https://doi.org/10.1007/s10708-020-10272-7

30. Nyetanyane, J.: Indigenous knowledge mobile based application that quantifies farmers' season predictions with the help of scientific knowledge. In: Masinde, M., Bagula, A. (eds.) Emerging Technologies for Developing Countries. AFRICATEK 2022. Lecture Notes of the Institute for Computer Sciences, Social Informatics and Telecommunications Engineering, vol. 503. Springer, Cham (2023). https://doi.org/10.1007/978-3-031-35883-8_13

31. Mafongoya, O.M.P.L., Jiri, O., Mubaya, C.P.: Using indigenous knowledge for seasonal quality prediction in managing climate risk in sub-Saharan Africa. In: Mafongoya, O.C., Ajayi, P.L. (eds.) Indigenous Knowledge Systems and Climate Change Management in Africa, Wageningen, CTA, pp. 43–66 (2017)

32. Papageorgiou, E.I., Papandrianos, N.I., Karagianni, G., Kyriazopoulos, G.C., Sfyras, D.: 2009 IEEE International Conference on Fuzzy Systems : Proceedings ICC Jeju, Jeju Island, Korea : 20–24 August 2009. IEEE (2009)

33. Kosko, B.: Fuzzy cognitive maps. Int. J. Man Mach. Stud. 24(1), 65–75 (1986). https://doi.org/10.1016/S0020-7373(86)80040-2

34. Axelrod, R.: Structure of Decision: The Cognitive Map of Political Elites. Princeton University Press, Princeton (1976)

35. Nguyen, H.T., Walker, E.A.: A First Course in Fuzzy Logic Front Cover (2018)

36. Gray, S.A., et al.: Using fuzzy cognitive mapping as a participatory approach to analyze change, preferred states, and perceived resilience of social-ecological systems. Ecol. Soc. 20(2), June 2015. https://doi.org/10.5751/ES-07396-200211

37. Mbele, M., Masinde, M.: Mitigating the impacts of environmental pollution in Lejweleputswa district through integration of local and scientific knowledge, pp. 77–88 (2020). https://doi.org/10.1007/978-3-030-51051-0_6

38. Groumpos, P.: Modelling COVID-19 using Fuzzy Cognitive Maps (FCM). EAI Endo. Trans. Bioeng. Bioinform. 1(2), 168728 (2021). https://doi.org/10.4108/eai.24-2-2021.168728

39. Nápoles, G., Espinosa, M.L., Grau, I., Vanhoof, K.: FCM expert: software tool for scenario analysis and pattern classification based on fuzzy cognitive maps. Int. J. Artif. Intell. Tools 27(7), November 2018. https://doi.org/10.1142/S0218213018600102

40. Papageorgiou, E., Papageorgiou, K., Dikopoulou, Z., Mouhrir, A.: A web-based tool for Fuzzy Cognitive Map Modeling. https://scholarsarchive.byu.edu/iemssconferencehttps://scholarsarchive.byu.edu/iemssconference/2018/Stream-C/73

41. Orang, O., de Lima e Silva, P.C., Guimarães, F.G.: Time series forecasting using fuzzy cognitive maps: a survey. Artif. Intell. Rev. (2022). https://doi.org/10.1007/s10462-022-10319-w

42. Mwagha, S.M.: A Visual Weather Lore Verification Tool Using Fuzzy Cognitive Maps Based on Computer Vision (2016)

43. Mwagha, S.M., Masinde, M.: Scientific Verification of Weather Lore for Drought Forecasting-the Role of Fuzzy Cognitive Mapping (2015). www.IST-Africa.org/Conference2015

44. Nozari, M.A., Ghadikolaei, A.S., Govindan, K., Akbari, V.: Analysis of the sharing economy effect on sustainability in the transportation sector using fuzzy cognitive mapping. J. Clean Prod. 311, August 2021. https://doi.org/10.1016/j.jclepro.2021.127331

Integration of IK, Satellite Imagery Data, Weather Data and Time Series Models in Season Behaviour Predictions. Case of Swayimane, KZN, South Africa

John Nyetanyane[✉]

Central University of Technology, Bloemfontein, South Africa
jnyetanyane@cut.ac.za

Abstract. Impacts of climate change continue to cripple the livelihood of many South Africans by sabotaging the rainfed agricultural systems that they rely heavily on. Despite the value of the indigenous knowledge (IK) in tackling the impacts of climate change, it continues to lose value and precision in season behaviour predictions. In this paper, the IK is integrated with scientific knowledge to enhance the season predictions by small scale farmers. This is achieved by quantifying the collection and processing of IK indicators. Secondly, collect and process the regional weather data (rain and average temperature) from the weather station close to the region of interest and satellite data(vegetation cover, waterbodies cover and soil moisture cover) collected within the region of interest. Thirdly, train the following time series models: Long Short Term Memory (LSTM) network, Seasonal Auto Regressive Moving Average (SARIMA) and Holt Winter's model on the historical weather and satellite data and perform rainy season predictions for scientific perspective. Fourthly, categorize the historical data into warm and cold rainy season periods when normal, below normal and above normal rains were experienced. Fifthly, develop the mobile application that will use the categorized historical data to complement the observation of IK indicators. Lastly, integrate the predictions made via the IK's perspective with the ones performed via the scientific perspective to come up with more robust season predictions.

Keywords: Indigenous knowledge · certainty level · LSTM · SARIMA · TES · Holt Winter's model

1 Introduction

Impacts of climate change continue to demoralize the livelihood of the planet earth's habitats. This is primarily observed in an agricultural sector which is the key to food, water, shelter and many other resources to support the human kind. Rainfed agricultures run by small holder farmers are in fragile state especially in South Africa that remains technologically developing and financially critical [4]. Despite the value that brought by the indigenous knowledge in season behaviour predictions, its accuracy continue to

M. Masinde et al. (Eds.): AFRICATEK 2023, LNICST 520, pp. 165–184, 2024.
https://doi.org/10.1007/978-3-031-63999-9_10

shrink as years progress due to among others climate vagaries, deforestation, pollution and many more. The seasonal climate forecasts on the other side are failing the farmers due to accessibility, interpretation and most importantly they are not locally scaled due to lack and sparse distribution of weather stations and rain gauges [1].

This paper aims at integrating the IK with scientific knowledge to come up with robust season predictions. This is achieved by first quantifying the collection and processing of the IK indicators and their observations. Collect and prepare the historical weather data and satellite data. Train the three time series models: Seasonal Autoregressive Integrated Moving Average (SARIMA), Long Short Term Memory (LSTM) network and Holt Winter's model on the historical data to come up with seasonal predictions for the scientific perspective. Categorize the historical data into warm and cold rainy season periods when normal, below normal and above normal rains were experienced. Further, develop the mobile based application that will use the categorized historical data to complement the predictions that will be made by the farmers using their IK system. The IK's perspective prediction will be integrated with the forecasts made for scientific perspective to come up with more robust predictions.

From the predictions that will be generated, farmers will be able to conclude on the possible season outcome by observing changes in the time series of rain, temperature, waterbodies, soil moisture and vegetation greenness cover.

2 Literature Review

The impacts of climate change continue to engulf the agricultural sector globally and worse in Sub-Saharan Africa which is primarily constituted by the small-holder farmers who are mostly in marginal locations with low level of technology and lack of essential farming resources [2, 21]. Majority of these farmers have claimed to have experienced excessive weather patterns that have resulted in prolonged wet, hot, dry weather conditions that result in crop damage, death of livestock, soil erosion, bush fires, poor plant germination, pests, lower incomes, and deterioration of infrastructure [2].

The government in association with the meteorologists are continuing to provide farmers with seasonal climate forecasts as an adaptation strategy to climate change. These forecasts have been doing well in predictions of rainfall and temperature anomalies to many places around the world. These areas have extensively benefited to food security, drought mitigation and adjustments of cropping decisions by many farmers [3].Despite the value of these forecasts, they are not doing justice to the localities that are remote from the weather stations. This is due to the limited number and sparse distribution of these stations in Africa [1, 22]. The seasonal climate forecasts can be complemented with local based knowledge and the local based land cover features and how they behave throughout the season. Tracking changes of the vegetation, water surfaces and soil moisture covers will help in explaining the precipitation and temperature given that these features are good proxy of the weather parameters. According to [5] increased sensitivity of these landcover features to precipitation and the use of remote sensing technologies can help to bridge the gap between the forecasts local farmers expect in their areas and what is provided by the weather stations.

The computation of the remote sensed land cover features is possible through ratioing which is a multi-satellite image manipulation enhancement technique that mathematically manipulates different spectral bands of the satellite image to generate new information that is not included in any single band. Ratioing gave birth to numerous indices that are now used to remotely explain the behaviour of vegetation, water and land resources to combat the impacts of climate change. For instance, The Normalized Difference Vegetation Index (NDVI) is a vegetation index that is used primarily to distinguish between healthy and stressed vegetation cover using red and near-infrared(NIR) bands [6]. The Macfeers' Normalized Difference Water Index (NDWI) and Normalized Difference Moisture Index (NDMI) on the other hand are primarily used to map water surfaces and moisture content on leaves and soil respectively [7].

There are number of projects conducted that are similar to the current study. The first project conducted by [8] was about the development of the IK mobile based application that quantifies the farmers' season predictions with the help of scientific data. The focus of the research was more on how the IK season predictions can be systematically explained with the help of scientific data. This is also part of the current study with respect to the IK's perspective in season behaviour prediction. The second study carried out by [9]was based on foreseeing of the season transition from one state to the other using the IK with vegetation data and temperature data. Few researches are presented where both IK and scientific knowledge are integrated: [10] proposed a way in which farmers' knowledge and scientific knowledge on tree species and soil fertility assessment can be combined to improve farmers' cropping decisions. [11] integrated both science and IK to diagnose types of hazards in diverse environmental and cultural settings. [12] presented the integration of IK, artificial intelligence and Information Technology to forecast an early onset of droughts in Western Africa to enhance adaptive capacities of the communities. [13] proposed a middleware that integrates the heterogeneous data sources with IK based on unified ontology for an accurate Internet of Things(IoT) Based Drought Early Warning System(DEWS). [14] proposed the participatory geographic information systems as an organizational platform for the integration of traditional and scientific knowledge in contemporary fire and fuel management. [15] emphasized on the integration of local knowledge and science to address the economic consequences of driftwood harvest in a changing climate. [16] proposed the Intelligent Agro-climate Decision Support tool for small scale farmers where they investigate the effectiveness of the integration of IK interpreted with fuzzy inference systems, mobile phone technology and smart sensors to enhance farmers decisions support systems. [17] proposed the use of Fuzzy Inference Rules System that integrates the local farmers' knowledge of soil and its fertility. Finally, [18] proposed an artificial intelligence technique called fuzzy cognitive maps to scientifically validate the farmers' indigenous knowledge on weather lore and the results have stimulated the opportunity for integrating consistent weather lore with modern systems of weather prediction and in enhancing applications offering decision support relying on weather effects.

3 Methodology

The action-based research methodology was adopted with the aim to identify the problem and come up with the solution to mitigate or lessen the effects of the problem. In this context, the researcher's aim was to evaluate the effectiveness of the IK in season behaviour predictions by small-scale farmers in Swayimane region in uMgungundlovu district KZN, South Africa. The 100 questionnaires were disseminated to the farmers and 88 of them were returned. From the analysis that was made, farmers rely heavily on the IK. Further, despite how important this knowledge system is to them, it continues to lose accuracy in predictions as most farmers claim failing to anticipate onset, magnitude, distribution and cessation of rains and temperature throughout the season. This is attributed to the change in climate that has caused shift of season patterns and erratic rains behaviour.

The framework presented below was followed to integrate these knowledge systems (IK and scientific knowledge) and present their integration via the mobile-based application (Figs. 1 and 2).

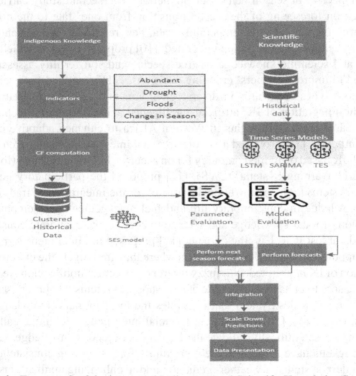

Fig. 1. Framework of the integrated Indigenous and Scientific Knowledge Systems

The indigenous and scientific approaches will be discussed separately and their integration later on.

3.1 Scientific Approach

3.1.1 Satellite Imagery and Weather Data Processing

An approximate of 400 free weekly Sentinel 2 satellite images between 2013 and 2021 were collected from USGS and Scihub Copernicus website. The multispectral bands of these images were ranging between band 1 (Coastal aerosol) and band 12 (short wave infrared (SWIR)). The temporal resolution of the satellite images was roughly 7 days with spatial resolution of 10 m in the visible part of the spectral bands and the NIR band. The Quantum Geographic Information System (QGIS) was used to process the satellite images. The Semi-Automatic Classification (SCP) and Base map plugins were installed into QGIS to aid in pre-processing of the images. Among tasks that were performed using these tools is band clipping, which is the process where set of pixels that represent the region of interest are extracted from the image with coarse spatial resolution. The clipped images were further calibrated by reducing the atmospheric effects. The images with high cloudy pixels were calibrated through cloud masking and mosaic where cloudy pixels in one image are replaced by noncloudy pixels in another image that is having a close temporal resolution as the one that is currently being calibrated.

Below is the satellite image representing the surface reflectance after applying the atmospheric corrections.

Fig. 2. Swayimane's satellite image

For every image, the raster calculator was used to compute the healthy vegetation cover represented by NDVI values of 0.3 and above using Red and NIR bands. The water surfaces cover and soil moisture cover were also computed using Macfeeter's NDWI and NDMI respectively. The Macfeeter's NDWI has the reflectance values ranging between -1 and $+ 1$ where positive values denote waterbodies and 0 or negative values denote non-water bodies features such as soil and vegetation. The NDMI on the other side has values ranging between -1 to $+ 1$, where the lowest values indicate low vegetation or soil water content, and the highest ones correspond to high water content. These pixel cover values were recorded together with the images' acquisition dates. The daily rain and average temperature data ranging between 1993 to 2021 were extracted from the weather station close to the region of interest. Given that there were less number of missed data, this was simply corrected by imputing the blank cells with the average data of a given column.

3.1.2   Time Series Analysis and Forecasting

The time series data (rain, average temp, waterbodies, vegetation greenness and soil moisture cover values) were loaded from the computer's directory and were manipulated using Anaconda IDE.

Three well-known time series models namely Holt Winter's model, SARIMA and LSTM were trained and evaluated using the historical data.

The time series data were split into training and validation sets as shown below (Table 1).

Table 1. Training and validation data table

Data	Training set	Test
Weather data	1993–2018	2019–2021
Satellite imagery data	2013–2018	2019–2021

The training set was used to train the model while the testing set was used to evaluate the performance of the model in predicting future values.

3.1.2.1. Background and Implementation of Holt Winter's Model

This model is also known as Tripple Exponential Smoothing (TES) is an extension of Double Exponential Smoothing and Single Exponential Smoothing models. It was assigned the name TES given its capacity to handle series with level, trend and seasonality components. Before forecasting using this model, the behaviour of the trend and seasonality must first be identified. Both trend and seasonality can either be additive or multiplicative in nature. An additive trend is observed when rate of change in the data is constant over time and can be represented by a linear graph. The multiplicative trend on the other side is observed when the rate of change in data is either increasing or decreasing exponentially over time and it can be represented by a non-linear graph. Below is the Holt Winter's additive forecast that is composed of an additive trend and multiplicative seasonality.

$$F_t = L_t + T_t + S_t = \left[\alpha \frac{y_t}{S_{t-m}} + (1-\alpha)L_{t-1} + T_{t-1} \right] +$$

$$\left[\beta(L_t - L_{t-1}+) + (1-\beta)T_{t-1} \right] + \left[\alpha \frac{y_t}{L_t} + (1-\gamma)S_{t-m} \right] \tag{1}$$

The model was imported from the Stats Model library. To fit the model, the training set, the trend and seasonal type which can both either be additive or multiplicative were passed as parameters to the model. The trend and seasonality types were applied interchangeably for each time series data and the Akaike Information Criterion(AIC) metric was computed.

For each training set, the best model was selected based on the minimum AIC value. The best models were used to forecast the number of units or rows equivalent to the ones of the test sets. Both the models' forecast and test sets are plotted for each time series data where the orange signal represents the predictions and the blue represents the actual data (Figs. 3, 4, 5, 6, and 7).

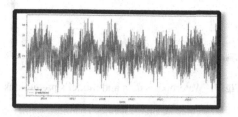

Fig. 3. Temperature data and model's predictions

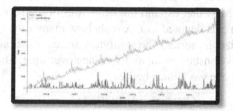

Fig. 4. Rain data and model's predictions

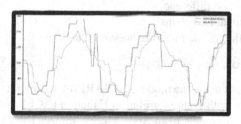

Fig. 5. Soil data and model's predictions

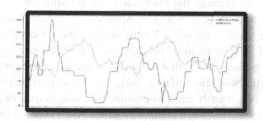

Fig. 6. Vegetation data and model's predictions

The Root Mean Squared Error (RMSE) was computed for each time series data.

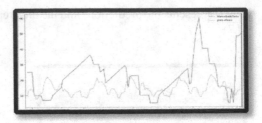

Fig. 7. Waterbodies data and model's predictions

3.1.2.2. Background and Implementation of SARIMA Model

SARIMA is an Auto Regressive Integrate Moving Average (ARIMA) model with seasonality. An ARIMA model is composed of two distinct models Auto Regressive (AR) and Moving Average (MA) that explain the behaviour of the series from two different angles. The integration part denoted as I, reveals how many times the differencing was performed to stationarize the series. The stationary series is the one with no increasing or decreasing trend, has constant mean and variance over time. The SARIMA model is presented with 7 parameters as shown below:

$$ARIMA(\text{p, d, q})(\text{P, D, Q})_m$$

where (m) is the seasonal factor (number of periods it takes for seasonality to repeat).

P-number of seasonal AR terms
D -number of seasonal differences
Q-number of seasonal MA terms
The general equation of the model is presented as

$$ARIMA(\text{p, d, q})(\text{P, D, Q})_m = \mu + \sum_{i=1}^{p} y_i f_{t-i} + \sum_{i=1}^{q} \theta_i \epsilon_{t-i} + \sum_{i=1}^{P} \phi_j f_{t-si} + \sum_{i}^{q} = 1 \mu_j \, \epsilon_{t-sj} + \epsilon_t \quad (2)$$

To perform forecasts using the model, the SARIMA model identified as SARIMAX was imported together with Auto Correlation Function (ACF) and Partial Auto Correlation Function (PACF) models from Stats Model library. The daily rain and average temperature were aggregated into weeks using the Mean function. This was performed to minimize the model fitting process which is considered resource heavy computation.

The first step was to evaluate the stationarity of the time series data to determine if transformation has to be done or not. The Augmented Dickey Fuller (ADF) test was performed to test the stationarity of each time series data. To conclude that the series is stationery, the null hypothesis must be rejected, and alternative hypothesis must be accepted. The null hypothesis states that the series in question is not stationery by nature and the alternative hypothesis states that the series is stationery by nature. The P-statistic value is the one that is primarily used to evaluate the stationarity of the series. If it is less than 5%, the series is considered stationery, otherwise it is considered not stationery and as a result, the transformation techniques will be implemented to stationeries the series. The data were evaluated and were concluded to be stationary. The next step was to determine the order movement of the SARIMA model for each time series.

The autocorrelation plots (ACF and PACF) were created for all the time series data. However, the accurate estimation of the lags for SARIMA through visual observation was complicated due to massive number of parameters that need to be estimated. To get around the selection of optimal model parameters, the function that uses nested loops to test wide range of candidate values representing model parameters was used. For each iteration, model fitting is performed, and the AIC matrix is computed.

The model for each time series that showed the minimum error rate was selected. Each model was used to forecast the number of units or weeks equivalent to test sets as illustrated below where the blue line represents the actual data in test sample and the orange line represents the model predictions (Figs. 8, 9, 10, 11 and 12).

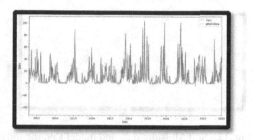

Fig. 8. Rain data and model's predictions

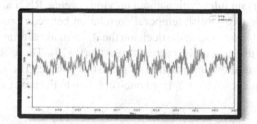

Fig. 9. Temperature data and the model's predictions

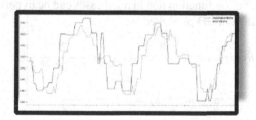

Fig. 10. Vegetation data and model's predictions

The RMSE was computed for each time series data.

3.1.2.3. Background and Implementation of LSTM RNN Model

The traditional Recurrent Neural Network (RNN) has been widely used for processing sequential data. These networks are fundamentally different from "vanilla" Neural Networks (NN) also known as feedforward NN that go for input and output, in one direction

Fig. 11. Waterbodies data and model's predictions

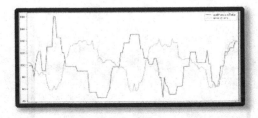

Fig. 12. Soil Moisture data and model's predictions

and are unable to maintain information about previous events. RNN are sequence-based models which are able to establish temporal correlation between previous information and current information and as such the decision the RNN made at time step t–1 can influence the decision it will reach at the current time step(t) [23]. These RNN architectures have loops in them that allow information to persist over time. The network computes the internal state update denoted as h_t from one-time step to the next as illustrated below.

$$h_t = f_w \left(W_{hh}^T h_{t-1} + W_{xh}^T X_t + b_t \right) \tag{3}$$

Where W_{hh}^T and W_{xh}^T are weights, h_{t-1} is the previous state, X_t is the current input and b_t is the bias, f_w is an activation function that in most cases can be hyperbolic tangent(tanh) or logistic sigmoid function (σ) presented as:

$$hyperbolic : f(x) = \tanh(x) = \frac{2}{1 + e^{-2x}} - 1 \tag{4}$$

$$tangent : f(x) = \sigma(x) = \frac{1}{1 + e^{-x}} \tag{5}$$

The hyperbolic tangent squashes the results (x) into –1 to 1, while the sigmoid function squashes the results(x) into 0 and 1.

The output y_t is the product of the current internal state and some weight vector.

$$y_t = W_{hy}^T h_t \tag{6}$$

The RNN uses backpropagation through time (BPTT) to train itself, this is where the model's output at time t, is compared to the ground output at time t and weights are adjusted based on the magnitude of the error to minimize it to its optimal. This is illustrated below:

$$e_t = (y_t - \hat{y}_t) \tag{7}$$

$$\Delta w_t = n\frac{de_t}{dw_t} \tag{8}$$

$$w_t = w_t + \Delta w_t \tag{9}$$

During the process of BPTT, the model suffers from gradient vanish and exploding problems due to number of multiplications that occurs resulting into model's inability to learn long term dependencies [20]. This is where LSTM RNN come into place by eliminating the traditional RNN problems. The LSTM consists of internal memory cell state and gates that solves vanishing gradient and exploding problems. The previous hidden state (h_{t-1}) and the current input X_t are fed to the sigmoid activation function of the forget gate. The gate will decide what information to keep or to throw away. Values close to 0 will be thrown while those close to 1 will be kept.

$$f_t = o\left(W_{fx}X_t + W_{fh}h_{t-1} + b_f\right) \tag{10}$$

The input gate receives the previous hidden state and the current input and uses the sigmoid function to decide what information to update

$$i_t = \sigma(W_{ix}X_t + W_{ih}h_{t-1} + b_i) \tag{11}$$

To compute the candidate cell state, the previous hidden state and the current input are fed to the tangent function which will squash the values between -1 and 1.

$$g_t = tanh\left(W_{gx}X_t + W_{gh}h_{t-1} + b_g\right) \tag{12}$$

The current cell state will be computed as the (product of candidate cell state and the input gate's output) added to the (product of the previous cell state and the forget gate's output) as shown below:

$$c_t = g_t \cdot i_t + c_{t-1} \cdot f_t \tag{13}$$

The output gate is computed using the previous hidden state and the current input

$$o_t = \sigma(W_{ox}X_t + W_{oh}h_{t-1} + b_o) \tag{14}$$

The current hidden state is computed as the product of the output from the output gate and the cell state that is first squashed to the tangent function.

$$h_t = tanh(c_t) \cdot o_t \tag{15}$$

The current hidden state and cell state are then carried to the next time step.

The key reason for using LSTM is that the cell state sum activities over time which can overcome vanishing gradient and better capture long term dependencies of time series [20].

To perform forecasting, the model was loaded from the Stats Model library. Given that the LSTM is sensitive to the scale of the data, the MinMax scaler function was applied to transform the time series data into a range of 0 and 1. Smallest values were close to 0, while largest values were close to 1. To prepare data for model fitting, train and test sets were further processed by splitting each sample into dependent and independent features based on timestamp that will be provided as an argument to the function. To predict y(t) considered as dependent variable, the model will first learn from the following regressed independent features y(t–1), y(t–2), y(t–3)......y(t–n). The number of independent features depends on the time stamp provided. The LSTM model will be expected to learn the independent features and predict the dependent feature for both train and test samples of every time series.

The stacked LSTM model with three hidden layers and output layer was created.

The model was compiled with RMSE loss function and 'Adam' optimizer. The model fit was performed for every time series' generated samples. The model was used to predict the dependent features in both train and test sets of every time series. To evaluate the model's performance, the data were rescaled back to original form. Below is the model's predictions plots for each time series where the blue signal represents the actual data, the orange signal represents the predictions made on training set and the green signal represents the predictions made on the test sets (Figs. 13, 14, 15, 16 and 17).

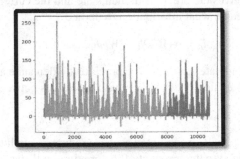

Fig. 13. Rain data predictions using LSTM

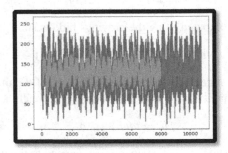

Fig. 14. Temperature data predictions using LSTM

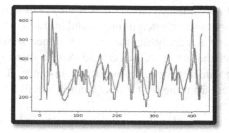

Fig. 15. Soil moisture predictions using LSTM

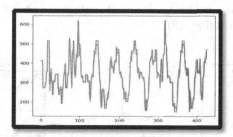

Fig. 16. Water surface data predictions using LSTM

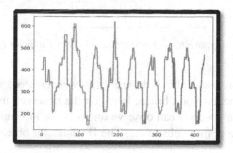

Fig. 17. Vegetation data predictions using LSTM

3.1.2.4. Conclusion on Models that Were Selected

The SARIMA $(1,0,1)$ $(1,0,2)$ model was identified as the best model to forecast weather data with average accuracy of 88.2%. The LSTM model was identified as the best model for satellite imagery data with average accuracy of 83.6%. These models were used to forecast the next 48 weeks. The data was stored in cloud database for further manipulation and integration.

3.2 Manipulation of the Historical Data to Complement the IK Predictions

The historic weather and satellite imagery data of only warm rainy season(Sept.–Jan.) and cold rainy season (March to May) were extracted from the main historical database. The data were analyzed and were grouped based on how they behave throughout the season. For instance, some records were clustered into abundant rains, less rains and excessive rains periods by observing and analyzing the change in their series values. Further, the data were structured such that set of records can be extracted and manipulated based on the current week the mobile application is used. For instance, if the system is used in week 12, the historic data from the next week (week 13) will be extracted and further manipulated.

The historical data were stored in cloud database for later manipulation by the system.

3.3   IK System Development

To quantify the collection and processing of IK indicators' observations, the following class diagram was created (Fig. 18).

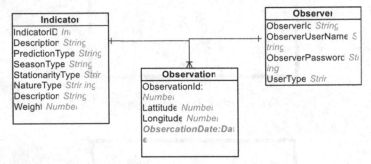

Fig. 18. Class diagram showing relationship between indicator and observer

From the diagram presented above, three entities were created, where the observation entity acts as an intermediary or a bridge between the observer and the indicator. This is due to the fact that an observer can observe one or more indicators and one indicator can be observed by one or more observers. The IK indicator object is comprised of the following properties:

Indicatorid: Uniquely identify an id,

IndicatorDesc: Describes the indicator

NatureType: describes the nature of an indicator which can either be meteorological, astronomical and environmental.

StationaryOrMotionType: Some indicators are in-motion or variable while others are fixed. For instance, birds or animal indicators will be different to trees indicators with respect to stationarity. The one that are in motion do not guarantee that their next observation will be on the same location at different time stamps in contrast to the ones that are fixed. This type of annotation will help in computation of time-stamp and location distance between two or more observations of the same indicator.

PredictionType: Indicators can predict either abundant rains, drought, floods or season changes.

SeasonType: Indicators are further clustered into either warm or cold season indicators.

Weight: The weight field measure the impact/accuracy the indicator has towards its prediction type.

The algorithm was developed to evaluate the registration of the IK indicators' observations. The aim of the algorithm was to ensure that indicators are registered strictly in the area of interest. If the indicator observation is registered for the first time, it will be accepted. However, if there are other observations already made of that indicator, the time stamp and location distance will be computed with the aim to avoid duplicate entries. The time stamp and location distance thresholds can be adjusted by an administrator of the mobile application. The role of an administrator is also to manage the indicators and their observations by performing the CRUD (create, read, update and delete) roles. The computation is also with respect to the nature and stationarity of the indicators. For instance, the location distance will apply between the two observations of a non-fixed environmental indicator. The timestamp distance will be sufficient for both the meteorological and astronomical indicators' observation given that they can be witnessed by everyone in the area. The Haversine equation presented below was used to compute the shortest distance between two points on an earth surface using latitude and longitude parameters.

$$d = 2r \, \sin^{-1}\left(\sqrt{\sin^2\left(\frac{x_2 - x_1}{2}\right) + \cos(x_1)\cos(x_2)\sin^2\left(\frac{y_2 - y_1}{2}\right)} \right) \qquad (16)$$

where r represents the radius $x1$ represents latitude of point A

$x2$ represents latitude of point B

$y1$ represents longitude of point A

$y2$ represents longitude of point B

The time stamp distance is computed as a days' difference between two dates.

3.3.1 Certainty Level Computation

The certainty level (CL) is about the sureness of the predicted season behaviour with respect to the observation of the indicators. It is computed using the qualifying indicators' observations taking into account number of times they were observed and the number of the observers. For instance, the indicator observation will qualify if it was observed two or more times by two or more observers. The threshold for the frequency values will be set by an administrator of the application.

The weight of the qualifying indicators will be summed to determine the season prediction type (abundant, floods or drought) that has a maximum value. The CL will be computed with respect to the winner prediction type. The CL is computed as a total weight of observed indicators divided by the sum of weights of all indicators that belong to the same prediction type and season type. If the CL is above a given threshold set by an administrator, IK will be integrated with the scientific knowledge. If it will be integrated, the categorized historical data will be extracted with respect to the prediction type and timestamp of when the prediction was made. For instance, if the predictions of abundant rains were made early in the warm rainy season, the historical data of the periods when the abundant rains were observed early during the warm rainy season will be extracted by the system and these data will be fed to the Single Exponential Smoothing (SES) model that will predict the next season data values. The selection of this model is due to the fact that it was easy to implement and its order movement parameter can be easily optimized by the system. Unlike other sophisticated models such as Double Exponential smoothing or Tripple Exponential Smoothing, this model is light in computational time given that only one parameter (its learning rate(alpha)) has to be optimized. The SES model is presented below

$$f_{t+1} = \alpha F_t + \sum_{i=1}^{n} a(1-a)^i F_{t-i} \qquad (17)$$

The predictions that will be made for the IK forecasts will be integrated with the predictions already generated for the scientific perspective.

3.3.2 Downscaling of the Season Predictions

At this stage the predictions are still in pixel area cover values for remote sensing data, in millimeters (mm) for rain data and in degree Celsius for temperature data. Hence, they are not presentable to the farmers. To scale down the predictions, number of algorithms were developed to extract the farmers' historic data and perform mathematical computations to scale the predictions to the range of 1 to 6, where 1 represents no change, 2- very less change, 3- less change, 4- normal change, 5-above normal change and 6 represents extreme change. For instance, to scale down the satellite imagery data, the average pixel area cover values of periods when farmers have experienced floods, abundant rains and drought will first be computed. The researcher's expectation is that during excessive rains periods, water surfaces and soil moisture cover average pixel values will be high than during abundant and drought seasons, however, that is what the algorithms will figure out.

To scale the temperature values, the average of temperature during warm rainy seasons and cold rainy seasons will be computed.

Below is the screenshot on how rainy season prediction will be presented to the user by showing movement of temperature(red series), water series (navy blue series) that represents the integration of rain, waterbodies and soil moisture series, and vegetation greenness (green series) data (Fig. 19).

3.3.3 System Demonstration

The screenshot below shows the menu screen that the farmer will be displayed with (Figs. 20 and 21).

The indicator observation will be registered as shown below where the user will select the season type which can either be warm or cold, the indicator's prediction type and the indicator that they have observed.

When the save button is clicked, the camera option will be opened for the environmental type of the indicators as illustrated below on Fig. 22.

The administrator will be able to conclude on the validity of the indicator observation with respect to the image and the indicator's description as illustrated on Fig. 23. Lastly, the system will use the observed indicators to compute the certainty level of the predicted season behaviour.

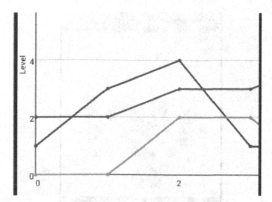

Fig. 19. Screenshot of the season prediction

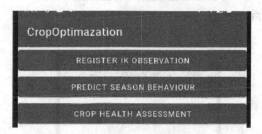

Fig. 20. Screenshot of the menu screen

Fig. 21. Screenshot showing the registration of the indicator observation

Fig. 22. Image capturing of environmental indicator

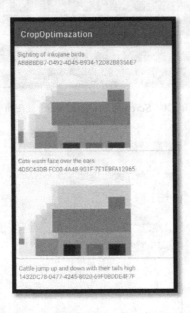

Fig. 23. Screenshot showing list of observed environmental indicators' images

4   Conclusion

This paper presented the integration of IK and SF approaches towards season behavior predictions. The development of this tool was motivated by the impacts of climate change and marginalization of the IK system, despite its contribution towards tackling the impacts of climate change. Despite the value brought by IK system, it is being directly and indirectly sabotaged for instance, through pollution and other human related activities where birds, animals, trees and insects that farmers use to build on the indigenous knowledge system are being sabotaged. Further, the indigenous knowledge continues to be overlooked by an upcoming generations who tend to adopt to the western life at an enormous rate while sideling their cultural life [19].

This paper has emphasized that the IK in season behavior predictions can be systematically collected and processed and also be integrated with the scientific forecasts to come up with more robust season predictions. Further, this paper has also emphasize the importance of the satellite imagery and ML technologies in mapping and predictions of the changes in land cover features to bridge the gap between the lack and sparse distribution of weather stations and what is expected by the farmers in local areas remote from the weather stations. The next approach will be to submit the prototype to the farmers in Swayimane region for evaluation. This process will help in identifying the strengths and weaknesses of the proposed application. Further, finding ways to improve it.

References

1. Masinde, M., Bagula, A., Muthama, N.J.: The role of ICTs in downscaling and up-scaling integrated weather forecasts for farmers in sub-Saharan Africa. In: Proceedings of the Fifth International Conference on Information and Communication Technologies and Development, pp. 122–129, March 2012
2. Mutekwa, V.T.: Climate change impacts and adaptation in the agricultural sector: the case of smallholder farmers in Zimbabwe. J. Sustain. Dev. Africa **11**(2), 237–256 (2009)
3. Meza, F.J., Hansen, J.W., Osgood, D.: Economic value of seasonal climate forecasts for agriculture: review of ex-ante assessments and recommendations for future research. J. Appl. Meteorol. Climatol. **47**(5), 1269–1286 (2008)
4. Fanadzo, M., Ncube, B.: Challenges and opportunities for revitalising smallholder irrigation schemes in South Africa. Water SA **44**(3), 436–447 (2018)
5. Richard, Y., Poccard, I.J.I.J.O.R.S.: A statistical study of NDVI sensitivity to seasonal and interannual rainfall variations in Southern Africa. Int. J. Remote Sens. **19**(15), 2907–2920 (1998)
6. Yengoh, G.T., Dent, D., Olsson, L., Tengberg, A.E., Tucker III, C.J.: Use of the Normalized Difference Vegetation Index (NDVI) to Assess Land Degradation at Multiple Scales: Current Status, Future Trends, and Practical Considerations. Springer (2015)
7. Al-Hakeem, R., Al-Kubaisi, Q.Y.: Detection of physical and chemical parameters using water indices (NDWI, MNDWI, NDMI, WRI, and AWEI) for Al-Abbasia River in Al-Najaf Al-Ashraf governorate using remote sensing and Geographic Information System (GIS) techniques. IRAQI J. Phys. **20**(4), 10–17 (2022)
8. Nyetanyane, J.: Indigenous knowledge mobile based application that quantifies farmers' season predictions with the help of scientific knowledge. In: Masinde, M., Bagula, A. (eds.) Emerging Technologies for Developing Countries. AFRICATEK 2022. Lecture Notes of the Institute for Computer Sciences, Social Informatics and Telecommunications Engineering, vol. 503. Springer, Cham (2023). https://doi.org/10.1007/978-3-031-35883-8_13
9. Nyetanyane, J., Masinde, M.: Foresee transition to agricultural season by integrating indigenous knowledge, satellite imagery, weather data and ARIMA family models to enable good crop establishment by small-scale farmers in Swayamani Region, KwaZulu-Natal, South Africa. In: 2020 2nd International Multidisciplinary Information Technology and Engineering Conference (IMITEC), pp. 1–7. IEEE, November 2020
10. Bukomeko, H., Jassogne, L., Tumwebaze, S.B., Eilu, G., Vaast, P.: Integrating local knowledge with tree diversity analyses to optimize on-farm tree species composition for ecosystem service delivery in coffee agroforestry systems of Uganda. Agrofor. Syst. **93**, 755–770 (2019)

11. Pareek, A., Trivedi, P.C.: Cultural values and indigenous knowledge of climate change and disaster prediction in Rajasthan, India (2011)
12. Masinde, E.M.: Bridge between African Indigenous knowledge and modern science on drought prediction (Doctoral dissertation, UNIVERSITY OF CAPE TOWN) 2012
13. Akanbi, A.K., Masinde, M.: Towards semantic integration of heterogeneous sensor data with indigenous knowledge for drought forecasting. In: Proceedings of the Doctoral Symposium of the 16th International Middleware Conference, p. 2. ACM, December 2015
14. McBride, B.B., et al.: Participatory geographic information systems as an organizational platform for the integration of traditional and scientific knowledge in contemporary fire and fuels management. J. Forest. **115**(1), 43–50 (2016)
15. Jones, C., Kielland, K., Hinzman, L., Schneider, W.: Integrating local knowledge and science: economic consequences of driftwood harvest in a changing climate. Ecol. Soc. **20**(1) (2015)
16. Thothela, N.P., Markus, E.D., Masinde, M., Abu-Mahfouz, A.M.: A survey of intelligent agro-climate decision support tool for small-scale farmers: an integration of indigenous knowledge, mobile phone technology and smart sensors. In: Fong, S., Dey, N., Joshi, A. (eds.) ICT Analysis and Applications. Lecture Notes in Networks and Systems, vol. 154. Springer, Singapore (2021). https://doi.org/10.1007/978-981-15-8354-4_71
17. Wenisch, S.M., Uma, G.V., Ramachandran, A.: Fuzzy inference system for an integrated knowledge management system. Int. J. Comput. Appl. **975**, 8887 (2010)
18. Mwagha, S.M., Masinde, M.: Scientific verification of weather lore for drought forecasting–the role of fuzzy cognitive mapping. In: Proceedings of the IST-Africa 2015 Conference, Lilongwe, Malawi, pp. 6–8, May 2015
19. Nyetanyane, J.: Indigenous knowledge crop health recommendation expert system for the upcoming generations. In: 2023 IST-Africa Conference (IST-Africa), pp. 1–8. IEEE, May 2023
20. Lindemann, B., Müller, T., Vietz, H., Jazdi, N., Weyrich, M.: A survey on long short-term memory networks for time series prediction. Proc. CIRP **99**, 650–655 (2021)
21. Ayanlade, A., Radeny, M., Morton, J.F.: Comparing smallholder farmers' perception of climate change with meteorological data: a case study from southwestern Nigeria. Weather Clim. Extrem. **15**, 24–33 (2017)
22. Dinku, T., Hailemariam, K., Maidment, R., Tarnavsky, E., Connor, S.: Combined use of satellite estimates and rain gauge observations to generate high-quality historical rainfall time series over Ethiopia. Int. J. Climatol. **34**(7), 2489–2504 (2014)
23. Kong, W., Dong, Z.Y., Jia, Y., Hill, D.J., Xu, Y., Zhang, Y.: Short-term residential load forecasting based on LSTM recurrent neural network. IEEE Trans. Smart Grid **10**(1), 841–851 (2017)

State-of-the-Art Review on Recent Trends in Automatic Speech Recognition

Abdou Karim Kandji[1]([✉]) [iD], Cheikh Ba[1] [iD], and Samba Ndiaye[2] [iD]

[1] University of Gaston Berger, Saint-Louis, Senegal
{kandji.abdou-karim1,cheikh2.ba}@ugb.edu.sn
[2] Cheikh Anta Diop University, Dakar, Senegal
samba.ndiaye@ucad.edu.sn

Abstract. In the ever-changing technological landscape, speech recognition stands out as a growing discipline within the field of natural language processing (NLP). This major breakthrough in human-machine interfaces has dramatically reshaped the way we interact with the digital systems and intelligent environments around us. Speech recognition, as a cornerstone of this revolution, aims to accurately and quickly translate the complex modulations of the human voice into text, thus opening up a multitude of applications ranging from virtual assistants and voice control systems to digital devices, communication aid and automated transcription. It will also facilitate illiterate people's access to various digital services and improve financial inclusion. This article dives deep into the state of the art in speech recognition, exploring technological advances, cutting-edge algorithmic models, deep learning methodologies, and persistent challenges driving research such as low-resource languages, multilingual models and innovation in this constantly evolving field. By taking a close look at the progress made, current gaps and future prospects, this review aims to offer a comprehensive overview of the most recent and relevant developments in speech recognition.

Keywords: Automatic Speech Recognition · End-to-End models · Multilingual speech recognition · Low-resource languages · African Languages

1 Introduction

Automatic speech recognition (ASR) is the act of transcribing the human voice represented in a waveform into text. The text produced should respect grammatical rules of the language.

Here are the main tasks needed to perform speech-to-text transcription:

(1) Capturing the audio signal: It is necessary to have a microphone or an audio recording device in order to capture the audio of the speech;
(2) Signal pre-processing: A pre-processing phase of the audio signal is necessary in order to reduce or even eliminate the noise contained in the signal (background noise, environmental noise, etc.);

© ICST Institute for Computer Sciences, Social Informatics and Telecommunications Engineering 2024
Published by Springer Nature Switzerland AG 2024. All Rights Reserved
M. Masinde et al. (Eds.): AFRICATEK 2023, LNICST 520, pp. 185–203, 2024.
https://doi.org/10.1007/978-3-031-63999-9_11

(3) Segmenting speech: In this stage, it is necessary to segment the speech audio signal into short elements such that each element represents a phoneme which is defined as a sound unit of spoken speech. Each segment is then associated with one or more phonetic labels which represent labels associated with human speech sounds;

(4) Recognizing speech: In this task, the goal is to identify the spoken word(s) based on the phonetic labels associated with the acoustic representation of speech;

(5) Correction or post-processing: Last step is dedicated for correction of any error or inconsistency introduced in the previous step. This may include correcting mistranscribed word errors. A linguistic model is responsible for doing this processing.

It is important to note that the quality of the transcription depends on several factors, including the quality of the input audio, the performance of the speech recognition engine used and the possible post-processing steps with the language model. The traditional approach to speech recognition was essentially based on Bayesian statistical models during the 1970s. This approach consisted of three modules: *acoustics, phonetics* and *linguistics*.

The first two tasks listed earlier require using a recording microphone and then applying the Fourier transform for signal pre-processing. The acoustic module is responsible for processing task (3), then the phonetics module will in turn solve task (4). Finally, the last task (5) is processed by the linguistics module. After defining the different tasks necessary for voice recognition, then showing the solutions proposed for solving these tasks, we will present the evolution of the technology from the traditional approach to the present days.

From the 90s to the 2000s, a so-called 'hybrid' model combining a neural network model (for text recognition) and an HMM-based model (for sequential alignment) emerged. One of the disadvantages of traditional models is that they require the implementation and training of separate components, making the development of new speech recognition technologies difficult and expensive. In conclusion, this model requires a lot of expertise on each module as well as expert linguistic knowledge to make it work. It also requires separate training and design process. To overcome these drawbacks, the last decade has seen the appearance of *'End-to-End'* models which have the ability to take an audio sequence as input and produce a sequence of characters as output, thanks to a single neural network which offers a simpler and efficient approach compared to traditional models. This eliminates the need to build intermediate components.

The 'End-to-End' models provided solutions for the tasks listed earlier. We can note as a solution to the sequence alignment task, the Connectionist Temporal Classification (CTC) [1] loss function which will learn to align the audio to the transcription. A special symbol is introduced to handle the size difference between the input sequence and the output sequence using following equation:

$$p(l|x) = \sum_{\pi \in \mathcal{B}^{-1}(l)} p(\pi|x) \tag{1}$$

It is also possible to join the acoustic and linguistic information, thanks to the RNN-T architecture [2].

The seq2seq architecture is also an approach for solving voice recognition tasks using an *'Encoder'* capable of encoding the acoustic signal and then translating the information produced by the Encoder into an output sequence using the '*Decoder*' via the attention mechanism [3].

However, we can note some limitations of the 'End-To-End' models such as:

- The CTC loss function assumes the independence of each word at the time of prediction, which can lead to inconsistent sentences;
- The attention mechanism is an auto-regressive model, and therefore it is able to produce only one token per time step, which results in a slow inference time;
- 'End-To-End' models require a large volume of data for its learning process.

Limits to CTCs and attention mechanism have been resolved with transducer models [2, 4].

To solve the limitations imposing a large volume of data, the following approaches have been proposed:

- Data augmentation techniques [5–7];
- Pre-training techniques, transfer learning [8, 9];
- Multitasking or multilingual learning techniques [10, 11];
- Unsupervised or self-supervised learning techniques [12, 13].

Another limit lies in low-resource African languages that have often been left behind in terms of research work. Resources in these languages are not only rare but they are even more so when it comes to specialized fields such as agriculture, finance or health. Current work [14–17] are mainly focused on language recognition in general and not in specific areas as mentioned.

In the next sections, we will start with the history of voice recognition going from the 1940s to the present days. Then we will detail the recent advances starting with monolingual then multilingual models, then we will end with models adapted to low-resource languages.

2 First Solutions Proposed in the Literature

2.1 Solutions Proposed in the 40s and 50s

The first automatic speech recognition solutions were developed in the late 1940s and early 1950s. A notable system, created by Bell Labs, was able to recognize any of 10 digits (0–9) spoken by a single speaker [18] with the system named Audrey. The system achieved an impressive 97 to 99% accuracy by selecting the model with the highest correlation coefficient with the input. The "Pattern matching" approach was used to compare each spoken word to a reference base and the choice was made according to the distance of the nearest word.

Authors of [19, 20] were the first to implement a phoneme recognition system capable of recognizing four vowels and five consonants.

2.2 Solutions Proposed in the 60s and 70s

Significant changes occurred during the late 1960s and early 1970s. The Shoebox project (1961) powered by IBM made it possible to perform arithmetic calculations with the recognition of sixteen words which are the digits 0 to 9 as well as arithmetic operations such as "plus", "minus", or "total".

We can cite the appearance of many feature extraction algorithms such as the Fast Fourier Transform (FFT) [21], the application of cepstral processing [22] or LPC for speech coding [23].

Another innovation during the 70s is based on models called Hidden Markov Models (HMM). [24, 25] have applied HMM models to various problems.

2.3 Solutions Proposed in the 80s and 90s

The association of HMM models with models named Gaussian Mixture Models (GMM) gained popularity in the 90s. During the same period, experiments were carried out with neural networks capable of predicting phonemes as well as performing other tasks related to speech processing. This constituted an alternative to HMM/GMM. Architectures have been created from neural networks such as the Time-Delay Neural Network (TDNN), models based on convolution networks [26, 27], and Recurrent neural network (RNN) [28].

There has also been the emergence of hybrid HMM/MLP models where the multilayer perceptron network is trained to recognize phonemes and extract a vector representation from them and then link it to the input of the HMM/GMM model [29].

The hybrid models showed performances close to the HMM/GMM models, however, their problem was related to their training speed which was very slow on CPU.

Performance at the time was limited to a layer containing 4000 units which was insufficient for consistent speech recognition.

2.4 Solutions Proposed in the 2000s and 2010s

The decades that followed saw the emergence of graphics cards, which made it possible to develop multi-layered neural networks. In 2009, the performances approached the HMM/GMM models on simple voice recognition tasks [30]. Then, in 2012, the performance of the hybrid systems ended up surpassing the traditional HMM/GMM systems [31, 32].

In 2006, the first works using the CTC loss function were carried out [1] as well as the RNN-Transducer in 2012 [2, 4].

Then appeared the End-To-End approach by rescoring [33] and by recognition [34] with advancements such as beam search [35]. The architecture of encoder-decoders based on the attention mechanism appeared in 2014 [36, 37]. The popular system called Listen, Attend and Spell (LAS) [3] appeared in the same period.

An alternative to RNNs named Transformer [38] started to appear in the speech field in 2018.

3   Recent Solutions Proposed in the Literature

3.1   Monolingual Approach

The last decade has seen the rise of models based on neural networks called 'End-To-End' [3, 39, 11]. Compared to traditional models which were based on HMM/GMM [30] and which required to train several components such as an acoustic model, a lexicon model as well as a language model. These 'End-To-End' models have also taken over the hybrid models [31, 32]. The notable difference of 'End-To-End' models is that they have the ability to take an audio sequence as input and produce a sequence of characters as output thanks to a single neural network.

One of the disadvantages of traditional models is that they require the implementation and training of separate components, making the development of new speech recognition technologies difficult and expensive. Furthermore, expertise is needed for every module that constitutes this model.

Hence the need to train a neural network called "End-To-End" [39] i.e., a single system capable of managing all the features listed earlier. It must also be able to learn a new language from scratch without making major changes to the system.

In 2016, End-To-End models being essentially based on attention mechanisms using RNN networks [39], as well as LSTM networks [3, 11] or both combined [3].

The model named "Listen, Attend and Spell" [3] consists of two sub-modules which are the listener and the speller. The listener encodes the acoustic information in order to be able to listen to the signal. The speller is an attention-based decoder. The Listen function of the listener takes as input a signal x and returns a representation noted $h = h_1, \ldots, h_U$ while the AttendAndSpell function receives data h to output a probability of character sequences noted P(y/x). The Listen function is a bidirectional LSTM or Bidirectional Long Short-Term Memory RNN (BLSTM) having a pyramidal structure. The disadvantage of using a single BLSTM resides in the difficulty of convergence of the model even after a month of training.

To overcome this limitation, the authors of [3] developed a pyramidal BLSTM denoted pBLSTM. In addition to reducing information, the model's neural network will be able to capture non-linear representations of the data. The pyramid structure also participates in reducing the computational complexity and therefore the time required for learning. To train the model, the functions Listen and AttendAndSpell are jointly trained by maximizing the probability of predicting the next character based on the previous one. The decoding phase of an acoustic representation is performed by the beam search algorithm.

Nevertheless, the LAS model produced less efficient results compared to the CLDNN-HMM [40] reference model. The results also showed a performance degradation on short utterances (2 words max) and also on longer utterances.

Another model called Deep Speech 2 capable of voice recognition of English and Mandarin was also presented during the same period by [39]. The architecture of Deep Speech 2 (DS2) is an RNN trained to consume spectrograms representing the audio signal in order to generate transcriptions in textual form. The model is responsible for generating graphemes for each language. The proposed model is an RNN composed of several hidden layers. The architecture is structured with one or more convolutional layers followed by one or more recurrent layers, followed by one or more dense layers.

The model is trained using the CTC loss function. The benchmark of the model is performed on two datasets which are the Wall Street Journal (WSJ) and LibriSpeech corpus [41].

On WSJ 92, the DS2 model exceeds human performance with a Word Error Rate (WER) of 3.60% compared to 5.03% for humans. On WSJ 93, DS2 is still better with a score of 4.98% compared to 8.08% for the human.

DS2 outperforms human on LibriSpeech test-clean [41] with a score of 5.33% but on the other hand gives lower performance on LibriSpeech test-other [41] with a score of 13.25% compared to human which is at 12.69%.

In 2019, a new End-To-End model named Jasper published by [42] achieved state-of-the-art (SOTA) results on the popular LibriSpeech dataset [41]. Jasper consists of an input convolution layer followed by blocks and then three consecutive convolutional layers. At the output of the model, we find a CTC layer.

A variant of Jasper called Jasper Dense Residual (DR) has also been proposed and which has the particularity of adding the output of each convolution block to the input of all the following blocks.

On the LibriSpeech dataset [41], the Jasper DR 10x5 model was trained on 400 epochs and achieved a SOTA performance on the test-clean subset with a WER score of 2.95%. A newer Jasper-based model named Jasper DR 10x5 + Time/Freq Masks was able to further improve performance with a WER 2.84%.

Authors of [43] focuses on sequence-to-sequence type models called Transformer [38] in order to carry out a comparison study with RNN models.

The experiments resulted in a significant performance improvement to the benefit of the Transformer model on several tasks compared to the RNN. The proposed solution is based on the sequence-to-sequence (S2S) method consisting of an encoder and a decoder. The S2S method is a neural network capable of learning to transform a source sequence denoted X into a target sequence denoted Y.

In the speech translation task, the Transformer improves the baseline RNN BLEU score with a score of 17.2%.

However, the Transformer model [38] shows some limitations in the decoding of filterbank features, namely a longer processing time compared to RNN. The comparative study showed better performance for the Transformer compared to the RNN, especially in the ASR task.

In 2020, [44] trained a model based on the LibriSpeech dataset [41] in conjunction with a model capable of generating pseudo-labeling from unlabeled audio datasets. The unlabeled dataset that was used is named LibriVox resulting in over 53,000 h of audio data. For the labeled dataset, LibriSpeech [41] was used. The Transformer model with GCNN + Transf LM produced as WER 2.09% on test-clean and 4.11% on test-other.

Also in 2020, [12] showed for the first time the principle of learning representations based solely on speech and then a fine-tining phase based on the transcription of speech. This methodology made it possible to surpass the performances obtained through semi-supervised models. The model in question named wav2vec 2.0 is based on the masking of speech portions through the latent space in order to find the hidden portions by solving a contrastive task. This task is obtained from the quantification of latent representations.

The experiments carried out on the Librispeech annotated dataset [41] made it possible to obtain 1.8%/3.3% as the WER score on the clean/other samples. It only takes 100 times less annotated data for wav2vec 2.0 to surpass the state of the art. With ten minutes of labeled data for a pre-trained model on a 53k hour (unlabeled) dataset to score 4.8%/8.2% WER.

During this same period, [45] published a paper presenting the Conformer model which surpassed the state of the art. The authors demonstrated that the combination between a convolution model (CNN) and a Transformer-based model [38] made it possible to respectively capture local and global dependencies from an audio sequence with efficient parameters.

The release of the Conformer model has significantly improved state-of-the-art performance. The limitation of transformers [38] identified by the authors is the low capacity for extracting local information from the audio signal of speech. While CNNs have an inability to capture global signal information.

The proposed solution to address the limitations identified by the authors is to combine Transformers and CNNs in order to learn information in a local as well as a global context.

With a language model, Conformer in its large version with 118M parameters outperforms the state of the art with 1.9% WER on testclean and 3.9% WER on testother of LibriSpeech [41].

ContextNet presented by [46] is a model that aims to improve the performance of CNN models in the speech recognition task. The main flaw of CNNs is that it is limited in learning the overall context of a given audio signal because it is only able to capture a small window in the time domain. The authors identified this limitation as the reason why CNN-based models perform worse compared to RNN or Transformer-based models.

To enable the CNN model to capture the global context of the signal, the authors introduced a new concept called squeeze-and-excitation (SE) which is introduced in a CNN and constitutes the ContextNet model. By introducing the SE in a convolutional layer, we allow the model to have access to the global information context.

Three different versions of ContextNet have been evaluated on LibriSpeech. The small (alpha = 0.5), medium (alpha = 1) and large (alpha = 2) versions. The large ContextNet(L) model with a Language Model (LM) outperformed the state of the art with 1.9% WER on testclean and 4.1% WER on testother from LibriSpeech.

In [13] the authors explore the field of unsupervised pre-training by combining speech and text within a single model. The proposed solution is called Speech and Language Model (SLAM) which is a model based on Conformer [45] and trained by coupling text and speech with cost functions such as SpanBERT [47] for the textual part and w2v-BERT [48] for the speech part.

For the speech recognition task, the model pre-trained with w2v-bert XL produces results comparable to the state of the art with 1.6% on the test set and 2.9% on test-other of LibriSpeech.

There are currently two major approaches to improve the automatic speech recognition task based on a large number of unlabeled speech. The first strategy is called self-training, also known as pseudo-labeling, which consists in initially training a *Teacher* model from labeled data. Then, the *Teacher* model is used to generate labels on unlabeled data. The combination of labeled and pseudo-labeled data is then used to train a *Student* model. The pseudo-labeling process can be reused several times in order to improve the quality of the *Teacher* model.

The second strategy is to use the method called self-supervised pre-training. This involves pre-training a model from unlabeled data in order to initialize it on a good basis, then fine-tuning it on a labeled dataset.

In the work presented, the authors [48] have implemented a model named w2v-BERT which combines two approaches exploiting self-supervised pre-training as presented in the literature as wav2vec2.0 [12] and BERT [49]. w2v-BERT uses the method called contrastive task taken from wav2vec2.0 in order to obtain a finite number of discriminative voice units. Then, it uses the result obtained in a second method called Masked Language Model (MLM) proposed by BERT for learning contextualized speech representation. w2v-BERT is composed of an encoder called Convolution Subsampling responsible for encoding speech features. A module called contrastive module responsible for discretizing the features encoded in a finite number of discriminative vocal units. And finally, a module called masked prediction module which aims to extract contextualized speech representations.

w2v-BERT XXL outperforms the Conformer [45], HuBERT [50], w2v-Conformer and wav2vec2.0 [12] models by displaying as scores on the test set 1.4% of WER and 2.5% of WER on the test-other of the LibriSpeech dataset. These results make w2v-BERT the actual state-of-the-art model as shown on Table 1. The authors mentioned as a perspective, the evaluation of w2v-BERT in a low-resource environment.

Implementing applications covering spoken languages with few or no resources is a real challenge. [50] propose as a solution a model called Hidden unit BERT (HuBERT) capable of using the clustering approach to generate labels and then train the model in the style of BERT [49]. The objective is to predict hidden units of the acoustic signal. Note that these units are classes generated after clustering a k-means model.

Pre-trained models are based on the wav2vec2.0 architecture.

The results obtained on low resource configurations reveal better scores for the HuBERT X-LARGE model compared to other models in the literature such as wav2vec2.0 and DiscreteBERT [51]. The results of HuBERT are close but less efficient than those of wav2vec2.0 + self-training on LibriSpeech 960h with a WER score of 1.8% on test-clean and 2.9% on test-other.

The approach proposed by [52] is the combination of two learning methods, which are iterative self-training and pre-training. Different versions of models are pre-trained and then trained afterwards in self-training mode. The unlabeled dataset will be used at each stage of the process i.e., used for pre-training and then used again for generating pseudo-labels by the *Teacher* model for training the *Student* model.

The ASR system is based on the Conformer model without the relative positional embedding layer in order to speed up the training process. Four versions of Conformer were used namely, Conformer L (100M), XL (600M), XXL (1B) and XXL +. Four generations of models have been trained (Gen0 to Gen3).

The best results were obtained with the 4th generation Gen3 Conformer XXL + model which combines pre-training and self-training with 1.4% WER on the test set and 2.6% WER on the test-other from LibriSpeech.

Table 1. Comparison of the Librispeech ASR benchmark

Paper	Year	Base model	Test-clean / Test-other
Deep speech 2 [39]	2016	Bi-RNN + CTC	4.3 / 13.2
ESPnet Transformer [43]	2019	Transformer	2.6 / 5.7
Jasper [42]	2019	CNN + CTC	2.8 / 7.8
SpecAugment [7]	2019	LAS with LM	2.2 / 5.2
Semi-supervised Transformer [44]	2020	Transformer + LM	2.1 / 4.1
wav2vec 2.0 [12]	2020	Transformer + CTC	1.8 / 3.3
Conformer [45]	2020	Conformer	1.9 / 3.9
ContextNet [46]	2020	CNN-RNN-Transducer	1.9 / 4.1
Conformer + NST + SpecAugment [52]	2020	Conformer	1.4 / 2.6
SLAM [13]	2021	Conformer	1.6 / 2.9
HuBERT [50]	2021	Transformer + BERT	1.8 / 2.9
W2v-BERT [48]	**2021**	**wav2vec 2.0 + BERT**	**1.4 / 2.5**

After having compared state of the art on monolingual models, we will present in the next section, models capable of recognizing and transcribing several languages.

3.2 Multilingual Approach

A multilingual version of wave2vec2.0 named XLSR was presented by [53]. The results showed improvements from the multilingual model compared to the monolingual models, i.e., models trained on a single language.

The solution is based on the wave2vec2.0 architecture [12] with audio data from several languages in order to take advantage of the sharing of representations learned through these various languages. The large model built by the authors named XLSR-53 was trained on 53 languages by combining all the BABEL [54], CommonVoice [55] and Multilingual LibriSpeech datasets [56]. The CTC loss function was used in the fine-tuning phase.

Analysis of latent speech representations revealed that the multilingual model has the ability to share common knowledge especially from close languages. The authors [10] highlighted the limitations of unsupervised or self-supervised pre-training methods that require little or no labeling such as the Wav2Vec2.0 model [12]. Indeed, this model needs to be fine-tuned to be able to adapt to a specific task (e.g., voice recognition). On the other hand, the task of fine-tuning requires very technical skills because of its complexity.

The authors [10] further emphasize the goal of a speech recognition system which must be able to generalize to any domain without requiring fine-tuning tasks on each domain-specific dataset. To address the problems listed above, [10] proposed a model named *Whisper* which was trained by supervised learning on 680,000 h of labeled audio data. The authors were able to demonstrate that models trained on such a large amount of data manage to generalize by zero-shot on any dataset, that is to say without having to resort to fine-tuning on a specific dataset. Note that the dataset includes 97 different languages. The Whisper model is mainly based on the Transformer encoder-decoder architecture [38].

This resulted in a dataset diversified by its data whose distributions are varied as well as environments, languages and actors. To evaluate Whisper, zero-shot technique was used to measure the generalization quality of the model on datasets on which it has never been trained.

- ASR task: Across 14 different datasets, Whisper Large outperforms wave2vec2.0 averaging 12.9% WER versus 29.5% WER. Note that on LibriSpeech test-clean, Whisper displays the same performance as wave2vec2.0, i.e., 2.7% of WER;
- Multilingual speech recognition task: Zero-Shot Whisper outperforms state-of-the-art models on the MLS corpus with 8.1% WER, but does much less than XLSR and mSLAM-CTC on VoxPopuli [57];

To build a model capable of learning multilingual and multimodal representations from hundreds of different languages, [58] proposed an improvement of the SLAM model [13]. The proposed model named mSLAM has the particularity of learning several languages compared to its predecessor SLAM. To avoid interference between modalities, the mSLAM model was trained with the CTC loss function on the speech-text pair of a dataset. The model is based on the SLAM architecture [13] by combining, together, pre-training based on unlabeled speech dataset with w2v-BERT [48] and unlabeled text with spanBERT[47]. The Translation Language Modeling (TLM) method was used on the labeled dataset coupling speech and transcription. The TLM method introduced by [59] aims to improve cross-language pre-training by extending to the Masked Language Modeling (MLM) method, which is more suitable for monolingual texts. TLM will concatenate the sentences of a source language and a target language in parallel and then randomly hide words in each language. To predict the hidden word in a specific language, the model will be able to rely on the representation from the parallel language.

One of the key challenges for Google is to be able to extend voice technologies to several languages. This results in enough data to be able to train high quality models. The task of manually labeling data from low-resource languages is a big challenge for supervised learning both in terms of time and cost. The objective of this study [60] is to manage to produce in the long term, a universal model of voice recognition capable of covering all the languages spoken in the world.

The approach used by the authors [60] is mainly based on the construction of a model called Universal Speech Models (USMs) trained on large datasets of three types which are unlabeled audio data, unlabeled textual data and data pairs (audio-text). The construction of the model is based on three steps such as unsupervised pre-training, a supervised pre-training with multiple objectives and supervised training on specific tasks such as ASR and AST. The solution is based on the large model named Conformer [45] with 2 billion parameters. The USM model and its variants outperform Whisper [10] on all multilingual datasets. USM also outperforms Whisper on all low-resource languages in the FLEURS dataset [61].

Recent scientific studies have focused on expanding the language coverage of speech processing technologies. However, current technologies are limited to the recognition of a hundred languages which is very low compared to more than 7000 languages spoken in the world. To address this problem, the authors of the article [62] constructed a new dataset comprising 1107 labeled languages and another dataset comprising 3809 languages in unlabeled audio format. A multilingual model called Massively Multilingual Speech (MMS) was created for the occasion from the new datasets to cover the recognition and speech synthesis of 1107 languages, as well as the identification of 4017 languages. The architecture of the MMS model is based on wav2vec2.0 [12].

The experiments are based on the pre-trained wav2vec2.0 model on several languages implemented with the fairseq tool [63]. The MMS model was finetuned on 61 languages in the FLEURS [61] dataset and was compared to the XLS-R model [53]. MMS outperforms XLS-R [53] on most languages, especially low-resource languages. On the ASR task, MMS was finetuned on the MMS-lab labeled dataset using the CTC criterion. The model was first compared to Whisper [10] and the results showed better performance for MMS in 31 out of 54 languages (FLEUR-54 dataset [61]). Regarding Google-USM [60], MMS slightly outperforms USM. Table 2 compares state-of-the-art multilingual models.

Table 3 compares number of supported languages by each model.

Table 2. Comparison on Multilingual LibriSpeech, VoxPopuli and FLEURS benchmark. All results are reported with the WER score except for the FLEURS dataset which is in Character Error Rate (CER).

Model	Year	MLS	VoxPopuli	FLEURS
MMS [62]	2023	8.7	10.3	6.2
USM [60]	2023	-	-	6.5
Whisper [10]	2022	8.1	15.2	-
XLSR [53]	2020	10.9	10.6	-
mSLAM [58]	2022	9.7	9.1	-

3.3 Automatic Speech Recognition for Low-Resource Languages

This article [15] presents the steps that were necessary to collect data from four sub-Saharan African languages such as Swahili, Hausa, Amharic and Wolof. The authors

Table 3. Number of languages supported

Model	Supported languages
MMS [62]	1162
USM [60]	102
Whisper [10]	99
XLSR [53]	53
mSLAM [58]	51

specifically focused on Wolof by setting up the very first voice recognition system for this low-resource West African language. Access to technologies is mainly done through mobile phones or smartphones. Speech technology is an essential mean to reduce the gap for illiterate people, both in the field of health, food and in social networks. It is in this sense that the project named ALFFA was initiated in order to develop ASR and Text-To-Speech (TTS) technologies for African languages. Note that the ALFFA project brought together profiles in various fields such as experts in technology and also in linguistics. Wolof is spoken in Senegal, Gambia and Mauritania. This language is spoken by more than 10 million people. Kaldi software was used to build the speech recognition system. The ASR for Swahili was trained over ten hours of audio and evaluated over 1.8 h. The language model contains approximately 28 million words. For Hausa, the model was trained on seven hours of data and tested on one hour. The language model has a size of 41000 words. The Amharic meanwhile was trained on twenty hours of data and tested on two hours. The language model is created using 3-g and the text has been segmented into morphemes. The studies in this article are mainly focused on the Wolof spoken in Dakar the capital of Senegal.

The construction of the audio corpus in Wolof was carried out by selecting 6000 utterances at random. Eighteen people (ten men and eight women) were selected from different socio-professional categories. These eighteen people were responsible for making voice recordings of 1000 utterances extracted from the 6000 mentioned earlier. The age of the people varies from 24 to 48 years old and the microphone used for the recording is a Samson G-track in an environment containing no noise.

A total of 18,000 utterances were recorded, representing 21 h and 22 min of audio signal. Two language models were set up and the tool named Phonetisaurus was used to transform the vocabulary into phonemes. Kaldi was used to build the ASR model. Three acoustic models have been constructed, namely HMM/GMM which is a hidden Markovian model coupled with a Gaussian model. Another model named SGMM or subspace Gaussian mixture model and a last one based on DNN deep neural networks. For the HMM/GMM model, it receives as input 133 MFCCs and 16.8 h of data. The DNN model was trained with the same MFCCs used for the GMM models. The DNN was fine-tuned with the Stochastic Gradient Descent (SGD).

The performances of the different models were around 30% WER. The best WER score of 27.21% was obtained on the LM2 language model with the DNN model. The limits are essentially on so-called diatric data which refers to a word which can take several forms. For example, the word "jél" which can also be written "jël" and which means "to take". One track mentioned in the paper would be to standardize the text by choosing only one form for all the words referring to several representations.

This article [64] studies the technique of learning transfer to a low-resource language such as Amharic. The transfer of learning took place through two high-resource languages (English and Mandarin) towards the target, which is Amharic. The results showed a strong reduction in the WER error rate. The best result was obtained from the English language.

A TDNN (Time Delay Deep Neural Network) neural network is proposed as a baseline. The alignment of text and voice data is performed by a GMM-HMM model before being injected into a neural network.

Amharic corpus contains 20 h of training data and 2 h of test data from 100 native speakers. English corpus containing 100 h for English-1 set and 460 h for English-2 set. 5.4 h are dedicated to the test set They are sourced from OpenSLR[1]. Mandarin corpus containing 178 h including 85% dedicated to the train set and the rest for the test set. It is sourced from Beijing Shell Technology.

The best results were obtained with English-2 as the source language with a WER score of 25.5% compared to the baseline which is 38.72%.

The authors [65] carried out experiments on the contribution of multilingual models on low-resource languages. Four low-resource Ethiopian languages as target were considered such as Amharic, Oromo, Tigrana and Wolaytta. What motivated the development of multilingual systems is justified by the number of high-resource languages which are not widespread and which require colossal means for their development. The idea is to take advantage of these languages in order to develop voice recognition models requiring few resources. The objective of this approach is to enable illiterate populations to benefit from being able to access digital services, mainly in rural areas, through their phones. The proposed solution is the implementation of multilingual models based on a corpus of more than 20 languages in order to build an ASR system for four Ethiopian languages.

The neural network is based on the Factored Time Delay Neural Networks with additional Convolutional layers (CNN-TDNNf) model. To train this model, the data is first aligned (voice and text) using an HMM-GMM model. The source dataset used is the GlobalPhone (GP) [66] which is a multilingual corpus covering 20 languages. For the Amharic language we have AMH2005 containing 20 h of training with 11k utterances. AMH2020 is used as the second corpus. Note that Amharic data was collected in Ethiopia as well as for Oromo, Tigrana and Wolaytta. All models were built using the Kaldi ASR toolkit. Tri-gram language models have been developed for each target language. The 1st experiment carried out led to the training of a multilingual ML22 model on the GP corpus. The 2nd named ML23 (22 languages + 1 Ethiopian) was trained by adding an Ethiopian language in the train data. The 3rd named ML25 (22 languages + 3 Ethiopian) was trained by adding three Ethiopian languages. The last experiment named ML26 (22 languages + 4 Ethiopian) was trained by adding four Ethiopian languages. Two models from transfer learning were built and named ML22_Ada and ML26_Ada.

---

[1] http://www.openslr.org/.

The best multilingual model on the Amharic language was obtained with ML22_Ada with 8.21% of WER. On Tigrina we have the MonoLing model which scores 16.82% WER. On Oromo, ML22_Ada wins with 32% WER. Finally, on Wolaytta the MonoLing model produces better results with 23.23% WER. We can conclude that training a model whose source and target language are close enough produces good results.

In this article the author [17] presents the creation of two datasets, one of which is labeled for ten African languages and the other for four African languages. The contribution of this paper is intended to reduce the digital divide within illiterate populations located in Sub-Saharan Africa. The work presents the exploitation of resources from radio archives for low-resource languages and the use of self-supervised methods based on wav2vec [67] to train models capable of solving speech recognition tasks intended for these languages. The Architecture of the West African wav2vec (WAwav2vec) model is based on wav2vec which is used for the feature extraction part.

On the Multilingual Speech Recognition task which consists in identifying 105 classes of utterances on four languages, WAwav2vec and wav2vec give similar results. The virtual assistant only understands contact management vocabulary, it would be possible to extend it in the field of micro-finance, agriculture and education. It would be useful to take advantage of the abundance of radio data to train the encoder to identify other nearby languages.

Much effort has gone into developing ASR models for so-called "high-resource" languages such as English, Mandarin and Japanese. However, the so-called "low-resource" models are much less robust due to an insufficient number of training data. The other point raised by the authors [9] is related to the multilingual models which have been tested in the literature and which produce limited results due to the non-proximity of the languages chosen for training.

To provide a solution to the points mentioned above, the authors have set up a multilingual model dedicated to low-resource Turkish languages. Ten Turkish languages were considered in the study such as: Azerbaijani, Bashkir, Chuvash, Kazakh, Kyrgyz, Sakha, Tatar, Turkish, Uyghur, and Uzbek. The models are based on a dataset created by the authors containing 218 h of speech transcribed into the Turkish language. The models are based on the Conformer model architecture.

The dataset created by the authors is called Turkish Speech Corpus (TSC) which is composed of 218 h of speech in Turkish. CVC includes ten different Turkish languages and one language in English. Russian language comes from OpenSTT. Data augmentation techniques were used such as speed perturbation and spectral augmentation. For the experiments, 22 models were trained in total (13 monolingual and 9 multilingual). All models were trained in Pytorch with the ESPnet framework. The monolingual models were trained with 1 NVIDIA DGX A100 GPU card (40 GB), the multilingual ones required four GPUs of the same type. The language model used is based on Transformer.

We can observe as a result that the multilingual models outperform the monolingual ones. The model trained only on Turkish languages (all_turkic) also outperforms those trained on non-Turkish languages (English, Russian). This proves that the proximity of the language has a positive impact on the model.

The authors [14] made a contribution to the modeling of the ASR task for low-resource Congolese languages. Would it be possible to surpass the state of the art with the wav2vec2.0 model on the Lingala? Would pre-training on large datasets be a solution to reduce the amount of data to label on a low-resource language? Would it be possible to benefit from the proximity of languages in order to develop efficient multilingual models?

To answer these questions, the authors proposed various solutions such as the creation of two datasets named *Congolese Speech Radio Corpus* and *Linguala Read Speech Corpus*, establishment of a baseline from the collected data and creation of a multilingual model from four languages spoken mainly in Congo.

The developed solution is based on wav2vec2.0 [12].

Two baselines were considered for the experiments such as GMM-HMM (T-DNN) and DeepSpeech 2 [39].Whisper medium [10] model was also used. For self-supervised experimentation, the BASE model wav2vec2.0 was used. The 1st experiment consisted in pre-training wav2vec2.0 on the Congolese Speech Radio dataset. For the second experiment wav2vec2.0 was finetuned in two scenarios: fine-tuning of the pre-trained model on four Congolese languages on Linguala Read Speech Corpus and fine-tuning of XLSR-53 and XLS-R multilingual models respectively on Linguala Read Speech Corpus. The tools used are HuggingFace and Fairseq. The best model is the multilingual version CdWav2Vec pre-trained on Congolese Speech Radio corpus and fine-tuned on Linguala Read Speech Corpus which obtains a WER score of 21.4%. The results prove that the pre-trained multilingual models show better performance than the monolingual ones. This is due to the richness of the representation of close languages which is transferable to target languages close to the source languages.

4 Conclusion

We reviewed the history of automatic speech recognition starting from traditional systems requiring the implementation of several models such as the acoustic model, then the phonetic model and finally the linguistic model. We have seen that these systems have limitations that so-called *"End-to-End"* systems try to simplify thanks to the development of neural networks. Nowadays, state-of-the-art models tend to offer multilingual approaches in order to model the largest possible number of spoken languages which is around 7000 [68] and, to allow illiterate people to be able to interact with all kinds of application from their native languages. Our future work will mainly focus on African languages, considered as low-resources due to the scarcity of their digitized data in order to allow people speaking African languages to be able to interact with digital services specifically related to financial sector.

Acknowledgements. This work is part of the ongoing PhD training supported by the Partnership for skills in Applied Sciences, Engineering and Technology (PASET) - Regional Scholarship and Innovation Fund (RSIF).

References

1. Graves, A., Fernández, S., Gomez, F., Schmidhuber, J.: Connectionist temporal classification: labelling unsegmented sequence data with recurrent neural networks. In: ACM International Conference Proceeding Series (2006)

2. Graves, A.: Sequence Transduction with Recurrent Neural Networks (2012)
3. Chan, W., Jaitly, N., Le, Q.V., Vinyals, O.: Listen, Attend and Spell (2015). https://doi.org/10.48550/arxiv.1508.01211
4. Graves, A., Mohamed, A.R., Hinton, G.: Speech recognition with deep recurrent neural networks. In: ICASSP, IEEE International Conference on Acoustics, Speech and Signal Processing – Proceedings (2013)
5. Sriram, A., Auli, M., Baevski, A.: Wav2Vec-Aug: Improved self-supervised training with limited data (2022). https://doi.org/10.48550/arxiv.2206.13654
6. Park, D.S., Chan, W., Zhang, Y., et al.: SpecAugment: a Simple Data Augmentation Method for Automatic Speech Recognition (2019). https://doi.org/10.21437/interspeech.2019-2680
7. Park, D.S., Zhang, Y., Chiu, C.-C., et al.: SpecAugment on Large Scale Datasets (2019). https://doi.org/10.48550/arxiv.1912.05533
8. Yi, C., Wang, J., Cheng, N., et al.: Applying Wav2vec2.0 to Speech Recognition in Various Low-resource Languages (2020). https://doi.org/10.48550/arxiv.2012.12121
9. Mussakhojayeva, S., Dauletbek, K., Yeshpanov, R., Varol, H.A.: Multilingual speech recognition for Turkic languages. Information 14, 74 (2023). https://doi.org/10.3390/info14020074
10. Radford, A., Wook Kim, J., Xu, T., et al.: Robust Speech Recognition via Large-Scale Weak Supervision (2022). https://cdn.openai.com/papers/whisper.pdf. Accessed 23 Sep 2022
11. Kim, S., Hori, T., Watanabe, S.: Joint CTC-Attention based End-to-End Speech Recognition using Multi-task Learning (2016). https://doi.org/10.48550/arxiv.1609.06773
12. Baevski, A., Zhou, H., Mohamed, A., Auli, M.: wav2vec 2.0: a Framework for Self-Supervised Learning of Speech Representations (2020). https://doi.org/10.48550/arxiv.2006.11477
13. Bapna, A., Chung, Y., Wu, N., et al.: SLAM: a Unified Encoder for Speech and Language Modeling via Speech-Text Joint Pre-Training (2021)
14. Kimanuka, U., wa Maina, C., Büyük, O.: Speech recognition datasets for low-resource congolese languages. In: 4th Workshop on African Natural Language Processing (2023)
15. Gauthier, E., Besacier, L., Voisin, S., et al.: Collecting resources in Sub-Saharan African languages for automatic speech recognition: a case study of Wolof. In: Proceedings of the Tenth International Conference on Language Resources and Evaluation (LREC 2016). European Language Resources Association (ELRA), Portorož, Slovenia, pp. 3863–3867 (2016)
16. Gauthier, E., Séga Wade, P., Moudenc, T., et al.: Preuve de concept d'un bot vocal dialoguant en wolof (Proof-of-Concept of a Voicebot Speaking Wolof). In: Actes de la 29e Conférence sur le Traitement Automatique des Langues Naturelles, Volume 1 : conférence principale. ATALA, Avignon, France, pp. 403–412 (2022)
17. Doumbouya, M., Einstein, L., Piech, C.: Using Radio Archives for Low-Resource Speech Recognition: Towards an Intelligent Virtual Assistant for Illiterate Users (2021). https://doi.org/10.48550/arxiv.2104.13083
18. Davis, K.H., Biddulph, R., Balashek, S.: Automatic recognition of spoken digits. J. Acoust. Soc. Am. 24 (1952). https://doi.org/10.1121/1.1906946
19. Fry, D.B.: Theoretical aspects of mechanical speech recognition. J. Br. Inst. Radio Eng. 19 (1959). https://doi.org/10.1049/jbire.1959.0026
20. Denes, P.: The design and operation of the mechanical speech recognizer at University College London. J. Br. Inst. Radio Eng. 19 (1959). https://doi.org/10.1049/jbire.1959.0027
21. Cooley, J.W., Tukey, J.W.: An algorithm for the machine calculation of complex Fourier series. Math. Comput. 19 (1965). https://doi.org/10.1090/s0025-5718-1965-0178586-1
22. Oppenheim, A.V., Schafer, R.W., Stockham, T.G.: Nonlinear filtering of multiplied and convolved signals. Proc. IEEE 56 (1968). https://doi.org/10.1109/PROC.1968.6570
23. Atal, B.S., Hanauer, S.L.: Speech analysis and synthesis by linear prediction of the speech wave. J Acoust. Soc. Am. 50 (1971). https://doi.org/10.1121/1.1912679

24. Baum, L.E., Petrie, T.: Statistical inference for probabilistic functions of finite state Markov chains. Ann. Math. Stat. **37** (1966). https://doi.org/10.1214/aoms/1177699147
25. Baum, L.B., Eagon, J.A.: An inequality with applications to statistical estimation for probabilistic functions of Markov processes and to a model for ecology. Bull. Am. Math. Soc. **73** (1967). https://doi.org/10.1090/S0002-9904-1967-11751-8
26. Waibel, A., Hanazawa, T., Hinton, G., et al.: Phoneme recognition using time-delay neural networks. IEEE Trans. Acoust. **37** (1989). https://doi.org/10.1109/29.21701
27. Lang, K.J., Waibel, A.H., Hinton, G.E.: A time-delay neural network architecture for isolated word recognition. Neural Netw. **3** (1990). https://doi.org/10.1016/0893-6080(90)90044-L
28. Robinson, T., Fallside, F.: A recurrent error propagation network speech recognition system. Comput. Speech Lang. **5** (1991). https://doi.org/10.1016/0885-2308(91)90010-N
29. Morgan, N., Bourlard, H.: Continuous speech recognition using multilayer perceptrons with hidden Markov models. In: ICASSP, IEEE International Conference on Acoustics, Speech and Signal Processing – Proceedings (1990)
30. Mohamed, A.-R., Dahl, G., Hinton, G.: Deep belief networks for phone recognition. Scholarpedia **4** (2009). https://doi.org/10.4249/scholarpedia.5947
31. Jaitly, N., Nguyen, P., Senior, A., Vanhoucke, V.: Application of pretrained deep neural networks to large vocabulary speech recognition. In: 13th Annual Conference of the International Speech Communication Association 2012, INTERSPEECH 2012 (2012)
32. Dahl, G.E., Yu, D., Deng, L., Acero, A.: Context-dependent pre-trained deep neural networks for large-vocabulary speech recognition. IEEE Trans. Audio Speech Lang. Process. **20** (2012). https://doi.org/10.1109/TASL.2011.2134090
33. Graves, A., Jaitly, N.: Towards end-to-end speech recognition with recurrent neural networks. In: 31st International Conference on Machine Learning, ICML 2014 (2014)
34. Maas, A.L., Xie, Z., Jurafsky, D., Ng, A.Y.: Lexicon-free conversational speech recognition with neural networks. In: NAACL HLT 2015 - 2015 Conference of the North American Chapter of the Association for Computational Linguistics: Human Language Technologies, Proceedings of the Conference (2015)
35. Hannun, A.Y., Maas, A.L., Jurafsky, D., Ng, A.Y.: First-Pass Large Vocabulary Continuous Speech Recognition using Bi-Directional Recurrent DNNs (2014)
36. Chorowski, J., Bahdanau, D., Cho, K., Bengio, Y.: End-to-end Continuous Speech Recognition using Attention-based Recurrent NN: First Results (2014)
37. Bahdanau, D., Chorowski, J., Serdyuk, D., et al.: End-to-End Attention-based Large Vocabulary Speech Recognition. In: ICASSP, IEEE International Conference on Acoustics, Speech and Signal Processing - Proceedings 2016 May, pp. 4945–4949 (2015). https://doi.org/10.1109/ICASSP.2016.7472618
38. Vaswani, A., Shazeer, N., Parmar, N., et al.: Attention is all you need. Adv. Neural Inf. Process. Syst. 5999–6009, December 2017)
39. Amodei, D., Ananthanarayanan, S., Anubhai, R., et al.: Deep speech 2: end-to-end speech recognition in English and Mandarin. In: 33rd International Conference on Machine Learning, ICML 2016, pp. 312–321 (2016)
40. Sainath, T.N., Vinyals, O., Senior, A., Sak, H.: Convolutional, long short-term memory, fully connected deep neural networks. In: ICASSP, IEEE International Conference on Acoustics, Speech and Signal Processing – Proceedings, pp. 4580–4584, August 2015. https://doi.org/10.1109/ICASSP.2015.7178838
41. Panayotov, V., Chen, G., Povey, D., Khudanpur, S.: Librispeech: an ASR corpus based on public domain audio books. In: ICASSP, IEEE International Conference on Acoustics, Speech and Signal Processing – Proceedings, pp. 5206–5210, August 2015. https://doi.org/10.1109/ICASSP.2015.7178964
42. Li, J., Lavrukhin, V., Ginsburg, B., et al.: Jasper: an End-to-End Convolutional Neural Acoustic Model (2019). https://doi.org/10.48550/arxiv.1904.03288

43. Karita, S., Chen, N., Hayashi, T., et al.: A Comparative Study on Transformer Vs RNN in Speech Applications
44. Synnaeve, G., Xu, Q., Kahn, J., et al.: End-to-end ASR: from supervised to semi-supervised learning with modern architectures a preprint (2020)
45. Gulati, A., Qin, J., Chiu, C.-C., et al.: Conformer: convolution-augmented transformer for speech recognition (2020). https://doi.org/10.48550/arxiv.2005.08100
46. Han, W., Zhang, Z., Zhang, Y., et al.: ContextNet: improving convolutional neural networks for automatic speech recognition with global context (2020). https://doi.org/10.48550/arxiv.2005.03191
47. Joshi, M., Chen, D., Liu, Y., et al.: SpanBERT: improving pre-training by representing and predicting spans. Trans. Assoc. Comput. Linguist. **8**, 64–77 (2019). https://doi.org/10.1162/tacl_a_00300
48. Chung, Y.A., Zhang, Y., Han, W., et al.: W2v-BERT: combining contrastive learning and masked language modeling for self-supervised speech pre-training. In: 2021 IEEE Automatic Speech Recognition and Understanding Workshop, ASRU 2021 – Proceedings, pp. 244–250 (2021). https://doi.org/10.1109/ASRU51503.2021.9688253
49. Devlin, J., Chang, M.W., Lee, K., Toutanova, K.: BERT: pre-training of deep bidirectional transformers for language understanding. In: NAACL HLT 2019 - 2019 Conference of the North American Chapter of the Association for Computational Linguistics: Human Language Technologies - Proceedings of the Conference, vol. 1, pp. 4171–4186 (2018)
50. Hsu, W.N., Bolte, B., Tsai, Y.H.H., et al.: HuBERT: Self-supervised speech representation learning by masked prediction of hidden units. IEEE/ACM Trans. Audio Speech Lang. Process. **29**, 3451–3460 (2021). https://doi.org/10.1109/TASLP.2021.3122291
51. Baevski, A., Auli, M., Mohamed, A.: Effectiveness of self-supervised pre-training for speech recognition (2019)
52. Zhang, Y., Qin, J., Park, D.S., et al.: Pushing the Limits of Semi-Supervised Learning for Automatic Speech Recognition (2020)
53. Conneau, A., Baevski, A., Collobert, R., et al.: Unsupervised cross-lingual representation learning for speech recognition (2020). https://doi.org/10.48550/arxiv.2006.13979
54. Gales, M., Knill, K., Ragni, A., Rath, S.: Speech recognition and keyword spotting for low-resource languages: Babel project research at CUED (2014)
55. Ardila, R., Branson, M., Davis, K., et al.: Common Voice: a massively-multilingual speech corpus. In: LREC 2020 - 12th International Conference on Language Resources and Evaluation, Conference Proceedings, pp. 4218–4222 (2019)
56. Pratap, V., Xu, Q., Sriram, A., et al.: MLS: a large-scale multilingual dataset for speech research. In: Proceedings of the Annual Conference of the International Speech Communication Association, INTERSPEECH 2020, pp. 2757–2761, October 2020 https://doi.org/10.21437/Interspeech.2020-2826
57. Wang, C., Rivière, M., Lee, A., et al.: VoxPopuli: a large-scale multilingual speech corpus for representation learning, semi-supervised learning and interpretation. In: ACL-IJCNLP 2021 - 59th Annual Meeting of the Association for Computational Linguistics and the 11th International Joint Conference on Natural Language Processing, Proceedings of the Conference, pp. 993–1003 (2021). https://doi.org/10.18653/v1/2021.acl-long.80
58. Bapna, A., Cherry, C., Zhang, Y., et al.: mSLAM: Massively multilingual joint pre-training for speech and text (2022)
59. Conneau, A., Lample, G.: Cross-lingual language model pretraining. Adv. Neural Inf. Process. Syst. **32** (2019)
60. Zhang, Y., Han, W., Qin, J., et al.: Google USM: scaling automatic speech recognition beyond 100 languages (2023)

61. Conneau, A., Ma, M., Khanuja, S., et al.: FLEURS: few-shot learning evaluation of universal representations of speech. In: 2022 IEEE Spoken Language Technology Workshop, SLT 2022 – Proceedings, pp. 798–805 (2022). https://doi.org/10.1109/SLT54892.2023.10023141
62. Pratap, V., Tjandra, A., Shi, B., et al.: Scaling speech technology to 1,000+ languages (2023)
63. Ott, M., Edunov, S., Baevski, A., et al.: fairseq: a fast, extensible toolkit for sequence modeling (2019). https://doi.org/10.48550/arxiv.1904.01038
64. Woldemariam, Y.: Transfer learning for less-resourced semitic languages speech recognition: the case of Amharic. In: Proceedings of the 1st Joint Workshop on Spoken Language Technologies for Under-resourced languages (SLTU) and Collaboration and Computing for Under-Resourced Languages (CCURL). European Language Resources association, Marseille, France, pp. 61–69 (2020)
65. Tachbelie, M.Y., Abate, S.T., Schultz, T.: Development of multilingual ASR using Global-Phone for less-resourced languages: the case of Ethiopian languages. In: INTERSPEECH (2020)
66. Schultz, T., Vu, N.T., Schlippe, T.: GlobalPhone: a multilingual text & speech database in 20 languages. In: ICASSP, IEEE International Conference on Acoustics, Speech and Signal Processing – Proceedings, pp. 8126–8130 (2013). https://doi.org/10.1109/ICASSP.2013.6639248
67. Schneider, S., Baevski, A., Collobert, R., Auli, M.: wav2vec: unsupervised pre-training for speech recognition. In: Proceedings of the Annual Conference of the International Speech Communication Association, INTERSPEECH 2019, pp. 3465–3469, September 2019. https://doi.org/10.21437/Interspeech.2019-1873
68. Ethnologue | Languages of the world. https://www.ethnologue.com/. Accessed 20 Aug 2023

Author Index

M. Masinde et al. (Eds.): AFRICATEK 2023, LNICST 520, p. 205, 2024.
https://doi.org/10.1007/978-3-031-63999-9

Printed in the United States
by Baker & Taylor Publisher Services